LEGAL INTERPRETING

INTERPRETER EDUCATION SERIES

Cynthia B. Roy, Series Editor

VOLUME 1	*Innovative Practices for Teaching Sign Language Interpreters*
VOLUME 2	*Advances in Teaching Sign Language Interpreters*
VOLUME 3	*New Approaches in Interpreter Education*
VOLUME 4	*International Perspectives on Sign Language Interpreter Education*
VOLUME 5	*In Our Hands: Educating Healthcare Interpreters*
VOLUME 6	*Service Learning in Interpreter Education: Strategies for Extending Student Involvement in the Deaf Community*
VOLUME 7	*Evolving Paradigms in Interpreter Education*
VOLUME 8	*Interpreter Education in the Digital Age: Innovation, Access, Change*
VOLUME 9	*Conversations with Interpreter Educators: Exploring Best Practices*
VOLUME 10	*The Next Generation of Research in Interpreter Education: Pursuing Evidence-Based Practices*
VOLUME 11	*The Role of the Educational Interpreter: Perceptions of Administrators and Teachers*
VOLUME 12	*Legal Interpreting: Teaching, Research, and Practice*

Legal Interpreting

Teaching, Research, and Practice

JEREMY L. BRUNSON, EDITOR

Gallaudet University Press
Washington, DC

Interpreter Education
A Series Edited by Cynthia B. Roy

Gallaudet University Press
gupress.gallaudet.edu

Gallaudet University Press is located on the traditional territories of Nacotchtank and Piscataway.

© 2022 by Gallaudet University
All rights reserved. Published 2022
Printed in the United States of America

ISBN 978-1-944838-98-0 (casebound)
ISBN 978-1-944838-99-7 (ebook)

Library of Congress Cataloging-in-Publication Data
Names: Brunson, Jeremy L., editor.
Title: Legal interpreting : teaching, research, and practice / Jeremy L. Brunson, editor.
Description: Washington, DC : Gallaudet University Press, 2022. | Series: Interpreter education series ; volume 12 | Includes bibliographical references and index. | Summary: "The collection focuses on key issues that should be considered by interpreter educators who are teaching students to interpret in a legal setting"—Provided by publisher.
Identifiers: LCCN 2021037943 (print) | LCCN 2021037944 (ebook) | ISBN 9781944838980 (hardcover) | ISBN 9781944838997 (ebook)
Subjects: LCSH: Court interpreting and translating—English-speaking countries. | Interpreters for the deaf—Training of—English-speaking countries. | Law—Translating—English-speaking countries. | Deaf—Legal status, laws, etc.—English-speaking countries.
Classification: LCC K2155 .L44 2022 (print) | LCC K2155 (ebook) | DDC 418/.0334—dc23
LC record available at https://lccn.loc.gov/2021037943
LC ebook record available at https://lccn.loc.gov/2021037944

∞ This paper meets the requirements of ANSI/NISO Z39.48–1992 (Permanence of Paper).

Cover description: Top of cover is black with white text reading, LEGAL INTERPRETING: TEACHING, RESEARCH AND PRACTICE; Jeremy L. Brunson, Editor. Bottom half of cover is an abstract art piece of colorful horizontal lines with rounded ends and grids of transparent dots. Colors include white, pink, blue, yellow, orange, green, and brown.

Cover design by Tracy Cox.

While the authors have made every effort to provide accurate internet addresses and other contact information at the time of publication, neither the publisher nor the authors assume any responsibility for errors or changes that occur after publication. Further, the publisher does not have any control over and does not assume any responsibility for third-party websites or their content.

CONTENTS

Editorial Advisory Board — vii
Signed Video Summaries — viii
Preface — ix

Part One: Applied

1. What Is Legal Interpreting? Introducing IPP Students to the Practice — 3
   Jeremy L. Brunson and Gino S. Gouby

2. Monitoring Interpretations: Analysis, Discretion, and Collaboration — 17
   Risa Shaw

3. Incorporating the Logic and Language of Attorneys Into Our Scope of Practice — 45
   Christopher Tester and Natalie Atlas

Part Two: Best Practices

4. Interpreters as Witnesses and the Experts Who Examine Them: The Pragmatics Behind the Politics — 73
   Carla M. Mathers

5. More Than Language Juggling: Measures to Be Added to Judiciary Interpreter Training in the 21st Century — 106
   Scott Robert Loos

Part Three: Research

6   Deaf Wisdom for Deaf Access   131
       Christopher Stone and Gene Mirus

7   *Justisigns:* Developing Research-Based Training Resources on Sign Language Interpreting in Police Settings in Europe   154
       Jemina Napier, Robert Skinner, Graham H. Turner, Lorraine Leeson, Teresa Lynch, Haaris Sheikh, Myriam Vermeerbergen, Heidi Salaets, Carolien Doggen, Tobias Haug, Barbara Bucher, Barbara Rossier, Michèle Berger, and Flurina Krähenbühl

8   Training Interpreters in Legal Settings: Applying Role-Space Theory in the Classroom   191
       Jérôme Devaux and Robert G. Lee

9   The Interactive Courtroom: The Deaf Defendant Watches How the Speaker Is Identified for Each Turn-At-Talk During a Team-Interpreted Event   219
       LeWana Clark

10   Training Legal Interpreters to Work With Deaf Jurors   246
       Jemina Napier, Debra Russell, Sandra Hale, David Spencer, and Mehera San Roque

11   Practical Professional Training: Building Capacity in Our Interpreting Communities   282
       Debra Russell

Contributors   309

Index   321

EDITORIAL ADVISORY BOARD

Jeremy L. Brunson
 Executive Director, Division of
  Equity, Diversity, and Inclusion
 Gallaudet University
 Washington, DC

Sharon Grigsby Hill
 Program Director
 American Sign Language
  Interpreting Program
 University of Houston
 Houston, Texas, United States

Maartje De Meulder
 Lecturer and Senior Researcher
 University of Applied Sciences
  Utrecht
 Utrecht, the Netherlands

Jemina Napier
 Chair of Intercultural
  Communication
 Department of Languages and
  Intercultural Studies
 Heriot-Watt University
 Edinburgh, Scotland, United
  Kingdom

Rico Peterson
 Assistant Dean and Director
 NTID Access Services
 National Technical Institute for
  the Deaf
 Rochester, New York, United
  States

Christopher Stone
 Reader in Interpreting and
  Translation
 Interpreting and Deaf Studies
 School of Social, Historical, and
  Political Studies
 University of Wolverhampton
 Wolverhampton, United
  Kingdom

Elizabeth A. Winston
 Director and Consultant
 Teaching Interpreter Educators
  and Mentors (TIEM) Center
 Loveland, Colorado, United
  States

Xiao Xiaoyan
 Associate Professor
 English Department/Conference
  Interpreting Program
 Xiamen University
 Xiamen, China

SIGNED VIDEO SUMMARIES

Scan or click the QR code at the beginning of select chapters to view a signed video summary. These videos can also be accessed by visiting the Gallaudet University Press YouTube channel under the playlist for this title.

PREFACE

ACCESS IS IMPORTANT in all aspects of one's life. And I am reluctant to attempt to rationalize the importance of one milieu in which interpreting occurs over another. Rather, I would like to point out the unique characteristics of interpreting in legal settings. The threat of most legal interactions is loss—loss of freedom, loss of property, loss of justice, or loss of life—are all potential outcomes of many legal interactions. Unfortunately, legal systems are not designed for those who do not speak the dominant language. The language of legal systems and members of the legal profession is often foreign to even those who grew up with direct access to the dominant language. It is not easy to gain access to this language in our everyday lives. These factors intersect in such a way that linguistic minorities are severely disadvantaged in legal events. Training for interpreters to provide access to legal settings, therefore, is paramount.

So, how can we teach interpreters to work effectively in legal encounters? Most interpreters and interpreting students learn about legal work through workshops and through trial and error. These workshops, which are extremely useful, rely on hands-on activities to hone a particular skill. The trial-and-error approach, which is far more detrimental to the process and all of the consumers, does not provide any checks and balances on the interpretation provided. To date, there has been no publication that provides a collection of work that focuses on best practices for teaching how to interpret in legal settings.

This collection focuses on issues and considerations of any person training others to interpret in a legal setting. It represents the work of scholars, practitioners, and deaf and nondeaf persons from the United Kingdom, Canada, and the United States. Provided here are the perspectives of different authors who are diversely located, both geographically and professionally, within the field of legal interpreting. It is intended for interpreter educators who teach future legal interpreters. It includes research-driven, experience-driven, and theoretical discussions on how to teach and assess legal interpreting. The topics covered in this volume include teaming in a courtroom, presenting to future legal interpreters, discourses used by deaf lawyers, designing assessment tools for legal settings, working with deaf jurors, working with police in Europe, training legal interpreters using role-space, interpreters as expert witnesses, and working as a monitor interpreter. The authors provide ways of teaching interpreting that are based in research, situated within lived experiences, and are theoretical in nature. The contributors are recognized leaders in the field of interpreting, interpreter training, and research. And when the collection is taken as a whole, a picture is provided of the current state of legal interpreting. Each contribution ends with a set of reflective questions and/or exercises for readers to use within their own practice of teaching. While not every issue facing legal interpreters is addressed in this volume, it does provide a discussion of some of the key topics.

THE CONTRIBUTIONS

The papers collected here fall into three broad categories: applied, best practices, and research. Produced from scholars and practitioners from the United States, Canada, and the United Kingdom, these contributions address the relevant issues still facing those wishing to train legal interpreters.

Applied

Jeremy L. Brunson and Gino S. Gouby begin the volume with a discussion of how educators can expose would-be interpreters to legal interpreting. Rather than focusing on the "how-to" of the work, they draw on the literature to explore the various issues that are relevant in this type of work. Touching on topics such as deaf interpreters (DIs), accuracy, role, trust, and assessment, to name a few, they also lay out some of the gaps in the current literature.

Being monitored is a critical part of legal interpreting. And in her chapter, Risa Shaw explains not only the importance of this role but also how it can be done successfully. She points out how the success of the interpretation requires a skilled monitor interpreter and collaboration among the attorneys, clients, and interpreters. The interpreter performing monitoring duties must be trained and adept at analyzing interpretations, describing their analysis, and discussing the potential implications of errors they detect in the proceedings' interpretation.

The authors of the next chapter, Christopher Tester and Natalie Atlas, discuss a framework for constructing successful arguments to maximize the potential for successful outcomes in any instance when an interpreter must advocate for whatever it is that will make the proceeding more effective for all stakeholders. The logic and language used by attorneys, specifically the IRAC (Issue, Rule, Application, Conclusion) approach, will frame the presentation of information and enable practitioners to recognize their own knowledge gaps. Along with the framework and research, the authors include examples of different ways to approach utilizing IRAC in order to provide interpreters with some language to "try on" so that they might gain the necessary confidence to address the court with a request and have it granted.

Best Practices

Carla M. Mathers's contribution posits the function and implication of the interpreter as an expert witness. A series of legal events that involved the Registry of Interpreters for the Deaf's (RID) then-Acting Executive Director Anna Witter-Merithew culminated in a letter from the National Association of the Deaf demanding that no staff or board member of the RID be allowed to provide expert testimony. The author does not opine on the merits or practicality of that directive; rather she discusses the Federal Rules of Civil Procedure that govern the use, payment, and requirements for expert witnesses in civil matters. Mathers also explores the logistics of expert witness work, including hiring, payment, report writing, subpoenas, disclosure obligations, and challenges faced by experts within the so-called soft sciences. Further explanation is provided about a far more common experience that legal interpreters have—being subpoenaed to testify regarding prior interpreting work. Mathers's goal is to assist interpreters, interpreting students, and educators in understanding the contours of the interpreter taking the stand to testify in a legal matter.

To date, little thought has been given to the fact that perhaps the innate skills of the bilingual interpreter are not enough to guarantee a viable pass rate among practitioners on assessment tools. In contrast to other professional fields, for example, nursing, medicine, accounting, or the law, the professional in this setting was expected to demonstrate abilities in ancillary aspects of the work they would be performing, in most cases as a requisite to even the administration of the exam. Therefore, Scott Robert Loos focuses on the assessment of interpreters. He poses a valid question, "How do we assess cultural literacy?" The concept of testing cultural literacy and the proper mastery of linguistic concepts in order to perform as a liaison in an intense and high-level forum has been neglected over the past 40 years, and even today is still being overlooked. Here, the author posits a more formalized curriculum to be required for professional admission into the field of interpreting, considering the challenges of the forum in which the individual must perform.

Research

Christopher Stone and Gene Mirus begin the section on research by exploring data from interviews with deaf lawyers and identifying the invisible work that deaf lawyers engage in when wishing to discuss the law with fellow experts. By better understanding how deaf American Sign Language (ASL) users with legal knowledge engage in legal discourse, then we are better able to understand how interpreters can craft an interpretation that suits the needs of deaf ASL users in general, and in so doing provide access to justice.

In the United States, it is illegal to prevent a person from serving as a juror based solely on their deafness. It is seen as a violation of the Americans With Disabilities Act. But little is known about how interpreters work in this setting. The collaboration between Jemina Napier and her collegueas has yielded insight into court judges and deaf people who serve on juries in the United States (Hale et al., 2017; Spencer et al., 2017) and deaf jury participation in jury deliberations in mock trials (Hale et al., 2014). These interdisciplinary studies conducted by sign language and spoken language interpreter researchers with legal scholars have also produced interdisciplinary curricula development. The authors provide evidence-based best practices in the training of legal interpreters to work with deaf jurors.

Jérôme Devaux and Robert G. Lee draw upon both empirical studies (e.g., Devaux, 2017) and theoretical approaches (e.g., Llewellyn-Jones & Lee, 2014) to outline the necessary components that aspiring legal interpreters need to be taught. They successfully argue that an awareness of these paralinguistic factors and being able to understand and articulate how the role-space is enacted by interpreters are key to successful interpreting.

In the following chapter, LeWana Clark reports in part from a larger study on nondeaf court interpreters that took place in 2017. A collective case study bounded by speaker identification was used to explore the relationship between two teaming models (the Rotate Model and Remain Model) and the type of discourse (monologic and dialogic). Only the presence, or absence, of the speaker identification marker was analyzed, not the interpreted content of the utterance. The author focuses solely on the dialogic/two-way discourse of a trial as the English-speaking witness testifies. The United States' Constitution provides the right for defendants to confront witnesses against them. This study questions the effects of long-held courtroom teaming practices such as the Rotate Model. This topic requires critical consideration for court interpreters because a larger question remains: If the interpretation from spoken

English into ASL lacks an unambiguous speaker identification marker for each turn-at-talk, is the deaf defendant's Sixth Amendment Constitutional right to confront witnesses compromised?

The next chapter is by Jemina Napier and colleagues who have been involved with a long-term project, *Justisigns*. The *Justisigns* project was an action research project funded by the European Commission Lifelong Learning program, and conducted by a consortium of hearing and deaf researchers across Europe who brought their own experiences as users and practitioners (Leeson et al., 2017). It represents a groundbreaking initiative that focused on providing qualified and qualifying sign language interpreters' new competencies in interpreting within police settings. The remit of the project was to develop training courses to be made available to sign language interpreters, legal professionals, and deaf sign language users in Ireland, Belgium, Switzerland, and the United Kingdom. In this chapter, the authors provide an overview of some of the key themes that emerged from the data, with respect to the barriers faced in providing access to justice, and will describe the development of three key training courses: (1) a professional development workshop for deaf interpreters (DIs); (2) a masterclass for deaf people, interpreters, and police officers together; and (3) a curriculum for credit-based courses for police officers and interpreters.

Debra Russell concludes this volume with an approach to providing sign language interpreters with the foundational skills necessary for legal discourse and courtroom experiences. Partnering with the professional association representing sign language interpreters, the Association of Sign Language Interpreters of Alberta (ASLIA), Russell recognized the need to enhance the capacity of interpreters to work in courts in Canada. They designed and delivered two major learning programs, and then the model was replicated with spoken language interpreters.

The contributions were chosen because of the nuanced ways in which they deal with pressing topics in the field of interpreting: power, privilege, and oppression. Each contribution in this volume can be understood as an interrogation of the various ways in which power, privilege, and oppression manifest within legal interpreting, and therefore must be contemplated in the training of legal interpreters. These contributions show how we are dealing with audism while interpreting for jurors and attorneys. They also show how we are participating in power when we are gatekeeping in interpreter education, or how our testimony as expert witnesses is an exercise of one's own power and privilege. And that using community building to develop training *with* rather than *for* interpreters is a way to combat power dynamics. Upon reading this volume, we are encouraged to step outside ourselves to see the taken-for-granted practices that are not universal when we attempt to develop an assessment that includes cultural sensitivity.

This collection is the first step in working through not only what the curricula for training legal interpreters are, but also provides insight into what legal interpreting scholars, practitioners, and consumers find the most relevant for legal interpreters to understand.

REFERENCES

Devaux, J. (2017). *Technologies in interpreter-mediated criminal court hearings: An Actor-Network Theory account of the interpreter's perception of her role-space* [Unpublished doctoral thesis]. University of Salford.

Hale, S., San Roque, M., Spencer, D., & Napier, J. (2017). Deaf citizens as jurors in Australian courts: Participating via professional interpreters. *International Journal of Speech, Language & the Law, 24*(2), 151–176. https://doi.org/10.1558/ijsll.32896

Leeson, L., Napier, J., Skinner, R., Lynch, T., Venturi, L. & Sheikh, H. (2017). Conducting research with deaf sign language users. In J. McKinley & H. Rose (Eds.), *Doing research in applied linguistics: Realities, dilemmas, and solutions* (pp. 134–145). Routledge.

Llewellyn-Jones, P., & Lee, R. G. (2014). *Redefining the role of the community interpreter: The concept of role-space.* SLI Press.

Spencer, D., San Roque, M., Hale, S., & Napier, J. (2017). The High Court considers participation of deaf people in jury duty. *Law Society Journal, 33,* 80–81.

Part One

Applied

1 WHAT IS LEGAL INTERPRETING? INTRODUCING IPP STUDENTS TO THE PRACTICE

Jeremy L. Brunson and Gino S. Gouby

EDITOR'S INTRODUCTION

> *Interpreting students are often eager to learn about legal interpreting. They want to know what's involved. They are curious about situations they may get to interpret and how to handle them. The conundrum that we as teachers and trainers are facing is that students are not ready to practice legal interpreting, let alone step into a courtroom. So how do we introduce them to legal interpreting, provide them with enough information so they can understand what's involved, and still dissuade them from attempting to enter the realm of legal interpreting too early? In their review of the literature on legal interpreting, Brunson and Gouby provide an outline for presenting information to interpreting students. Touching on topics such as deaf interpreters (DIs), defining legal interpreting, legalese, and several other relevant topics, Brunson and Gouby tackle this difficult subject.*

INTERPRETER PREPARATION PROGRAM (IPP) instructors often ask those of us who work providing legal interpreting to give talks and training to other individuals who would like to work in that arena one day. For some of us, this request fills us with unease. On the one hand, we remember sitting around with colleagues and having feverish discussions about why IPP students should not be talked to about legal work. "They aren't going to do it for many years." "This

---

Note. The order of the authors is alphabetical. Both authors contributed equally to the production of this essay.

time can be spent focusing on foundational interpreting skills." "They should focus on those areas they will interpret: educational, medical, vocational rehabilitation." "They are going to think they can do it." "Any discussion about legal interpreting for IPP students should aim to scare them into never ever doing this kind of work." All are comments we have either said or heard and typically agreed with over the years. However, we also remember how we wanted to learn about legal interpreting when we were training as an interpreter. We often wondered how it was different from other types of interpreting work. We remember thinking that it would be interesting to do even if we knew we didn't want to do it immediately.

What is our job, as experienced practitioners, educators, scholars, and future colleagues, if not to share what we have learned? So, rather than attempting to scare the students or reminding them that they are nowhere near ready to take on this kind of work, some of us have decided to share what it is we know and let them decide when they are ready to enter this area of interpreting. The authors have taken this approach. We have decided to empower them to make informed decisions.

As part of our discussions here with educators of would-be legal interpreters, we aim to encourage a dialogue on systematic analysis. Like the sociology of interpreting adopted by Brunson (2011), we discuss issues beyond the language work. Focusing on which sign expresses which word provides an incomplete picture of the work required to interpret. A systemic analysis requires that we begin to see, and teach others to see, our work is embedded in larger apparatuses (for further discussion, see Stone & Brunson, 2020). During our analysis, we hope to unpack the challenges and differences in legal interpreting. Access to various resources will aid in our ability to do our jobs and identify who is necessary and who is not (e.g., DIs, teams). Of course, we also want to explore how we, as practitioners, can perpetuate certain practices or challenge them.

In doing this, we have taken as our task to provide students with the findings of various studies. Our respective presentations have changed slightly over the years as more studies have been published. We have found this approach useful in that students get to see what legal interpreting is, discuss interesting anecdotes, and see where the gaps are in the literature. What we present here is an overview of our presentations to students. These are presentations that we have given independently of each other. However, over the years we have spoken about legal interpreting, attended each other's presentations, and find that many of the topics we discuss are similar.

WHAT DO WE CALL LEGAL?

We typically start our presentations with a question: "How well do you know the legal system in your country?" To this, we usually get, "I have had a speeding ticket." Or "I went through a divorce." We then follow up with a question about the characteristics of our legal system. Of course, people mention rights, judges, and jails. This is a time to get a feel for how the students think about the legal system. It never fails; it is always more limited than what the legal system actually is.

In states where there is interpreter licensure in place, such as Arizona, attempting to discuss the broad range of events that could be legal can be complicated. What we, as academics, educators, and practitioners, consider to be legal are not the same as those enshrined in statute. As we know, legal is far more than what occurs in the courtroom (see Bancroft et al., 2013; Benmaman, 1995; Hale, 1995; Marszalenko, 2014; Mathers, 2018; Pöchhacker, 1997; Walker & Shaw, 2011). However, in Arizona, where both of us have lived, "legal" is limited to court, attorney/client meetings, and police interactions (A.R.S. § 12-242). In this way, Arizona has done what most studies have done—limiting legal interpreting to a few moments in the legal process. Indeed, Monteoliva-Garcia (2018) found in her review of literature that most publications between 2008 and 2017 focused on courtroom interpreting.

Regardless of this limitation by state statute, educators should attempt to expand what it is that students may think of as legal. We use examples of contracts such as modern-day marriage. To be sure legal scholars still debate whether marriage is a status or a contract (Halley, 2010; Scott & Scott, 1998).

The myriad contract interactions and court-ordered evaluations are often left out of discussions of legal interpreting. But we think it is important to at least mention them to students during our presentations. We want them to begin to see how mundane events can be legal. Within a broader conceptualization of legal events something like an Individual Education Plan (IEP), in the United States, can be considered a legal contract (Brunson & Stone, 2021). Indeed, Campos (1998) suggests,

> Now law comes to us, whether we want it to or not. Legal modes of vocabulary and behavior pervade even the most quotidian social interactions; the work place, the school and even the home mimic the language of the law, and as a consequence replicate its conceptual schemes. (p. 5)

However, we warn students that we must not consider every part of human life to be legal just because the law interacts with it. This can be a challenge because the law intersects with nearly every part of our social, private, and professional lives.

What is typically missing are contracts (e.g., IEPs, marriages) and court-ordered counseling and evaluations. What makes these interpreted events legal, we argue in our presentations, is their proximity to the court. While the law permeates every part of our lives, for these events the influence of the law is far more tangible; that is, while interpreting in each of these events, the law dictates how the meeting is organized, who is present, what can be shared outside of the meeting and when, and the documents that must be kept as a record. Therefore, whereas typically these events do not occur in a courthouse and often do not have badged or judicial officers present, they are often considered legal by us and should be included in any lesson to would-be legal interpreters.

WHAT CAN WE LEARN FROM THE CURRENT LITERATURE?

The literature, from both sign language interpreting and spoken language interpreting, is filled with various issues that are relevant to legal interpreting. The topics that are discussed range from language-neutral issues such as legalese, rules of the courtroom, roles and responsibilities of interpreters, trust, and accuracy to language-specific issues such as interpreting for jurors, reasons for not doing legal interpreting, training, and DIs. We also discuss credentialing bodies that are of specific interest to the audience to whom we are presenting.

Legalese

Legalese, or the "register of English that is used by lawyers and judges specifically for legal proceedings" (Berk-Seligson, 2002, p. 16), is often too complicated for the untrained individual to comprehend. Butt (2001) suggests that legalese is unnecessarily complicated:

> Mysterious in form and expression, it is larded with law-Latin and Norman-French heavily dependent on the past, and unashamedly archaic. Antiquated words flourish—words such as *herein, therein, whereas*—words long lost to everyday language. A spurious sense of precision is conjured through liberal use of jargon and stilted formalism: *the said, aforesaid, the same, such* (used as an adjective). (p. 28)

Although Butt (2001) is talking about legal English, his point could apply to any country. Whether it is referred to as "legalese" or a formal register, the fact is that courts are linguistically inaccessible to many people who are not trained in the discourse. This occurs across the world. Given the "stilted" and "mysterious" forms of expression, it is no wonder that interpreters may find it difficult to (a) comprehend the language and (b) interpret that into another language that does not have a courtroom or legal discourse history.

People do not speak in their everyday lives as they do in legal encounters. However, even the language used in settings out of the court has legalese integration. Legal discourse is unique in that it is not intended to be understood by people outside the field of law. Napier and Spencer (2008) found in their experiment that although legal facts and concepts can be interpreted into Auslan, interpreters stated the "legalese" created difficulty for interpreting for a deaf juror.

Credentialing Bodies

In the United States, we have two credentialing bodies: the Board of Evaluators of Interpreters (BEI) and the Registry of Interpreters for the Deaf (RID). RID issues certifications for generalists and specialists through knowledge-based and skills-based assessments. The Certified Deaf Interpreter (CDI) certification, which has been criticized because some believe that it does not capture what DIs do (see Johnston, 2005), does not test for legal competency; however, many CDIs find themselves thrust into this arena immediately after passing their exam. The specialist certification for legal work is the Specialist Certificate—Legal (SC:L). In 2015, the RID suspended the SC:L exam, citing financial reasons (Roy et al., 2018). Before it was suspended the certification was awarded to deaf interpreters and nondeaf interpreters alike. This complicates issues for the courts as well. Trying to explain that DIs provide a unique addition to the interpreting work in legal settings is often challenged as they hold the same credential as nondeaf interpreters. Whether RID will reinstate the certification is yet to be seen. However, the conflating of deaf interpreters and nondeaf interpreters into a single certification system should be examined if we continue to argue for the unique skills brought to the work by DIs.

Rules of the Courtroom

Another unique characteristic of legal interpreting, specifically the work that occurs within a courtroom, is that it is rule governed (Fowler, 1995). Who can speak and when is predetermined by the culture and formality of the courtroom. In the United States, for example, the prosecution presents its case first in criminal cases. In a civil case, the burden of proof is on the plaintiff, and therefore they get to present their case first. In most cases, particularly criminal, where one is represented by counsel, they are unable to address the court directly. All noncourt officers must speak only through their legal representatives. Of course, there are exceptions to this rule, but only those familiar with the setting and its rules will know this. Most people who have business before the court will not know these rules.

Discussing these rules with students allows them to begin to see the distinction between this type of work and others. It also shows the students how they are not prepared for this kind of work since they are not familiar enough with the rules used in the court.

Accuracy

Discussing an overview of the characteristics of court processes and legal interactions lay the foundation for students. But many are still far more interested in the interpreting aspects of this type of work. Therefore, we discuss the issue of accuracy. Students are hyperaware of issues of accuracy. They often have rigid ideas about accuracy versus errors. We try to reframe their understanding by examining how accuracy is discussed in the literature:

> To achieve accuracy of interpretation, the interpreted version must not only convey the "general idea" of the message, but also the speaker's intentions. It must be uttered in a way that would achieve the same reaction in the Target Language (TL) listener as it would in the Source Language (SL) listener. (Hale, 1995, p. 202)

Furthermore, "accurate interpretation does not equate with literalness, and that linguistic omissions and additions are often required to ensure accuracy" (p. 211). The court sees accuracy differently from how interpreters see it. The court wants to know that what was said or signed was then interpreted verbatim in the target language. Students must understand this expectation and how to address it with the court.

Roles and Responsibilities

Another issue that many students want to focus on is their role. What are the role expectations of interpreters in legal events? Students are coached to arrive early and interpret everything that is said and signed. They have discussed many of these expectations during their codes of professional conduct discussions. What they may not realize yet is that there are other expectations that will come to bear on them in all settings, including legal. For example, the court considers legal interpreters to be officers of the court (Mathers, 2006). This conception comes with a host of expectations. Those expectations include legal and ethical obligations to the functioning of the judicial system as a whole. Students need to be reminded that their obligation to effectively provide access is determined by these legal and ethical obligations and not by the tenets of a professional organization, such as RID or BEI.

As students are discussing codes of professional conduct and acceptable behavior, their notion of role is often discussed. These discussions in the literature point to the complicated nature of all of our work. In reporting on a panel during a legal training in New South Wales, Australia, Foley (2006) found that lawyers and interpreters see their role differently ". . . they made the explicit point that the existence of the interpreter-client relationship does *not [sic]* entail any 'duty' or preference to that 'client' in the sense that it does for lawyers" (p. 99). Lee (2009) similarly found that although legal professionals recognize the important work that interpreters do, they have differing opinions about the role of the interpreter. Fowler (1997) found that the magistrates want interpreters to fix communication breakdowns. Instructors need to be sure to inform would-be legal interpreters of this expectation, and teach them how they need to respond to these paradigms.

Deaf Interpreters

Any discussion of legal work must include a discussion of DIs. Students are often surprised when we say that there are few studies on the difference in products between deaf and nondeaf interpreters. There is literature that identifies some of the settings in which DIs work. Of the few studies out there, many are conducted by nondeaf people and are small in scale. Russell's (2017) study of deaf interpreter (DI)/hearing interpreter (HI) teams identified strategies these interpreters used while teaming. However, the size and methodology—qualitative versus quantitative—make it difficult to generalize her findings. Some of the studies that have explored the work of DIs come from graduate theses. For example, Ressler

(1999) compared the work of DIs and HIs and found that there is no significant difference between their respective products in conference interpreting. Sforza (2014) found that deaf-deaf teams rely on their peripheral vision when working together. In another study, Ramsey (2015) found that the difference between the products of those interpreting the Miranda warnings could be explained, not by audiology, but longevity in the field. Perhaps larger studies would have similar findings. However, the other issue might be that we are asking the wrong questions about the work of DIs.

Typically, what we know is from anecdotal evidence of the inclusion of DIs, especially in the legal arena, which suggests that they play an important role in the interpretation process. Various writings (see Boudreault, 2005; Burns, 1999; Egnatovitch, 1999) have discussed examples of DI work that have been done in the past. However, the challenge remains—what is it that a DI does? Forestal (2005) wonders, "What do deaf interpreting processes entail?" and "Are deaf interpreters interpreting from ASL to ASL? What should that be called? Can that be considered as 'more' ASL?" (p. 255). She suggests that these, and several other questions, should be the focus of future research into the Deaf Interpreting profession. In his study of "in-vision"[1] interpreters, Stone (2009) found that DIs went about producing their translation/interpretation differently than did HIs. And his study documents the different prosodic markers used by DIs and HIs. However, he doesn't explore whether that different product is better or worse (see Brunson, 2011). Perhaps Stone is onto something. Rather than examining the product, perhaps our focus should be on process. What we do know is that these gaps in the literature about the work of DIs can make it difficult to justify to a court that they need to provide a DI. What we can talk about is the settings in which DIs are employed (e.g., medical, legal, educational, conference), with whom they are called on to work (e.g., children, foreign born, those who have experienced linguistic deprivation), and what that might mean for a particular legal case.

---

1. In the United States, we refer to this as "television interpreting."

Training

We then focus on studies that lay out why people are not doing this kind of work. For example, Roberson et al. (2011) found in their survey of 1,995 interpreters that the interpreters were unwilling to take on this type of work for different reasons. The largest group (*n* = 1,353) stated that they did not have legal training. We use this information to emphasize how experienced interpreters see the need for training. Walker and Shaw (2011) found that interpreters gave a similar reason for not taking on legal interpreting—they didn't feel they were prepared.

As part of our discussions of the rationale for not doing this type of work, we provide some reasons why it might be difficult to get the necessary training. The opportunity for hands-on training or even observations is limited. Not because there is not enough work. Rather, because the events are often short. Matters in court, if they proceed, are very short. An actual hearing, at least in the United States, can last less than 3 minutes. Other events, such as trials, can take much longer, but the likelihood that those events will be continued or vacated is rather low. Therefore, interpreters wishing to learn the craft of legal interpreting have very little opportunity to see actual interpreters doing this work. This is compounded when the language is a sign language. While we try to impress upon students that observing the courtroom with other cases is just as informative if not more informative than seeing an interpreter work, most students are not interested in that option.

The brief duration and sometimes infrequent occurrence of matters with a sign language interpreter is not the only barrier to learning and becoming comfortable with legal interpreting. There is also the issue of difficulties related to gaining access for research in a legal setting. This, of course, is not impossible. Scholars have produced studies that required access to legal settings (Berk-Seligson, 2002; Brunson, 2008; Leo, 1992, 1994, 1995; Moston et al., 1992). It is possible but difficult to do.

We conclude our chapter with a list of the issues that still remain unanswered:

1. Efficacy of DIs.
2. Use of notes for sign language interpreters.
3. How is access defined by legal professionals and the courts?
4. What are the minimum qualifications for this kind of work?
5. What is the role of credentialing bodies in maintaining ambiguity vis-à-vis specialist certifications?
6. And of course, what should be defined as legal work?

QUESTIONS AND APPLICATION

1. How is legal interpreting different from other types of interpreting we have discussed?
2. What steps will you take to be competent to begin legal interpreting?
3. The authors conclude with a list of several topics. Pick two of those and discuss why the authors might have included them in the list.

REFERENCES

Arizona Revised Statute 12-242. (Rev. 2000) *Arizona Interpreters for Deaf Persons*.

Bancroft, M., Bendana, L., Bruggeman, J., & Feuerle, L. (2013). Interpreting in the gray zone: Where community and legal interpreting intersect. *The International Journal for Translation & Interpreting, 5*(1), 94–113. https://doi.org/10.12807/ti.105201.2013.a05

Benmaman, V. (1995). Legal interpreting by any other name is still legal interpreting. In S. E. Carr, R. Roberts, A. Dufour, & D. Steyn (Eds.), *The critical link: Interpreters in the community* (pp. 179–190). John Benjamins.

Berk-Seligson, S. (2002). *The bilingual courtroom: Court interpretation in the judicial process*. The University of Chicago Press.

Boudreault, P. (2005). Deaf interpreters. *Benjamins Translation Library, 63*, 323. https://doi.org/10.1075/btl.63.17bou

Brunson, J. L. (2008). Your case will not be heard: Sign language interpreters as problematic accommodations in legal interactions. *Journal of*

Deaf Studies and Deaf Education, 13(1), 77–91. https:/doi.org/10.1093/deafed/enm032

Brunson, J. L. (2011). *Video relay service: Intricacies of sign language access.* Gallaudet University Press.

Brunson, J., & Stone, C. (2021). The sociological organization of K–12 educational interpreting by the individualized educational program. In E. A. Winston & S. B. Fitzmaurice (Eds.), *Advances in Educational Interpreting* (pp. 111–130). Gallaudet University Press.

Burns, T. (1999). Who needs a Deaf interpreter? I do! *RID Views, 16*(10), 7.

Butt, P. 2001. Legalese versus plain language. *Amicus Curiae*, (35), 28–32. https://doi.org/10.14296/ac.v2001i35.1332

Campos, P. F. (1998). *Jurismania: The madness of American law.* Oxford University Press.

Egnatovitch, R. (1999, November). Certified Deaf interpreters—WHY? *RID Views, 1*, 6.

Foley, T. (2006). Lawyers and legal interpreters: Different clients, different culture. *Interpreting, 8*(2), 97–104. https://doi.org/10.1075/intp.8.1.07fol

Forestal, E. (2005). The emerging professional: Deaf interpreters and their view and experiences on training. In M. Marschark, R. Peterson, & E. A. Winston (Eds.), *Sign language interpreting and interpreting education: Directions for research and practice* (pp. 235–258). Oxford University Press.

Fowler, Y. (1997). The courtroom interpreter: Paragon and intruder? In S. E. Carr, R. Roberts, A. DuFour, & D. Steyn (Eds.), *The critical link: Interpreters in the community* (pp. 191–200). John Benjamins.

Hale, S. (1995). The interpreter on trial: Pragmatics in court interpreting. In S. E. Carr, R. Roberts, A. Dufour, & D. Steyn (Eds.), *The critical link: Interpreters in the community* (pp. 201–214). John Benjamins.

Halley, J. (2010). Behind the law of marriage (I): From status/contract to the marriage system. *Unbound, 6*(1), 1–38. http://www.law.harvard.edu/faculty/jhalley/cv/1-behind_the_law_of_marriage.2.15.11.pdf

Johnston, E. (2005). Guest editorial: The field of certified deaf interpreting. *CIT News, 25*(2) 8–9. http://www.diinstitute.org/wp-content/uploads/2012/07/Johnston_CITNews.pdf

Lee, J. (2009). Conflicting views on court interpreting examined through surveys of legal professionals and court interpreters. *Interpreting, 11*(1), 35–56. https://doi.org/10.1075/intp.11.1.04lee

Leo, R. A. (1992). From coercion to deception: The changing nature of police interrogation in America. *Crime, Law and Social Change, 18,*

35–59. https://doi.org/10.1007/BF00230624

Leo, R. A. (1994). *Police interrogation in America: A study of violence, civility, and social change* [Unpublished doctoral dissertation]. University of California.

Leo, R. A. (1995). Trial and tribulations: Courts, ethnography, and the need for an evidentiary privilege for academic researchers. *American Sociologist, 26*, 113. https://doi.org/10.1007/BF02692013

Marszalenko, J. E. (2014). Three stages of interpreting in Japan's criminal process. *Language and Law/Linguagem e Direitto, 1*(1), 174–187.

Mathers, C. (2006). *Sign language interpreters in court: Understanding best practices.* AuthorHouse.

Mathers, C. (2018). Interpreting in legal contexts. In L. Roberson & S. Shaw (Eds.), *Sign language interpreting in the 21st century: An overview of the profession* (pp. 115–130). Gallaudet University Press.

Monteoliva-Garcia, E. (2018). Interpreting or other forms of language support? Experiences and decision-making among response and community police officers in Scotland. *Translation & Interpreting, 12*(1). https://doi.org/10.12807/ti.112201.2020.a03

Moston, S., Stephen, G. M., & Williamson, T. M. (1992). The effects of case characteristics on suspect behavior during police questioning. *British Journal of Criminology, 32*(1), 23–40. https://doi.org/10.1093/oxfordjournals.bjc.a048178

Napier, J., & Spencer, D. (2008). Guilty or not guilty? An inversitation of deaf jurors' access to court proceedings via sign language interpreting. In D. Russell & S. Hale (Eds.), *Interpreting in legal settings* (pp. 72–122). Gallaudet University Press.

Pöchhacker, F. (1997). "Is there anybody out there?" Community interpreting in Austria. In S. E. Carr, R. Roberts, A. Dufour, & D. Steyn (Eds.), *The critical link: Interpreters in the community* (pp. 215–226). John Benjamins.

Ramsey, C. (2015). *Discourse analyses of the Miranda warning* [Unpublished MA thesis]. Gallaudet University.

Ressler, C. (1999). A comparative analysis of a direct interpretation and an intermediary interpretation in American Sign Language. *Journal of Interpretation*, 71–102. http://www.interpnet.com/JIR/

Risler, A. (2007). A cognitive linguistic view of simultaneity in process signs in French Sign Language. In M. Vermeerbergen, L. Leeson, & O. Crasborn (Eds.), *Simultaneity in signed languages: Form and function* (pp. 73–101). John Benjamins.

Roberson, L., Russell, D., & Shaw, R. (2011). American sign language/English interpreting in legal settings: Current practices in North America. *Journal of Interpretation, 21*(1), article 6. http://digitalcommons.unf.edu/joi/vol21/iss1/6

Roy, C., Brunson, J. L., & Stone, C. (2018). *The academic foundations of interpreting studies: An introduction to its theories.* Gallaudet University Press.

Russell, D. (2017). Deaf/non-deaf interpreter teams: The complexity of professional practice. In C. Stone & L. Leeson (Eds.), *Interpreting and the politics of recognition* (pp. 138–158). Routledge.

Scott, E. S., & Scott, R. E. (1998). Marriage as relational contract. *Virginia Law Review, 84*(7), 1225–1334.

Sforza, S. (2014). DI(2) = Team interpreting. In R. Adam, C. Stone, S. D. Collins, & M. Metzger (Eds.), *Deaf interpreters at work: International insights* (pp. 19–28). Gallaudet University Press.

Stone, C. (2009). *Toward a Deaf translation norm.* Gallaudet University Press.

Stone, C., & Brunson, J. L. (2020). Sign language interpreting. In S. Laviosa & M. Gaonzalez-Davies (Eds.), *The Routledge handbook of translation and education* (pp. 367–384). Routledge.

Walker, J., & Shaw, S. (2011). Interpreter preparedness for specialized settings. *Journal of Interpretation, 21*(1). http://digitalcommons.unf.edu/joi

2 MONITORING INTERPRETATIONS: ANALYSIS, DISCRETION, AND COLLABORATION

Risa Shaw

EDITOR'S INTRODUCTION

Any interpreter who has worked in a courtroom knows that relying on another interpreter to monitor our work is ideal, though not always possible. What Shaw highlights here is the role and responsibilities of the monitor interpreter, what is required to effectively monitor, process and protocol for monitoring, a framework for error analysis, techniques for assessing errors and evaluating options, and recommendations for interpreters, interpreter educators, and attorneys. What is poignant in Shaw's discussion is the importance of collaboration—collaboration between the monitor and the other legal professionals. Furthermore, she makes a point to bring us back to the system in which we are working—the legal system and the importance of the "record" and that this information is applicable to any situation in which testimony is given.

EVERY INTERPRETER[1] in a legal setting, regardless of their role, is obligated by their professional ethics, their designation as an officer of the court, and their oath to make true and accurate interpretations. However, despite interpreters' best intentions and efforts, interpreting errors are inevitable—inherent in humans performing a cognitively demanding task intensively is the fact that they cannot do it at 100% accuracy and that they are not machines (Hale, 2004; Janzen & Shaffer, 2008; Morris, 1998). Qualified interpreters in any situ-

---

1. The term "interpreter" in this chapter refers to any interpreter, one who is deaf, hard of hearing, Coda, or not-deaf, and may apply to any language combination.

ation will note and remedy errors that they have made. This is no less true in legal situations. However, because of the nature of legal proceedings and what is at stake for the parties (e.g., liberty, custody of a child, liability, money), a monitor interpreter may be employed by the court, and/or by one or both of the parties to monitor the official court/proceedings interpreters. Monitoring is:

> A mechanism to help ensure the quality and accuracy of an interpretation. This is accomplished by analyzing an interpretation for accuracy and equivalency, noting discrepancies in the interpreted version (from the original message), and recommending ways in which to clarify or correct such inaccuracies. (Shaw, 2003)[2]

The legal system in the United States is an adversarial system. However, interpreters do not have to, and many would argue that they ethically cannot, operate from an adversarial position. An interpreter who works in legal settings[3] is an officer of the court, regardless of the interpreting role they play or whether they are publicly or privately retained (see González et al., 1991/2012, federal and state rules, and the federal and many state codes of conduct). As such, interpreters have more than one responsibility/role, and by virtue of their training they know which role attaches at any given time.[4] Regardless of who hires an interpreter for monitoring (prosecution, defense, or plaintiff's attorney, or the court), the monitor's responsibilities remain the same: to uphold the integrity of the judicial process by helping to ensure more accurate and effective interpretation.

---

2. Some of the information in this chapter comes from a small case study (participant observation—Patton, 2002; Reinharz & Davidson, 1992) in which I examined the experiences of attorneys and their deaf client in working with an interpreter who worked as a monitor interpreter with them. This study had approval from the Gallaudet University Institutional Review Board (IRB). I presented this study at Iron Sharpens Iron in Atlanta, GA, in 2003.

3. I would argue that the role of officer of the court and the obligation to follow the court code of conduct attaches in all legal settings regardless of whether the interpretation takes place in or out of court. See also Morris (1998).

4. An example of this is when an interpreter is monitoring and the proceedings interpreters fail to recognize a substantive error they have made. The monitor interpreter is obligated to bring the error to the attention of the parties/court regardless of whether the error is favorable or unfavorable to the party that hired the monitor.

Monitoring[5] is a critical role for interpreters to play because interpretation is by its nature such a complex and difficult task and because the stakes in legal settings are so high. The presence of a monitor interpreter should not be considered as a comment on the competence or ethics of the other interpreters involved. Rather, it is a way to manage the inevitable: Interpretation errors will be made and they must, if fairness and justice are to prevail, be recognized and corrected. Proceedings interpreters have the benefit of the presumption of regularity, that is, that they will perform accurately (see Federal Rules of Criminal Procedure 604). Monitoring functions as a "double check" to increase accuracy. It is never to undermine other interpreters.

Interpreters may be hired as interpreters for a legal case at different points in the process. Proceedings interpreters, no matter how qualified, competent, and well prepared for a case they may be, are nonetheless at a disadvantage because they usually have not been interpreting for either side of the specific case until they are called to interpret the proceedings. The preparation they undertake is crucial. However, this preparation is necessarily done in a condensed period of time, frequently without complete background and context, and also unfortunately, often only after sustained persistence by the interpreters simply to obtain the necessary information to make sense of a case as a whole. Their gestalt understanding of the case therefore will emerge as the work proceeds, even in the best-case scenario when they are well prepared and competent. Because of the pressure of interpretation, especially of simultaneous interpretation, proceedings interpreters may in the moment miss errors they have made (Hale, 2002, 2007; Russell, 2000, 2003), not from bad intent but merely because they lack a complete picture. Proceedings interpreters who have interpreted for either party prior to a proceeding

---

5. Monitoring should not be confused with team interpreting, about which relatively more research and writing have been done (see Cokely, 2003; Russell, 2000; Shaw, 1995). The role of the monitor interpreter is distinct in many respects. The monitor is closely following the process of the interpretation, but the monitor's goal is not primarily to help the proceedings interpreter correct their own work; it is to ensure an uncorrected error made by the proceedings interpreter(s) is corrected in some way regardless of whether the proceedings interpreter(s) realizes errors. (This difference may explain the discomfort some interpreters experience being monitored.)

are generally precluded from interpreting the proceeding. In contrast, the monitor typically has more background knowledge than the proceedings interpreters and is tasked specifically to watch for errors.

I have spoken with numerous interpreters who work as proceedings interpreters who are relieved when there is a qualified monitor interpreter working because they believe it helps them do their job more effectively and that if they do not recognize an error they make, there is another level of safety to catch it. This anecdotal evidence makes sense: An interpreter who is serious about their work and oath to interpret accurately will appreciate, not resent or resist, assistance in assuring accuracy.

Monitoring may be done by an interpreter who is hired specifically and solely for that function during a legal proceeding by the court or an attorney, or by an interpreter who is working with counsel and their client for the duration of a case. An interpreter may work with the attorney and client from the inception through completion of a case and perform the monitor function at mediation, arbitration, deposition, court hearings, and/or trial. The goal of all participants is that the nondominant language user(s) have access to full and accurate interpretation and, therefore, to the proceedings.

Monitoring is a vital role that can be taught. Still, it is not a role for everyone, nor does every interpreter currently have the skills needed to carry out this role. The judgment required to monitor evolves through practice and experience. The skill set required for an effective monitor interpreter can be thought of as an enhanced version of what a regular interpreter is doing in their self-monitoring. This leads to certain conclusions about who ought to consider themselves for a monitor role. The monitor role is appropriate for a seasoned interpreter who has had numerous years of experience honing their skills at monitoring their own and their teammates' work. This is not only about someone's skills as an interpreter per se. There are certain aspects of performing in any profession that evolve as a person practices it more, so it is to be expected that a person who has been interpreting, especially in the legal setting for a number of years, will have better facility with the monitoring task because of their hours of practice and their exposure to many different situations. This is what becoming a seasoned professional means. One can think about developing self-monitoring skills as preparation to step into roles such as the monitor later in one's career. In addition to the self-monitoring skills required of all interpreters, the monitor interpreter must be able to articulate what a particular error is and what the options for remedying it are. One must have the willingness to perform these tasks, and an adeptness and facility with the task that enables one to analyze and explain accurately, quickly, and effectively.

Monitoring interpretations ultimately benefits all parties in legal proceedings in the same way that fair proceedings ultimately benefit all parties (albeit in any given case, one party may benefit personally from an inaccurate interpretation). As an officer of the court, a monitor interpreter is obligated to note inaccuracies that occur regardless of whether they are "in favor" of the legal team with which the interpreter is working. In the adversarial context of legal settings, "Interpretation can be one non-adversarial aspect of litigation. All are served when the interpretation is accurate and of high quality. This is one common goal that all participants can share" (Shaw, 2003).

AUTHORITY SUPPORTING THE MONITOR FUNCTION

The practice of interpreters monitoring other interpreter's work has become more common over the years, in large part because participants in legal settings have become more aware of the presence and ill effects of inaccurate interpretation. There are no previous studies that focus specifically on monitoring interpretations. However, Russell (2000, 2003, 2005) interviewed nondeaf attorneys and judges, deaf witnesses, and interpreters who worked together in mock trials that she studied for her dissertation research. Russell's study provides us with invaluable information from the perspective of each of these participants about their views on the interpreting process and the experience of having worked with interpreters in a legal setting.

Authority supporting the use of monitor interpreters is found in various legal sources, including case law and law review articles. A 1953 case, *Lujan v. United States* notes a "counter interpreter" who was present at counsel table to make suggestions and corrections to the official interpretation. *People v. Mendes* also references a defense interpreter who challenged the official court interpreter's work. Both of these cases were affirmed on appeal for a variety of reasons, including in *Lujan v. United States*, because the "counter interpreter" had noticed only minor errors, and in *People v. Mendes*, because the court found the official and defense interpreters were generally in agreement; although the monitor interpreter corrected major errors, the fact that the errors were corrected obviated any prejudice to the defendant.

People v. Resendes held that the defense interpreter is party to privileged communications and the role is a potentially partisan one. Therefore, the defense interpreter should not be interpreting for other defendants or the court.

Chang and Araujo (1975) argue that there are three separate roles for interpreters to play in criminal proceedings and that one of the functions of the defense interpreter is to "serve to ensure the accuracy of the proceedings and witness interpreters" (p. 822). Chang and Araujo are quoted in several cases, including *People v. Aguilar* and *People v. Carreon*. *People v. Carreon* provides for a state constitutional right to a defense interpreter. *People v. Carreon* also finds that the defense interpreter's "presence may assist defense counsel in assuring that testimony is being accurately translated" (151 Cal. App. 3d at 851).

Reagan (1997) argues that attorneys hire interpreters as experts and that as such interpreters may provide evaluations, opinions, and advice to the attorney about matters related to interpreting issues. Specifically, she argues that the monitor function is an inherent part of the "counsel" interpreter's role and not an optional function.

LaVigne and Vernon (2003) state that even with a certified interpreter there will be errors, and the potential for lapses in accuracy must be remedied contemporaneously by continually monitoring the communication. They argue that a counsel table interpreter is the most efficient and effective way to ensure accuracy by performing the "important function of checking the interpretation and the communication process in general" (p. 921).

PRECONDITIONS FOR MONITORING

Monitoring interpretations does not happen in isolation. Its success depends on collaboration among all of the participants—attorneys, clients, judges, and interpreters. The monitor interpreter must be prepared to describe their role and function, including logistics and how they will carry out the work. This can be done by description and demonstration: describing what the monitor will be looking at and how they will analyze for accuracy, demonstrating how the monitor will take notes and use those notes, how they will signal the attorney for their immediate attention, and how they will inform the deaf client of errors that do not need to be corrected on the record. The monitor should also explain logistical considerations, including seating arrangements (e.g., the monitor must have full visual and auditory access to the proceeding and be in close proximity to the attorney to show the attorney written notes and/or speak with the attorney if immediate attention is needed, and have clear sightlines with the deaf client for private communication from others). This explanation should include describing what information the monitor interpreter may have that will aid the proceedings interpreters in their preparation and understanding in order to effectively interpret the proceeding. This information will usually be linguistic in nature and not case information. Proceedings interpreters should obtain case information directly from the attorneys and/or court. Although the monitor may know case information in their role as a monitor, it is usually not theirs to share. Therefore, the interpreter who has been working with counsel and their client should be knowledgeable and skilled in preparing with the proceedings interpreters in an appropriate and ethical manner.

In an ideal situation, the proceedings interpreters and a monitor interpreter would each be qualified for the role they accepted for the assignment. In addition, they would have a shared understanding of the task of interpreting.[6] The most important shared understanding is that errors are inevitable, even with appropriate preparation, and must be remedied.

Effective monitoring requires a certain way of conceptualizing interpreting and the specific roles of the various interpreters in a case and of what it means to be qualified and prepared for each of those roles. It takes soft and hard skills. It requires a collaborative approach, no ego attachment, inquisitiveness, willingness to be in a conversation about why one interpreted something a particular way, and nonattachment to being right, identification of an error, and willingness to consider whether it may have been an error or not. It takes the analytical skills to recognize errors and to assess what to do with that information. There are different kinds of preparation—getting enough information to determine whether one is an appropriate interpreter for the assignment, preparing oneself for the actual interpretation (information, with one's interpreter team), preparing the legal personnel and the deaf clients on how to work with the proceedings interpreters, the table interpreter, and the monitor function. Although interpreters are working in an adversarial setting, interpreting is nonadversarial. And interpreters need to foreground that their interpretation is accurate and not one that favors the person who hires them. All interpreters in legal settings ought to be able to view themselves as on the same team, working to make sure that the interpreting is accurate no matter whose interests the content may serve.

QUALIFICATIONS AND EXPERIENCES OF EFFECTIVE MONITORS

An interpreter must understand and be able to explain whether an error is a language error or an interpretation error. Their conceptualization must also include taking into consideration the context, which includes the people. So, for example, if a deaf person wants

---

6. Historically, the field of interpreting has conceptualized the task of interpreting in evolving ways. See Berk-Seligson (1990/2002), Mikkelson (2000, 2008), Morris (1998), Wadensjö (1998), Wilcox and Shaffer (2005).

signs in English word order with mouthing of the English words, then that must be the interpreter's linguistic goal. If the deaf person wants American Sign Language (ASL), then that is the linguistic goal. An interpreter must be able to meet the goal of the people they are working with. Their other vital skills include understanding the legal system and the specific case they are working on. They must possess interpersonal skills that allow them to obtain the case information for proper preparation and to stop the proceedings when necessary and explain the error (which means they have to understand when that is necessary). They must be skilled at both simultaneous and consecutive interpretation and be able to determine when one or the other, or a blended approach, is called for. They must be able to monitor their teammates' work (as the proceedings interpreter), and the proceedings interpreters have to work well together. If an interpreter's framework lacks any of these, there is likely to be tension between the proceedings interpreters and monitor when errors are made and subsequently dealt with.

The monitor interpreter must also work professionally and effectively with counsel and their client (or the court). Typically, a single interpreter is hired to monitor proceedings, and this is usually a hearing interpreter. However, when it is appropriate for the situation the hearing interpreter should insist on performing the work in a deaf/hearing team (Stewart et al., 2009). Attorneys generally prefer to minimize the number of people privy to their client's confidences and privileged communications when the monitoring falls under the umbrella of the role of counsel interpreter (interpreting for the attorney and their client, consulting and advising on interpretation issues, and helping to ensure accurate interpretation), so the necessity of a deaf/hearing team may require explanation.

Agreement among the interpreting team members about what constitutes an effective team, taking into consideration deaf and hearing interpreters and the number of interpreters, is necessary. All the interpreters would ideally understand their ethical duties, understand the legal system and jurisdiction in which they are working, understand what is required to prepare for the assignment, and carry out thorough preparation by obtaining the meetings and information they need and by educating and advising the legal personnel and deaf people involved in the case. Operating from this shared interpreting framework can allow for monitoring to happen as a regular part of the interpretation. All involved persons should expect that the proceedings interpreters will make errors and remedy them, and, during those times they might fail to recognize an error, the monitor interpreter should make note of the errors and remedy them in an appropriate manner.

PROTOCOL AND PROCESS

The proceedings interpreters and monitor interpreter should prepare anyone involved—judge, counsel, parties, witnesses—so that they understand that the most accurate and high quality of interpretation will occur when the proceedings interpreters and monitor interpreter are allowed to consult with one another prior to and during the proceedings to conduct the preparation they need to do together for effective interpretation. As previously stated, this is typically limited to sharing linguistic information. It also includes establishing protocol for when the monitor interpreter has identified errors that would be of use to the proceedings interpreters for clarity of their interpretation but do not rise to the level of requiring correction of the record. As a practical matter, not every judge or attorney will understand or agree to this arrangement. However, I have seen judges and attorneys allow for this, and once they experience the effectiveness and efficiency of it, they expect it in future cases. It is our ethical duty as interpreters to provide the most effective interpretations, and therefore it is our ethical duty to work with the legal personnel and deaf clients to help them understand on a practical level what that looks like. This can be accomplished through face-to-face meetings as well as through written/video correspondence. Interpreting conducted in this way provides one more level of information to the legal personnel so that they can make decisions in the best interest of the case and their clients (see Russell, 2002). If this practice is not allowed, then the interpreters make recommendations for how errors will be handled. All of this assumes a level of competence from all interpreters for the roles they have accepted in any given case.

CONSIDERATIONS FOR LESS-THAN-IDEAL CIRCUMSTANCES

I describe this "ideal case" from experience. It is not created out of whole cloth, and it is not impossible to achieve. It comes about when all interpreters are operating from a similar framework that includes the conceptualization of the task (Russell & Shaw, 2016) and strategies for carrying that out. In practice, it may not look the same in each case, but the goals remain the same: access to the legal system for the nondominant language user through accurate and ethical interpretation.

Unfortunately, and all too often, one or more of the hired interpreters may not be qualified for the role they accept. When this is the case for a proceedings interpreter, the monitor interpreter must inform the attorney or judge who hired them and make recommendations on how to move forward. Recommendations may include additional preparation meetings and materials, use of consecutive interpretation, adding deaf interpreters, replacing one or more of the interpreters, or postponing the proceedings. It is not up to the monitor interpreter to ensure that these changes will be made; however, it is up to the interpreter to advise and help make a record of interpreting issues.

In a deposition I worked where unqualified proceedings interpreters were hired, the attorneys stopped the proceedings, consulted with the deaf parties, monitor interpreter, opposing attorneys, and the proceedings interpreters. Ultimately, the attorneys and client decided to proceed with the deposition because their goal was not to use the transcripts for trial but to assess what damages should be dealt with. The opposing attorney agreed to accept all changes in the errata sheet that the attorney and their client made. One of the proceedings interpreters found a replacement interpreter, and the proceedings interpreters were asked to interpret in a consecutive manner, in an attempt to increase accuracy. However, they were not skilled in consecutive interpretation, and that instead created additional errors. The attorneys and client agreed that they would stop the deposition for content errors and correct the record contemporaneously and that the monitor would note all errors of grammar and tense and tone, which would be saved for the errata. Because of these decisions, the attorneys and their client spent two full days reviewing the transcripts, and they created 23 pages of errata. This is not a usual occurrence. The attorneys' attempt to save time cost more time than they had expected.

The deposition took nearly twice as long as the attorneys had planned, and in the end both sides agreed that they would not proceed with unqualified interpreters again because it was too time consuming and frustrating, especially for the deaf deponent. Even though they had "just wanted to get it over with," they said they would in the future postpone in order to retain qualified interpreters rather than muscling through and advise other attorneys and clients to do the same.

A different set of challenges are present when it is the monitor interpreter who is unqualified. The result of this may be that there is unfortunately no backup for the proceedings interpreter, which is no different than if there had been no monitor interpreter present, because if the monitor does not raise issue with any errors, then the monitor role is not actually being performed. However, when an unqualified monitor challenges the proceedings interpreters' work, the challenge must be addressed. Qualified proceedings interpreters are prepared to address challenges to their work in a professional manner. They consider and respond to the challenge. When an unqualified monitor repeatedly brings what they consider to be errors to the attention of attorneys and judges, it usually does not take long for the attorneys and judges to recognize a pattern of challenging the proceedings interpreters' work that is neither material or relevant. I have seen judges consult with the proceedings interpreters and consult with the attorneys on how to proceed once they determine that the monitor is not adding value to the interpretation. I have also frequently seen judges admonish monitor interpreters (and the attorneys with whom they are working) to stop wasting the court's time. I have even seen them tell the monitor that they will be excused from the courtroom if they bring forth something that does not have a bearing on the case again.

Open court cases allow us to observe interpreted proceedings, so sometimes we are not present in an interpreter role but simply as an observer to a proceeding. In such cases, we do not have an avenue to affect the work. However, we can advocate for more training and more accurate self-assessment. I have in several cases observed interpreters hired in the monitor role who may have been qualified for another interpreter assignment but were not for the ones I saw them in. This includes one table interpreter who chatted with the deaf person throughout the proceedings, chewed gum, laughed at points in the proceedings, and missed numerous errors that could have been corrected on the record. More commonly I see table interpreters whose goal seems to be to catch the proceedings interpreters making errors only that favor the client they are working with directly, or table interpreters who simply do not understand the function of the monitor role and/or do not have the training and skills to perform the function. Such work does not support the goal of having accurate, effective interpretation in the name of access for deaf parties, witnesses, or attorneys.

NUTS AND BOLTS OF WHAT AND HOW TO MONITOR

Since the job of the monitor is to recognize and remedy errors that the proceedings interpreters do not themselves recognize and/or remedy, the monitor must have the skills and abilities to do this. This is a skill set over and above that required for effective interpretation. All interpreters should have the skills to recognize when they have made errors, understand the possible impact of their errors, and know what their options are to correct them. However, the monitor interpreter must also have the judgment, which comes with training and experience,[7] to analyze with the accuracy and speed to monitor effectively.

---

7. See Dreyfus and Dreyfus (1986) for discussion of the mastery of skills.

Once a monitor interpreter has identified an error, this is the process that they should follow:

a. Determine the type of error (e.g., omission, addition, substitution, source language intrusion, anomaly, deception).[8] See below for descriptions and examples.

b. Assess the possible impact of the error (e.g., an inaccurate record, confusion by the deaf party, no one will know there is an error if left as is). Understanding the case is an essential factor in determining the impact of the error and whether an error is "substantive." We have used that word in the field without explication of how "substantive" is determined. I argue that materiality and relevance are key elements of determining the impact of an error and may be more useful than labeling an error substantive or not.

c. Consider options for dealing with the error (e.g., informing the deaf client at table, the attorney, the court, and/or the proceedings interpreters; making written notes; signing privately to the deaf client at table or publicly to the deaf client at table so the proceedings interpreters see it).

d. Determine the possible cause (e.g., slip of the tongue, fatigue, mode of interpretation, language use, lack of preparation) and possible repetition of the error (e.g., first time, repeated, may be consistent due to mode or language use or lack of preparation) may lead to which options the interpreter selects.

e. Implement an option(s) for remedying the error (e.g., one or more of the options listed in [c.] above), depending in part on where the attorney is located (e.g., at counsel's table, questioning a witness).

When I teach interpreters how to function as a monitor, we practice the steps listed above using a method of categorizing errors (also called miscues) listed below. I encourage interpreters to create a set of initials or symbols for each type of error, create a key of these shortcuts, and keep that key with their notes. In addition, we practice taking written notes on paper—some people take notes digitally now, though I do not recommend that in this circumstance—of

---

8. These categories have been modified based on the work of Cokely (1984), Napier (2003), and Taylor (1993). An error may fall into more than one of these categories.

the different types of errors while still watching the interpretation/ testimony. I recommend beginning the assignment with a pad of paper with pages that the monitor has already numbered and put the date on. Each time there is a break, end that section with the time and date, and begin the next section with the time and date when the proceedings begin again. Create a key with initials of the interpreters and anyone who will be speaking in order to identify the speakers and the interpreters. I encourage practicing how to watch language in use and write at the same time; this seems especially difficult for some people prior to practicing it.

FRAMEWORK FOR ERROR ANALYSIS: TYPES/CATEGORIES OF ERRORS

Below are examples of the categories of errors. As stated in footnote 8, errors may fall into more than one of these categories. ASL signs are represented in capital letters. L1 signifies the first lawyer; L2, the second lawyer; J, the judge; D, the deaf party; and I, the interpreter. As previously stated, this framework is based on Cokely (1984), Napier (2003), and Taylor (1993), and an error may fall into more than one category.

A. Omissions (information/meaning that was in the original is missing from the interpretation).

> L1: "Is it true that deaf people sometimes are very proficient in sign language and have trouble reading and writing the English language?"
>
> L2: Objection (no interpretation—this is an omission).
>
> J: Sustained.
>
> I: OBJECT. JUDGE SUPPORT, DROP QUESTION, ALL FINISH (it could be argued that this is also an addition or substitution or anomaly).

B. Additions (information/meaning that was not in the original is added in the interpretation).

> Example 1.
>
> Adding hesitations (or other affects) that are not in the original but are part

of the interpreter's processing.

Example 2.

D: "The car was blue I mean it was green."

I: "The car blue, I mean green and it was big."

There are many types of additions. Other additions may be when the interpreter reacts or adds their own opinion or attempts to repair an error but does so ineffectively thereby adding information/meaning that was not in the original.

C. Substitutions (information/meaning in the original is changed to other information/meaning in the interpretation).

L1: "You testified at the grand jury, right?"

D: "Yes. It was sometime last year."

L1: "Yes. February 15, 2001. Do you remember that testifying?"

I: (*interpretater asked if the witness remembered the date*).

D: "No" (*answered to not remembering the date*).

This interpretation error led to additional questioning about testifying at the grand jury.

There are many types of substitutions. Common errors in substituting include substituting the type of question asked, that is, substituting a wh-question with a yes/no question, changing the tense/when something happened, and changing the affect or tone.

D. Source language intrusions (the gloss of a word in one language is used in the other language when semantically they are different, however nuanced that difference may be). Underlined words indicate the source language intrusion in the examples below.

Example 1.

D: ME FEEL-LIKE MARRIED.

I: I <u>felt</u> like I was married.

This example was on a motion to recognize marital privilege[9] and could be argued that semantically "I felt like I was married" and "I considered myself married" to present different evidence.

Example 2.

D: DOCTOR, ME SEE DIFFERENT+++, 10 MONTHS.

I: "I had been <u>seeing</u> doctors for 10 months."

This example was in the context of providing testimony about getting improper diagnosis from two doctors and had the meaning of "I had been looking for the right doctor for 10 months."

E. Anomalies (the interpretation has information/meaning in it that cannot be accounted for).

Example 1.

I: ... And that's when I said: "Your Honor, I have been wrongfully arrested." *You mean, I have been fingerprinted?* (italicized language was not in the original and could not be accounted for) And—they said: "Yes, you better get a lawyer."

Example 2.

I: "Yes, yes. Nope."

The witness had said: "Yes, I asked for paper and a pen. The officers would not give it to me."

F. Deceptiveness (information/meaning that is linguistically sound and makes sense but is not what was said).

Example 1.

I: A description of the trauma to the head that was on the wrong area of the head.

Example 2.

I: Stating that they threw the drugs out the car window from the driver's side

---
9. This is an example of where legal relevance and materiality are at issue.

up and over the car (*when in fact how the drugs were thrown and from where they were thrown had not been stated yet, and these facts would be entered into evidence*).

ASSESSING IMPACT OF ERRORS, EVALUATING OPTIONS

Interpreters must be able to determine the possible impact of each error as they then consider how they will remedy it. The impact of an error that will create an inaccurate record affects those at the proceedings and can also affect work toward an appeal since the error would be memorialized in the transcript. The official record in a legal proceeding is of paramount importance. It is the basis for any appeal, and it establishes as a matter of law what happened in the proceeding. It is of vital importance to all parties, and the court, that the record be accurate. Therefore, any error that will create an inaccuracy in the record must be corrected on the record. Typically, when an error will create an inaccurate record, the error must be brought to the attention of the court, either directly from the proceedings interpreters to the judge or through counsel from the monitor interpreter. When there is a jury present, the interpreters or counsel will request to approach the bench and discuss the error outside of the hearing of the jurors.

Conversation with judges and attorneys prior to the start of a case about how they prefer to handle interpretation errors educates them that errors will occur and sets the stage for them to participate in how errors will be handled. The interpreters need to offer recommendations and state what they can and cannot do with errors. A judge who insisted that he be apprised of all errors, on or off the record, quickly changed his mind when he saw the type and scope of errors and how the interpreters could handle them without interrupting the court each time.

Whether the interpretation is on or off the record is often a determining factor in how the error will be corrected. The impact of an error that causes confusion or looks like a contradiction or would go unnoticed but is not creating a record has a narrower reach and a wider range of options for correction.

Whenever a deaf person is speaking and their discourse is creating a record, whether testimony or a conversation at the bench with the deaf person or whether a deaf lawyer is speaking in their role as counsel, all the interpreters (proceedings interpreters and the monitor interpreter) need to understand what is relevant and material. These are times when the record needs to be corrected.[10] The monitor interpreter must quickly assess if an error is material or relevant or simply is not what the deaf person said. Prior agreement with counsel will determine how the monitor interpreter informs the attorney when such an error occurs, and cues (e.g., one word whether spoken or written, such as "stop" or "now") for requiring immediate attention of counsel should be reserved for this type of error. The attorney may take a moment to consult with the monitor, or they may have already recognized that a possible error was made. It is the choice of the attorney as to how they will handle the error, with the knowledge that the interpreter is ethically bound, regardless of whether the error favors one side or the other, to ensure that the error is brought to the attention of the court/record. I have had to remind attorneys of my ethical duty, and each time counsel has then stopped the proceedings to deal with the error.

When the error will not create an inaccurate record, the monitor interpreter still has to determine the impact of the error and the need for immediacy of correction and relay this to the attorney and client so that they may decide if it will be handled quietly at table or if there is the need for a pause in the proceedings to consult about the error. Regardless of the impact or type of error, the monitor should make a note of the error in their own notes so that all errors are documented.

When the error is a "slip of the tongue" or grammatical or a one-time error, the monitor might inform the deaf client and the attorney via written notes, signing, whispering at the table, either signing privately to the deaf client at table or more publicly to the deaf cli-

---

10. If the proceedings interpreters are being videorecorded so that there is a record of the English-to-ASL interpretation, then all error corrections need to be made in the English-to-ASL interpretation as well. In addition, video recordings may be reviewed by the monitor for accuracy.

ent at table so the proceedings interpreters can see the error that is being corrected.

When the error is due to fatigue, mode of interpretation, language use, or lack of preparation, and repetition of that error is likely and/or ongoing, consultation with the attorney and deaf client needs to take place. A request for a recess, change in mode being used, change in interpreters for a specific portion of the proceedings, or additional preparation may be solutions. If the proceedings interpreters are not able to modify their work to lessen the errors (it may be quantity, frequency, and/or impact of errors), then a larger discussion may ensue. The monitor interpreter must be skilled and prepared to have that discussion, to offer solutions, and to discuss the impact that such errors continuing could have on the case and on the accuracy of the record.

After a deposition (or less frequently, on appeal), the monitor interpreter may be called to consult on review of the transcript and creation of the errata sheet. The notes the monitor made during the proceedings will be relied upon to do this. Sometimes, the attorneys will work from the monitor's notes and consult with the interpreter if they have questions about the notes without bringing the interpreter into a meeting. This can be done when the interpreter uses consistent words and symbols throughout their notes so that the interpreter, and the attorneys and their client(s), can all understand the timing, type, and import of the errors. The monitor's notes of the date and time, who was speaking when, and specific information about what was said and what the interpretation was, as well as what the import of the error was, will aid the attorneys and client in reviewing the transcript.

As mentioned earlier, I monitored a deposition that required two additional days of work with the attorneys and their deaf client on the errata. The deposition was long and riddled with errors, and we worked from the interpreter's notes to create the errata sheet for that deposition.

On a practical level, when working on the errata it is useful for the interpreter to have a dedicated copy to study and review, compare their notes against the transcript, note transcript page numbers on their notes for easy reference, and note on the transcript any errors found and notate why something is an error. This may happen in the presence of the attorneys and their client or prior to providing them with an assessment. If there is a meeting with the attorneys and their client, another interpreter will need to be hired to interpret that meeting because a monitor interpreter cannot perform another role simultaneously.

The monitor must inform the attorneys and their client what is necessary to change (the big picture, what is and isn't material or relevant), why should it be changed (taking into account both the client's and the interpreter's perspective), and whether or not the client was interpreted in a way that reflects what they actually said and how they would say what they said in another language. The attorneys and their client understand that the interpreter has information no one else has access to and they are relying on the monitor to provide them with this information.

In qualifying the proceedings interpreters, and sometimes also in preparing the attorneys and court to understand the role of a monitor, the monitor should have a sample voir dire in case the proceedings interpreters do not have one. The monitor should also be prepared with specific questions about errors and how the proceedings interpreters will handle them. The court and attorneys will often use that sample, verbatim, to voir dire the proceedings interpreters. Examples of counsel questions may include: "How will you handle errors in your interpretation?" "How will you handle a challenge to your interpretation if the monitor interpreter recognizes an error that you and your team do not recognize?" Responses such as "We have been interpreting for X years and we do not make errors," or "I have never had another interpreter challenge my work," provide room for further questioning and are red flags about the qualifications of the interpreters for work in a legal setting.

Monitor interpreters should always remind attorneys and their clients that the monitor is obligated to bring errors to the attention of the parties/court regardless of whose "favor" the error is in and regardless of who is paying the monitor. More than once, an attorney's immediate reaction to notification of an error that was favorable to their case was to discount it being brought to the attention of the court, yet a reminder that it was my ethical duty to do so alerted the attorney to ask to approach and invite me to inform the court of the error I had noted.

RECOMMENDATIONS[11]

Interpreters need focused training and skill development to be able to monitor effectively (AVLIC, 1994/2011; Hale, 2004; Mikkelson, 2014; Morris, 1998; Roberson et al., 2012; Stewart et al., 2009). In addition to training, attorneys and their deaf clients who have worked with monitor interpreters recommend that interpreters consider a number of factors that can make monitoring successful.

Recommendations for Interpreters

1. Demonstrate your trustworthiness and gain the trust of the deaf persons you work with.
2. Assess your qualifications and ability to do the interpretation. Know and respect your qualifications according to each specific assignment. If and when you find yourself in an assignment that is beyond your level of competency, remove and replace yourself. This is an ethical responsibility.
3. Consider and offer deaf-hearing teams of interpreters (AVLIC, 1994/2011; NCIEC, 2007; Russell & Shaw, 2016; Stewart et al., 2009).
4. Learn the skills needed for this specific function and continue to hone those skills.
5. Know and understand what the professional standards for interpreting are and abide by them. Incorporate monitoring as a standard practice by interpreters in legal proceedings.
6. Educate other interpreters about the function of monitoring.

---

11. This information is applicable to sign or spoken language interpreting, to deaf and nondeaf interpreters, to any situation in which testimony is given (arbitration, mediation, deposition, trial), and to any other situation in which the interpreters and/or parties deem monitoring to be necessary or appropriate to help achieve accurate interpretation.

7. Educate legal professionals in order to raise the standards in the field for both sign language and spoken language interpretation. Teach them, by example and providing information, about the acceptable standards and expectations.
8. Emphasize: (a) the importance of accuracy in the record; (b) how a record is created, and how it is used; (c) the dynamics of dispute resolution (knowing what to expect); and (d) collaborate with the deaf person(s) and attorney(s) to control the process and set the tone.
9. Understand the ethical standards that govern the attorney's work (most importantly, confidentiality and privilege), and the interplay between attorney ethical standards and interpreter ethical standards.

Recommendations for Interpreter Educators

1. Learn what the standards and practices are in the field.
2. Learn what skills needed, and who can teach them. Engage those educators.
3. Use education and training as a vehicle for changing the standards and the practices in the field.
    a. Teach interpreters who work in legal settings to understand the legal system and what their proper function in that system is, so that they do not overstep the bounds of their role as interpreters. In particular, interpreters need to understand the importance of the accuracy of the record, confidentiality, and attorney/client privileged communications.
    b. Teach interpreters how to interpret accurately, gain an understanding of the legal system and the jurisdictions in which they work, demonstrate respect for the participants' roles, understand and apply ethical standards, and help create equity in the interpreting standards that are expected in legal cases.

Recommendations for Attorneys

1. Do not settle for unqualified interpreters even when that means incurring additional cost and time.
2. Trust the deaf (non–English-speaking) client's assessment of the interpreter.
3. Know who your client is and what interpreting services will suit your client and the case.
4. Know that all interpreters are not created (or educated) equal. Learn what it means to be a qualified interpreter, seek them out, and hire them. Understand why interpreter consistency, familiarity, and preparation are important.
5. Encourage the use of deaf/hearing interpreting teams.
6. Learn how and when to use monitoring. Use monitor interpreters whenever testimony is interpreted (the interpretation is what creates the record).
7. Educate yourself about interpreting and interpreting issues interpreting in order to represent a non–English-speaking client well.
8. Expect the interpreter to provide guidance and consultation about interpreting issues.
9. Build and maintain a relationship with an interpreter with whom you can work well and who will be your regular interpreter for the case when possible. This will build client trust and rapport and will improve the quality of communication in your case, as the interpreter will not have to relearn people, facts, and issues. This will help minimize the number of people privy to your client's confidences and your privileged communications.
10. Educate yourself about interpretation at the outset of the representation—what the standards are, what the court has or should have available, and what your own needs and/or obligations are. Study literature on legal interpretation and use the information to explain to the court and/or the other side when interpretation issues arise (including use of attorney–client or monitoring interpreters in addition to official interpreters).
11. Understand the ethical standards that govern the interpreter's

work, and the interplay between attorney ethical standards and interpreter ethical standards.

CONCLUSION

A skilled monitor interpreter allows the attorney to focus on the job of representing the client without concern about the interpretation, protects the accuracy of the record, and ensures that the deaf client is receiving accurate information on what is being said in English and receiving effective interpretation services. Monitoring also provides a mechanism for real-time corrections—for example, whether the interpretation is creating a record or not, corrections to the record, corrections to the transcript (errata)—and helps to allay mistrust by opposing counsel and the court and, thus, can provide and create peace of mind for clients. Monitoring benefits all of the participants involved in the legal interaction. Interpreters should welcome monitoring of their work because effective monitoring can enhance the quality of the interpretation, thereby upholding the integrity of the legal process.

Effective monitoring requires skill, discretion, collaboration, judgment, and grace on the part of the monitor interpreter. The skills for this interpreting role can be learned and honed, though this role may not be for every interpreter. Advanced training, specific to this role, can produce a wider pool of qualified interpreters. This training includes working with effective monitor interpreters to gain the experience and develop the judgment required to perform the monitor functions. Integrating monitoring and standards for this role will elevate the standards of the interpreting field and provide greater access to deaf persons in legal settings.

QUESTIONS AND APPLICATION

1. What is the function of the monitor interpreter?
2. What is needed to effectively monitor interpretations?

3. What is the process and protocol for monitoring?
4. Discuss the function of the "record."
5. Why is accuracy important for the record? What are some ways that the record can be used by interpreters?
6. Discuss the similarities and differences between teaming and monitoring.
7. Discuss the framework for error analysis and the types or categories of errors.
8. What recommendations are provided for interpreters, interpreter educators, and attorneys?

REFERENCES

AVLIC. (1994/2011). *Interpreting legal discourse and working in legal settings: An AVLIC position paper. Association of Visual Language Interpreters of Canada.* http://www.avlic.ca/sites/default/files/docs/AVLIC-Interpreting_Legal_Discourse%26Working_in_Legal_Settings.pdf

Berk-Seligson, S. (1990/2002). *The bilingual courtroom: Court interpreters in the judicial process.* University of Chicago Press.

Chang, W., & Araujo, M. (1975). Interpreters for the defense: Due process for the non-English-speaking defendant. *California Law Review, 63,* 801–823.

Cokely, D. (1984). *Towards a sociolinguistic model of the interpreting process: Focus on ASL and English* [Unpublished dissertation]. Georgetown University.

Cokely, D. (2003). Interpreting in teams: A pilot study on requesting and offering support. *Journal of Interpretation* (pp. 49–93). RID Publications.

Dreyfus, S., & Dreyfus, H. (1986). *Mind over machine.* Free Press.

Fed. R. Crim.P. 604. https://www.law.cornell.edu/rules/fre/rule_604

González, R. D., Vásquez, V. F., & Mikkelson, H. (2012/1991). *Fundamentals of court interpretation: Theory, policy, and practice.* Carolina Academic Press.

Hale, S. (2002). How faithfully do court interpreters render the style of non-English speaking witness' testimonies? A data-based study of Spanish—English bilingual proceedings. *Discourse Studies, 4*(1), 25–47.

https://doi.org/10.1177/14614456020040010201
Hale, S. (2004). *Power and control in the courtroom: The discourse of court interpreting.* John Benjamins.
Hale, S. (2007). The challenges of court interpreting: Intricacies, responsibilities and ramifications. *Alternative Law Journal, 32*(4), 198–202. https://doi.org/10.1177/1037969X0703200402
Janzen, T., & Shaffer, B. (2008). Intersubjectivity in interpreted interactions: The interpreter's role in co-constructing meaning. In J. Zlatev, T. Rachine, C. Sinha, & E. Itkonen (Eds.), *The shared mind: Perspectives on intersubjectivity* (pp. 333–355). John Benjamins.
LaVigne, M., & Vernon, M. (2003). Interpreter isn't enough: Deafness, language, and due process. *Wisconsin Law Review, 5,* 843–935.
Lujan v. United States, 209 F.2d 190 [10th Cir. 1953].
Mikkelson, H. (2000). *Introduction to court interpreting.* St Jerome.
Mikkelson, H. (2008) Evolving views of the court interpreter's role: Between Scylla and Charybdis. In C. Valero-Garcés & A. Martin (Eds.), *Crossing borders in community interpreting: Definitions and dilemmas* (pp. 81–97). John Benjamins.
Mikkelson, H. (2014). *Introduction to court interpreting.* Routledge.
Morris, R. (1998). Justice in Jerusalem: Interpreting in Israeli legal proceedings. *Meta, 43*(1), 1–10. https://doi.org/10.7202/003669ar
Napier, J. (2003). A sociolinguistic analysis of the occurrence and types of omissions produced by Australian Sign Language-English interpreters. In M. Metzger, V. Dively, S. Collins, & R. Shaw (Eds.), *From topic boundaries to omission: New research on interpretation* (pp. 99–153). Gallaudet University Press.
NCIEC. (2007). *2007 National DI Survey.* NCIEC: National Consortium of Interpreter Education Centers. http://www.diinstitute.org/study-results-2/2007-national-di-survey/work-settings/
Patton, M. (2002). *Qualitative research and evaluation methods* (3rd ed.). Sage.
People v. Aguilar, 35 Cal. 3d 785 [Cal. S.Ct. 1984].
People v. Carreon, 151 Cal. App. 3d 559, 843 [Cal.App.1984].
People v. Mendes, 219 P.2d 1 [Cal. 1950].
People v. Resendes, 164 Cal. App. 3d 812 [Cal.App.1985].
Reagan, H. E. (1997). Considerations in litigating a civil case with non-English speaking clients. *American Jurisprudence Trials, 65,* 1.
Reinharz, S., & Davidman, L. (1992). *Feminist methods in social research.* Oxford University Press.
Roberson, L., Russell, D., & Shaw, R. (2012). A case for training signed language interpreters for legal specialization. *International Journal of*

preter Education, 4(2), 52–73.

Russell, D. (2000). *Interpreting in legal contexts: Simultaneous and consecutive interpreting* [Unpublished doctoral dissertation]. University of Calgary.

Russell, D. (2002). *Interpreting in legal contexts: Simultaneous and consecutive interpreting*. Linstok Press.

Russell, D. (2005). Consecutive interpreting. In T. Janzen (Ed.), *Topics in sign language interpreting* (pp. 135–164). John Benjamins.

Russell, D., & Shaw, R. (2016). Power and privilege: An exploration of decision-making of interpreters. *Journal of Interpretation, 25*(1), Article 7. https://digitalcommons.unf.edu/joi/vol25/iss1/7/

Shaw, R. (1995). A conversation: Written feedback notes while team interpreting. In E. Winston (Ed.), *The Proceedings from the Tenth National Convention of the Conference of Interpreter Trainers*. CIT.

Shaw, R. (2003). *Monitoring interpretations: Analysis, discretion and collaboration* [Paper presentation]. Conference of Legal Sign Language Interpreters, Atlanta, GA.

Stewart, K., Witter-Merrithew, A., & Cobb, M. (2009). *Best practices: American Sign Language and English interpretation within legal settings* [Working paper]. NCIEC: National Consortium of Interpreter Education Centers. http://www.interpretereducation.org/wp-content/uploads/2011/06/LegalBestPractices_NCIEC2009.pdf

Taylor, M. M. (1993). *Interpretation skills: English to American Sign Language*. Interpreting Consolidated.

Wadensjö, C. (1998). *Interpreting as interaction*. Addison-Wesley Longman.

Wilcox, S., & Shaffer, B. (2005). Toward a cognitive model of interpreting. In T. Janzen (Ed.), *Topics in sign language interpreting* (pp. 27–50). John Benjamins.

3 INCORPORATING THE LOGIC AND LANGUAGE OF ATTORNEYS INTO OUR SCOPE OF PRACTICE

Christopher Tester and Natalie Atlas

EDITOR'S INTRODUCTION

Interpreters deal in discourse. The goal of any interpreter is to understand what is being said and make it accessible to another person. Tester and Atlas reinforce this idea by exploring how it is that lawyers and judges make arguments in the courtroom. If we can include frameworks such as the Issue, Rule, Application/Analysis, and Conclusion (IRAC) in interpreter education, we are able to assist interpreters in this setting mentally prepare for their court assignments. It also provides a way for interpreters to situate information that will enable the recipient to follow along with the procedures easier.

A SEASONED AND WELL-TRAINED hearing legal interpreter sits in a courtroom waiting for their case to be called. They arrived early, read the case file, and met the Deaf defendant in the hallway for a communication check (after receiving permission from defendant's attorney). Because they would not be interpreting during this conversation, and in the interest of trust and transparency, the interpreter had a prepared list of talking points that they removed from their portfolio and offered to counsel. They then introduce themselves to the Deaf defendant and informed them about the intent of the chat, making sure to mention that it was in their best interest to say nothing related to the case. After about 5 minutes, the Deaf defendant and the interpreter agreed that they were able to understand each other.

Once the case was called, the interpreter took their place in the well and was sworn in. This brief process conferred upon them the mantle of officer of the court, with all its duties and responsibilities. Feeling calm, confident, and flexible, they interpreted the judge's litany followed by the first question from the judge to the defendant. It quickly became apparent to the interpreter that the defendant had become markedly emotional since the communication check. This impacted the defendant's signing to such a degree that the interpreter did not understand the defendant's response.

> Interpreter: "Your honor, the interpreter would request permission to interpret the question again as she did not fully understand the response."
>
> Judge: "Granted."

The second time, the interpreter still could not adequately understand the response and was therefore unable to adhere to the section of the interpreter's oath that demands accuracy. They knew they couldn't continue without a Deaf interpreter partner. Taking a deep breath, the interpreter reached into their metaphorical toolbox and pulled out the IRAC. They were going to need it.

ADDRESSING THE GAP

The opening scenario presents two issues; recognizing the need to work with a Deaf interpreter partner, and how to verbalize a request to the judge for a Deaf interpreter in an appropriate manner. This chapter will introduce some new research on Deaf interpreters, defining their role and function. It then will elaborate on IRAC as a tool that can be used both inside and outside the courtroom. IRAC is the acronym for Issue, Rule, Application/Analysis, and Conclusion, the four stages of a structured way to create and organize a legal analysis (CUNY School of Law, n.d.). It has been described as a "rational approach to thinking and problem solving.... a 'logical linear pattern' and 'an orderly and structured method of legal reasoning'" (Burton, 2016). Last, we offer some sample language and scenarios for practice.

For the purpose of the chapter, the major focus is on using IRAC to argue in court for a Deaf interpreter. However, it will also be shown throughout that IRAC can be a fundamental tool for both Deaf and hearing interpreters to make a clear and direct request based on facts and professional practice in virtually any setting. We begin by defining Deaf interpreters.

DEAF INTERPRETERS

A Deaf interpreter is an individual who is Deaf and is trained as a sign language interpreter. This is a growing sector in the sign language interpreting profession and in research (Adam et al., 2014; Boudreault, 2005; Forestal, 2005, 2014; Stone, 2009; Tester, 2018, 2021). Deaf interpreters and Deaf clients of interpreting services share a similar language, culture, and knowledge of the Deaf world (Adam et al., 2014; Forestal, 2005; Stone, 2009). They also share the experience of being Deaf and "navigating" the non-Deaf world (Howard, 2014; Tester, 2021).

Deaf interpreters may work between two languages (Boudreault, 2005; Stone, 2009) (interlingual interpreting) or within the same language, possibly between different discourse communities or communities who do not share a frame of reference (intralingual interpreting) (Boudreault, 2005; Tester, 2021). Furthermore, Deaf interpreters not only draw on language but also employ semiotic resources such as gestures, drawings, and props (Tester, 2021). An interpretation may incorporate a mixed-use of communicative strategies, utilizing both American Sign Language (ASL) and pictures or index cards to support the interpretation and ensure accuracy (Tester, 2021).

When qualified and trained Deaf interpreters are hired to work in the courtroom, the premise is that a Deaf interpreter will work with Deaf individuals who have language issues (Boudreault, 2005; Mathers, 2009; Tester, 2018, 2021; Tuck, 2010). These clients are Deaf people who have an ability to communicate to a limited extent but never fully acquired any language (ASL or English) due to numerous factors including but not limited to education (LaVigne & Vernon, 2003; Tester, 2018), regional variations of ASL, and country of origin (Mathers, 2009; Tester, 2018). This suggests that "a significant portion of the Deaf population is best served by the provision of a Deaf-hearing interpreting team accommodation" (Mathers, 2009, p. 6). In the United States, the practice of having Deaf interpreters work in the court system alongside hearing ASL interpreters is becoming a more widely accepted practice (Mathers & Witter-Merithew, 2014; Roberson et al., 2011; Stewart et al., 2009; Tester, 2018).

A recent trend has shifted away from the Deaf individual's language as the sole justification for a Deaf interpreter. The rationale is now expanding to include the Deaf individual's experience (or lack of experience) in navigating the court system, along with the emotional toll the court process extracts on a person (Tester, 2021). Deaf interpreters are also hired when there are complicated court cases involving multiple Deaf parties, or highly sensitive content (Tester, 2018). Some Deaf interpreters have argued that since they have had the direct experience of moving through the world without the ability to hear, they are in possession of different insights on navigating the court system which provides an additional benefit to the Deaf party (Tester, 2019).

In the courtroom, the Deaf and hearing interpreters work as a team, and at first glance it appears to be a relay process. The hearing interpreter listens to the source message in English, then interprets that message in some form of ASL to the Deaf interpreter who then works closely with the hearing interpreter to produce a context-rich and meaningful interpretation for the Deaf person (LaVigne & Vernon, 2003; Mathers, 2009; Tester, 2018, 2021; Wilcox, 1995). Furthermore, Mathers and Witter-Merrithew (2014) suggest that Deaf interpreters function as gatekeepers, ensuring that Deaf clients are comfortable and aware of the process and its ramifications, as well as having access to contextualized information.

This chapter is built around the example of a hearing interpreter working alone and making a request to the court to bring in a Deaf interpreter partner. However, research has shown that it is not necessarily the hearing interpreter who bears the burden of making that request. Sometimes the Deaf interpreter is already in place or requested by someone else (Tester, 2018).

In Tester's 2015 study, a hearing interpreter participant explained that in their city, a group of court specialized interpreters established their own criteria, which led to specific protocols for putting a Deaf-hearing interpreting team in place (Tester, 2018). For example, any Deaf witness testimony or proceedings involving Deaf children would trigger staffing with a Deaf-hearing team (Tester, 2018, 2019). These specialized interpreters initially automatically assigned Deaf-hearing teams for all arraignments, but this was found to be difficult to manage and not always successful. Currently, a hearing and Deaf interpreting team work together at arraignments, with the Deaf interpreter acting as a monitor of the process to see if a modification to communication is required. Together, the team decides whether this particular client should have a Deaf-hearing team for future appearances (Tester, 2018). These are examples of protocols some courts have put in place, though they vary by state and court system.

COMPETENCIES OF THE LEGAL INTERPRETER

Many interpreters are daunted by the prospect of asking the court for anything, and while hearing legal interpreters may effectively identify moments when it is necessary to advocate for a Deaf-hearing team, research indicates that they can let the moment pass without taking action (Tester, 2018). While the reasons for this can be ascribed to a variety of factors, including lack of confidence or hesitation to disrupt the process (Russell & Shaw, 2016; Tester, 2018), part of the problem can stem from a lack of facility with spoken English. Hearing interpreters often become tongue-tied as they attempt to effectively communicate the need for a Deaf interpreter, even though they know that appropriate staffing will allow for the most effective administration of justice. Furthermore, some may not even know how to explain the role of a Deaf interpreter. These necessary skills—being in full command of an understanding and ability to articulate what we do and what we need in order to be effective, is not limited to interpreters who can hear. Deaf interpreters need training as well in order to confidently make requests for anything that will make their work more successful. So, for both Deaf and hearing interpreters, IRAC can be an invaluable scaffold. Some of the exercises and resources at the end of this chapter are designed to be used toward developing these competencies.

All too often, interpreters who do not possess the necessary qualifications or training continue to work in the judicial system due to the court's lack of understanding of what effective interpreters actually do (Hale, 2006). Hale (2007) argues that "no amount of oath swearing can guarantee high quality interpreting from an interpreter who does not have the necessary competency" (p. 198). While the oath is a powerful tool for court interpreters, the interpretation will fail if the sworn practitioner is not competent. A crucial ingredient for the interpreter to begin to achieve competency is a thorough understanding of the court system and its language, along with being a competent bilingual (Hale, 2007; Mathers, 2009; Tester, 2018).

One obstacle to rendering accurately interpreted work is the court's often-flawed understanding of the role of interpreters (Hale, 2006, 2007; Jacobsen, 2012; Russell, 2005). Part of the problem can be attributed to some judges' and attorneys' expectation that the message will be interpreted "verbatim," without understanding the intent of "interpreting faithfully" (Hale, 2006, 2007). Interpreting "verbatim" comes from the court's long-held perception of the interpreter as coding machine, unaware that the interpreter is creating meaning-based interpretations. Contrary to the court's belief and desire for the interpreter to be "physically invisible and vocally silent," the court interpreter has an active verbal role. Furthermore, "the interpreter's verbal role is tied to the linguistic control of the legitimate participants in judicial proceedings" (Berk-Seligson, 1999, p. 54). This can conflict with the court's misguided desire for a monologic interpreting process when the judge speaks directly to any Deaf witness (Tester, 2021).

Due to the challenges described above, it is vital for the interpreter to develop legal analysis and reasoning skills. IRAC is a tool that court interpreters can utilize to develop and strengthen legal reasoning. Its application is not limited only to requesting a Deaf interpreter team; it can be applied when requesting permission to use specific materials such as drawings, pictures from the case file, or other communication aids that will improve the Deaf individual's ability to receive due process.

We would be remiss if we did not address power and privilege. In the courtroom, the interpreter has far more of both than any Deaf defendant. As Russell and Shaw observed in their 2016 study,

> The participants provided numerous examples demonstrating that when interpreters are aware of their own power and privilege ... they are able to choose to make professional decisions that may impact the power dynamics in interactions in appropriate and positive ways. Alternatively, interpreters may consciously or unconsciously misuse their professional and/or personal power. (p. 11)

Legal interpreters bear the responsibility of owning and exercising their power and privilege in the interest of effective communication and the administration of justice. Interpreters must develop personal awareness of power and privilege in all interactions, which allows them to have a stronger sense of agency (Russell & Shaw, 2016). Part of the legal interpreter's responsibility is to recognize, for example, that the Deaf individual cannot approach the bench and make a request. They have neither the power nor the privilege to do so. The interpreter is responsible for effective communication and must be able to observe, identify, and recommend appropriate modifications (Mathers, 2006; Stewart et al., 2009; Stewart, 2012). Unfortunately, there are still far too many legal interpreters who feel that they have "no say over what a court will or won't do" (Russell & Shaw, 2016, pp. 22–23). There are myriad factors that may impede effective communication in the courtroom, and the interpreter has a duty to address all such issues (See NCSC model code of professional responsibility as an example).

IRAC: AN INTRODUCTION

Much has been written about the logic used to create successful arguments in court. This chapter does not attempt to parse the plethora of strategies that are used by attorneys; there are just too many. Burton (2016) presented over 40 acronyms that are used in law schools to teach legal reasoning as a type of problem-solving (Burton, 2016, p. 2). To avoid drowning in alphabet soup, we focus on a single logical framework—IRAC (see Figure 1), which has been one of the primary frameworks for problem-based questions in law for the last 40 years (Burton, 2016), and has proven itself an invaluable tool when convincing the court to provide appropriate accommodations for a Deaf party (Atlas & Tester, 2016; Mathers, 2016).

IRAC is formulaic, and interpreters appreciate having a scaffold to work from to accomplish a goal. IRAC is a tool that aids learners in understanding and examining information and making an informed decision (Bittner, 1990). When applied in the law school setting, students utilize this template to develop legal reasoning in assessment tasks; IRAC has become a simple and structured tool for educational purposes (Burton, 2016, 2017; Neumann et al., 2017). Legal reasoning is defined as a "practice of identifying the legal rules and processes of relevance to a particular legal issue and applying those rules and processes . . . to generate an appropriate response to the

Issue	Rule	Application/ Analysis	Conclusion
Frame the legal issue in the factual problem. Can be constructed as a question.	Include definitions from statute and case law.	Make a linkage between the elements of the law and the factual problem.	Reach a convincing conclusion on all of the legal issues in the factual problem based on strong support from statute and case law.
		Identify additional facts required.	Be prepared to justify why alternative conclusions were not reached.

Figure 1. IRAC defined. (Adapted from Burton, 2017)

issue" (Kift et al., 2010, p. 18). Furthermore, when law students are evaluated on their analyses, they are graded on how well they can "identify genuine issues, determine the governing rules, state those rules accurately, and apply the rules to the facts" (Neumann et al., 2017, p. 124). Clearly, it is a tried and true method of legal reasoning. When employed by legal interpreters, IRAC becomes a means to develop legal reasoning and articulate an argument.

When he wrote, "throughout the law, planning is essential to success" (Neumann et al., 2017, p. 125), it is likely that Neumann did not have courtroom interpreters in mind. However, he was spot on when it comes to our profession. Interpreting in a courtroom can be high stress and high stakes. Many of the players are at cross purposes, and the ethics and principles that inform the interpreter's decisions differ radically from those for community interpreting. In order for legal interpreters to advocate successfully for reasonable accommodation, it is in the best interest of the process for us to not only learn the lingua franca of the courtroom but also to be able to construct an argument in a manner that is familiar to the audience. Legal reasoning is often described as thinking like a lawyer (Burton, 2016, p. 1). Learning how to think like a lawyer takes time, training, and practice. Fluency with documentation that will support your argument also requires preparedness; for example, knowing the pertinent laws of your state and carrying a copy with relevant sections highlighted. For a more thorough understanding of the expectations of competencies of a legal interpreter, read *Toward Effective Practice: Specialist Competencies of the Interpreter Practicing within Court and Legal Settings from NCIEC* (Stewart, 2012).

IRAC seems simple on its surface. The first thing we do is present the issue. Next, we present a rule that will support our request. Then we take the facts at hand and apply the rule, and wrap it up by requesting whatever is needed to resolve the issue. ". . . . (F)irst, articulate an important legal issue or question; next, state and explain the relevant legal rule; next, apply the rule to your facts; finally, conclude by explicitly answering the question or taking a position on the issue" (CUNY School of Law, n.d.). However, you will see that it takes practice to parse each element and gain facility in expressing them in a manner that is succinct, thorough, and readily understood by the court.

Returning to the opening example, after receiving permission to approach the bench, the interpreter stated the following, utilizing IRAC structure:

> Your honor, there is an interpreting issue here, as not all Deaf people are easy to understand by interpreters who can hear. This can be for a variety of reasons, none of which have anything to do with my interpreting competence. As you are probably aware, the law in NJ states that if an interpretation can benefit from the addition of an intermediary interpreter, then one must be provided. I am not able to understand this defendant well enough to render an accurate interpretation; therefore, I would ask that you adjourn this matter until correct staffing can be put in place.

This example should not be read as prescriptive. It has been included to illustrate how this interpreter approached the bench. The end result was that the judge ordered the matter adjourned until it could be staffed appropriately. It is worth noting that after going off the record, the judge called the interpreter back to the bench, thanked them for informing the court that communication was not successful, and speculated aloud with a measure of concern about how many times similar things have occurred in his court, which the judge would have no way of knowing if the interpreter didn't speak up.

IRAC Defined

Issue

The issue is the answer to the question "Why are we here?" which will most assuredly be at the forefront of the judge's and attorneys' minds as you stand at the bench. When presenting an argument using IRAC as scaffolding, it is necessary for the issue to be stated in a general fashion, and ideally for that statement to include the desired outcome so the court might be more inclined to accede to the request (Mathers, 2016).

In the scenario that opened this section, the issue is that for a variety of reasons, not all Deaf people are readily understood by all interpreters who can hear, and the question is whether the matter should be adjourned in order to locate a Deaf interpreter.

Rule

The rule is the authority you select to justify the need for a Deaf-hearing team. You can use case law, ethical codes, the oath, state or Federal Constitution, federal or state statutes, and even your cumulative experience if nothing else seems to fit.

As indicated above, your myriad choices include the Federal Constitution; for example, the sixth Amendment says a defendant has the right to confront and cross-examine witnesses against them. If there are any communication issues between the interpreter and the Deaf person, then the defendant cannot (1) confront, (2) cross-examine, or (3) assist counsel in their defense.

There are two ways that a rule can be perceived by the court: binding authority (e.g., statute or a precedential case) or persuasive authority (e.g., law review articles, hornbooks, "my over 35 years of experience . . ."). The strength of your argument depends on the strength of the rule (Burton, 2016, 2017; Mathers, 2016; Neumann et al., 2017). Critical thinking is necessary in order to determine which authority you will use to support your argument.

Familiarize yourself with your state's laws and policies regarding interpreters and interpreting in court. You will likely find strong authority there. For example, statutes in California, Michigan, Maine, and New Jersey put the onus of determining the need for a Deaf interpreter on the interpreter who can hear (Mathers, 2009; Tester, 2018). For a full discussion of individual state statutes and how they can be used to support an argument for a Deaf-hearing team, read Mathers (2009) *The Deaf Interpreter in Court: An Accommodation That Is More Than Reasonable*.

Keep copies of any pertinent statutes in your portfolio, along with a copy of the National Center for State Courts' (NCSC, 1995) Model Code of Professional Responsibility for Interpreters in the

Judiciary whose tenets offer justification for resolving numerous issues. If you are challenged, it can be helpful to have such documents readily available to show the court.

One solid "go to" justification for numerous issues is the interpreter's oath. This is another document you should have in your portfolio. Some courts do not remember to swear in the interpreter; having a copy of the oath to give to the clerk or bailiff or whoever is responsible for swearing in the interpreter allows you to ensure that you are sworn in without risking embarrassment to the court (a thing you do not ever want to do, a lesson one of the authors learned the hard way). Until we are sworn in, we are not officers of the court. The Federal Rules of Evidence explicitly state that interpreters must take an oath; therefore, once sworn in, the oath can be a strong rule (Mathers, 2016). The most important thing to keep in mind as you are constructing your argument is that you need to find the strongest rule that fits the issue.

Application/Analysis

Application (or Analysis) is taking the rule you have chosen and applying it to the current situation. This is the most important step of IRAC. Here, you develop the answer to the issue you raised. As you are building the argument in your mind, you will also be considering how to present it to the court, and one buzzword that works well as you tie it together is "Here" (Mathers, 2016), as in "Here we have a Deaf person who the interpreter understood prior to the start of proceedings, however, something unexpected has happened and she can no longer understand him well enough to abide by her oath."

Conclusion

The conclusion is where the facts, authority, and analysis that you have crafted come together and create a logical need for some kind of action on the part of the court. A helpful buzzword for the conclusion section is "Therefore" (Mathers, 2016), as in "Therefore this matter should be adjourned until proper staffing can be put in place."

Language Samples

Returning once again to the scenario at the beginning of this section, the trigger to utilize IRAC is that once the proceedings are underway, the interpreter realizes they do not understand the Deaf individual well enough to interpret accurately and is unable to uphold their oath. This could be framed in the following fashion: whether the court should provide a Deaf/hearing team for a person who is using nonstandard ASL (Atlas & Tester, 2016; Mathers, 2016). For more language samples, see the Questions and Application section at the end of the chapter.

CRITIQUE

IRAC has been criticized for being overly rigid (Turner, 2015). However, this criticism arises when examining IRAC as a tool for written legal analysis. These critics argue that IRAC can lead law students or lawyers to overwriting while making a complex legal analysis too simple. That may be true, but it rests outside the scope of this chapter. For our purposes, simplification is the desired outcome. As interpreters, not attorneys, an attempt at a complicated and nuanced analysis is outside our scope of practice. Therefore, this critique does not apply.

APPLICATION TO INTERPRETERS

At this point, you might feel a bit overwhelmed and may even be thinking, "I'm an interpreter, not a lawyer—and I have no desire to learn how to think or speak like one." However, once you begin to master this strategy, you will find it worth the time spent learning it.

Many of us are trained to educate our hearing clients about Deaf culture and other elements, which can contribute to a more effective communication environment. Unfortunately, much of what we are taught about our role as sometime educators does not transfer to the courtroom. The court does not care about Deaf culture, whether someone feels comfortable, and so on. The court is only concerned with facts and the reasoning utilizing those facts (Mathers, 2016). This does not mean that we never function as educators in court; explaining to the judge, for example, why interpreting verbatim is impossible. Still, that is a fact-based teaching. Attempting to convince the court to bring in a Deaf interpreter because it will potentially make the defendant feel less stressed by having another Deaf person in the room is not an argument that will carry any weight in this setting.

One of the most important elements in creating a strong argument using IRAC is preparation. It bears noting, however, that preparation is only one part of the equation; an interpreter, whether Deaf or hearing, must also be fast on their feet as they gauge whether the argument is working, and making adjustments if it is not. It also requires the ability to think quickly and critically (Stewart et al., 2009; Stewart, 2012) and move back and forth between the micro (the specific facts) and the macro (the overall goal). "Active preparation, not simply knowing the details of the assignment, but cognitively and strategically preparing for the linguistic and interactional features of the event and considering whether they are qualified to perform the expected task, can ensure the interpretation is as effective as possible in a given situation" (Russell & Shaw, 2016, p. 7). So, the 'micro' in this quote consists of "the details of the assignment" and the 'macro' encompasses "the linguistic and interactional features of the event" that includes the possible outcomes for the Deaf defendant whose life and liberty are at stake. It is also important for the interpreter to know when it is time to give up, preferably before inciting the ire of the judge (e.g., when the judge begins to look irritated, or you find yourself repeating the same points). Even if the argument is failing, it is crucial to continue all negotiations on the record. If there is a later challenge to the interpreter's request or the judge's decision, having a record of the negotiation will provide both clarification and protection.

Some food for thought and part of the "macro" piece of your preparation. If you are unable to persuade the judge of the need for a Deaf interpreter after exhausting every strategy you can think of, what do you do? (See the Questions and Application section for an anecdote about how one of the authors responded after failing to elicit agreement from the court.)

An important element to bear in mind when addressing the court is so obvious it can be easily overlooked. The judge and the attorneys are human beings who may be in a good mood or a bad mood. Maybe they got stuck in traffic that morning, maybe they are dealing with problems at home, and although none of this can be known by the interpreter as they approach the bench, it is crucial to remember how people normally interact.

When exercising our privilege in speaking to the court, remember to be sensitive to the human element. We interpreters can get so caught up in making sure our argument is strong and effective that the end result can sound robotic or like we're giving a lecture. Be aware of your facial expressions. As you approach the bench, you can easily project, just by using your face, "I wish we didn't have to have this conversation." Do not immediately launch into your argument. First, take the temperature of the players. Even a quiet "Good morning, your honor. How are you?" can make all the difference in the success or failure of your request. Be sensitive to ordinary human dynamics throughout your interchange. This is another lesson one of the authors learned the hard way when a judge filed a complaint about her with the state's Administrative Office of the Court. The complaint was not about the content of what the interpreter said; the way it was said was unacceptable to the judge. The judge's impression was that they were being lectured, which they did not appreciate.

Become facile with the elements of IRAC so you can present them with the appropriate tone. It would behoove you NOT to memorize the entirety of any of the language samples that are presented here, though there are certain key phrases that you may want to commit to memory. With practice, you will develop the confidence to speak naturally.

CONCLUSION

This chapter introduced and provided examples of how IRAC has become a useful tool in developing court sign language interpreters' legal analysis and reasoning. However, surveying educational materials and training to see when and where it is taught is outside the scope of this chapter. The authors believe, however, that IRAC should be part of any core curriculum for developing the interpreter's analysis and legal reasoning skills. It does not need to be limited to courtroom interpreters; it would benefit any practitioner to develop case analysis skills (Bittner, 1990). There are many possible situations wherein an interpreter might be called upon to justify a decision or request. IRAC has been suggested to be used to develop the interpreter's case study analysis skills and can be used to analyze media, social science subjects, and other areas (Bittner, 1990).

Anecdotally, Deaf interpreters often begin their interpreting careers within the legal setting, and very often in the courtroom. While it is expected that Deaf interpreters also complete legal training after Deaf interpreter training, in some regions this is not possible due to limited resources, availability of training, or a limited pool of qualified Deaf interpreters. Deaf interpreters face barriers in employment and having stronger language to articulate the issues, like the provision of interpreting services, is helpful. Furthermore, a part of the Deaf interpreter's competency is to match communication style (Boudreault, 2005; NCIEC Deaf Interpreter Work Team, 2010; Tester, 2019). Utilizing IRAC could become an additional resource to support articulating the need for the communication assessment that Deaf interpreters, as a part of their role, are expected to conduct. Yet the 2016 Deaf Interpreter Curriculum does not offer this specific type of training. The curriculum's focus is training Deaf individuals in becoming interpreters and does not include legal interpreting training.

Learning and teaching IRAC is one way to maximize the success of individual assignments, foster our profession, and enhance legal reasoning skills.

QUESTIONS AND APPLICATION

Modeling the Language: Exercises for Practice and Discussion

For each of the following samples, discuss whether you think they are effective or ineffective. If they are effective, or if parts are effective, talk about why. If parts are ineffective, how might they be phrased differently to improve them? Also note that our profession is shifting away from talking about standard ASL versus nonstandard ASL, or using terms such as "minimal language skills." While this discussion is outside the scope of this chapter, we urge you to be mindful of the way you describe an individual's use of language. The way we talk about our clients will directly impact how they are perceived by the court.

For Deaf interpreters, as you practice, remember to videotape yourself so you can go back and see the language you use. For hearing interpreters, speak out loud to see how your language hits the ear. You will also find value in recording yourself as you speak. While you practice, use different scenarios that trigger the need for a Deaf interpreter (one is offered at the end of this section). Take the scenarios through the IRAC process. The sample that this chapter is based on is only one of the countless issues that could possibly be resolved using this logic. You can also find many case studies on the Internet to use for practice as you develop your IRAC analysis skills. A simple google search using the terms "legal cases for analysis practice" brings up a host of resources.

Language Samples

> Sample 1: "Your honor, the issue here is whether an intermediary interpreter would make the interpretation more accurate. Due to the many variations in sign language, not all interpreters are able to understand all Deaf people without the assistance of an intermediary. The variation in language can occur for a host of reasons, including where the Deaf person grew up, where they were educated, where and how they learned and use sign language, just to mention a few. This is not an uncommon occurrence, and New Jersey law states that

when a qualified interpreter determines that an intermediary interpreter would benefit from the accuracy of the communication, he or she bears the responsibility to inform the court. Here we have a such a situation, where I am unable to understand this Deaf individual well enough to uphold the section of my oath that requires the highest degree of accuracy. Therefore, I would respectfully request that this matter be adjourned until it can be appropriately staffed."

Sample 2: "The defendant and I do not use the same language." (Mathers, 2016)

Sample 3: "Your honor, the issue is. . . . " (Mathers, 2016)

Sample 4: "Like any language, ASL has style variations. This interpreter has not been trained in this particular/rare/uncommon variation used by this witness. There are Deaf interpreters who are trained in that variation."

The following language samples have been taken from a 2016 survey and have not been altered in any way.

Sample 5: This case/client requires the use of a linguistic specialist in order to ensure the accuracy of the record. If the participant is the defendant, I also include a reference to sixth amendment protections. If the situation is a civil matter, I cite the ADA and the relevant state laws. (Atlas & Tester, 2016, respondent 1)

Sample 6: Your honor the interpreter requests a moment? May I approach? Your honor, I have had the opportunity to meet with the defendant as required to establish communication and understanding between myself, the defendant and court. In meeting with the defendant, I was not able to establish a clear understanding of communications between myself and the defendant. It is my recommendation and standard practice that a certified Deaf interpreter be assigned to work on the case alongside the ASL interpreter. Having learned ASL at a college level the linguistical range required in this case is beyond the scope of a second language learner. A CDI in a native language user who, if brought in on the case, could establish clear communication assuring the court of accuracy in the interpretation.

(Atlas & Tester, 2016, respondent 5)

Sample 7: We need a specialist added to this trial team (arraignment >> any sentencing, to ensure the clarity of information to the [deaf party..but say if defendant, plaintiff etc]. This will protect the integrity of the record, access to communication and make sure all parties understand proceedings on all levels from English to ASL and ASL to English. . . . (this is a poorly worded question . . . not sure your goal I could say more or less. This is more to requesting a CDI . . . but there are tons of other things to request). (Atlas & Tester, 2016, respondent 8)

Sample 8: This Deaf person has a highly individualized (or idiosyncratic) communication system that I am not able to fully understand. They will be best served by bringing in a Deaf interpreter to guarantee maximum understanding and allow them full participation at your hearing. I cannot promise they are answering knowingly or intelligently without a Deaf interpreter team. (Atlas & Tester, 2016, respondent 10)

Sample 9: I believe this situation requires the language skills of a native speaker of ASL. This person is referred to as a Certified Deaf Interpreter in the Code of Evidence for California. Do you already have a list of CDIs or would you like some recommendations of colleagues I have worked with in the past? (Atlas & Tester, 2016, respondent 13)

Sample 10: As a professional sign language interpreter, I am certified in using the most common established signs used among deaf individuals. The client here today uses a unique individualistic or idiosyncratic form of sign language different from the established norm. In order for communication to be effective and thus ensure the accuracy of the record, the interpreter is requesting the court to engage the services of a certified language specialist who possesses the necessary education, training and specialized skills to ensure the effectiveness of communication. (Atlas & Tester, 2016, respondent 15)

Resources for Citing Rules in IRAC

The following are additional survey responses from practicing legal interpreters (Atlas & Tester, 2016) to this question: Are there any resources that you commonly use or refer to when making this request (to bring in a Deaf interpreter)? What are they?

For the reader—can you envision other scenarios where these resources could be used? Are there any that are not fully satisfactory? If not, why not, and which resources or rules might you use instead to strengthen your argument?

> RID best practice papers. Precedent. (Atlas & Tester, 2016, respondent 3)

> "I don't have anything that I commonly refer to." (Atlas & Tester, 2016, respondent 14)

> RID SPP; NAJIT team interpreting bulletin; NCSC Canon. (Atlas & Tester, 2016, respondent 15)

> "Sometimes I refer them to NAD (the attorneys there whose names I can't think of right now) or Elaine Gardner who used to work for the Washington Lawyer's Committee on Civil Rights. Point is, I'll use attorneys as resources more than anything else." (Atlas & Tester, 2016, respondent 11)

Anecdote—When IRAC Fails

One of the authors arrived at an assignment where a Deaf individual was to provide a statement about a series of domestic violence incidents. While this interpretation was not going to take place in court, she knew that the document generated by this communication would become a legal instrument and likely be presented in court as evidence. During the communication check, it became clear to the interpreter that the services of a Deaf interpreter would be necessary. The interpreter immediately informed the person conducting the interview, using the IRAC framework to explain the need (in a more casual register than she would have used inside a courtroom). In spite of the explanation, the interviewer insisted that the interpreter "do the best she could." The interpreter respectfully stated that she could not proceed, explaining again that whatever document was generated by the interpretation would certainly be inaccurate. The interviewer left and returned with her supervisor who exerted additional pressure on the interpreter to facilitate the interview. The interpreter repeated her reasons for declining to continue. The supervisor then asked the interpreter to wait a moment and returned shortly with a judge who, after hearing the full rationale for her unwillingness to interpret the interview without a Deaf interpreter, proceeded to order her to do it anyway. The interpreter's response? "Your honor, with all due respect to the court, it is impossible for me to accurately interpret this individual's statement. Are you ordering me to knowingly interpret inaccurately?" The judge was clearly flummoxed and furious and while the interpreter stood quietly awaiting his response; her heart was pounding because she knew he could incarcerate her for refusing to follow his order. After about a minute of consideration, he turned to the interpreter and said, "Fine. Just go." And she did.

Scenario for IRAC Practice

In spite of repeated requests to the hiring party for preparation information for an upcoming assignment at a state court, all you are able to ascertain is the name of the Deaf person and that the matter has something to do with probation.

> Question: What are the possible scenarios you can think of that fit with this extremely limited information?

Once you arrive at the interpreters' unit, you are still unable to get any additional information other than a courtroom number. When you ask if this is a hearing regarding violation of probation, you are told that they don't know. As you walk to the court, you consider every possible scenario regarding probation. It occurs to you that most probation matters are handled in a different location in the courthouse and involve a probation officer or a hearing officer, not a judge. This leads you to believe that the likeliest scenario is a hearing on a violation of probation.

Upon entering the courtroom and identifying yourself to the appropriate staff, you are asked to interpret a brief meeting between the public defender and their client. They are meeting for the first time.

It is not until you ask the public defender about the nature of the meeting and matter that you are informed that this "probation" assignment is an arraignment for murder.

REFERENCES

Adam, R., Aro, M., Druetta, J. C., Dunne, S., & Klintberg, J. (2014). Deaf interpreters: An introduction. In R. Adam, C. Stone, S. D. Collins, & M. Metzger (Eds.), *Deaf interpreters at work: International insights* (pp. 1–18). Gallaudet University Press.

Atlas, N., & Tester, C. (2016). *Effective strategies to articulate, advocate and argue for appropriate staffing in legal settings* [Presentation]. Registry of Interpreters for the Deaf Region 1 Conference, July 2016.

Berk-Seligson, S. (1999). *The bilingual courtroom: Court interpreters in the judicial process* (2nd ed.). The University of Chicago Press.

Bittner, M. (1990). The IRAC method of case study analysis. *Social Studies, 81*(5), 227–230. https://doi.org/10.1080/00377996.1990.9957530

Boudreault, P. (2005). Deaf interpreters. In T. Janzen (Ed.), *Topics in signed language interpreting: Theory and practice* (pp. 323–355). John Benjamins.

Burton, K. (2016). Teaching and assessing problem solving: An example of an incremental approach to using IRAC in legal education. *Journal of University Teaching & Learning Practice, 13*(5). https://ro.uow.edu.au/jutlp/vol13/iss5/20

Burton, K. (2017). Assessment rubric on IRAC (Issue, Rule, Application, Conclusion). *Journal of Learning Design, 10*(2), 12. https://doi.org/10.5204/jld.v10i2.229

CUNY School of Law. (n.d.). *IRAC and CRRACC*. https://www.law.cuny.edu/legal-writing/students/irac-crracc/irac-crracc-1/

Forestal, E. (2005). The emerging professionals: Deaf interpreters and their views and experiences on training. In M. Marschark, R. Peterson, & E. A. Winston (Eds.), *Sign language interpreting and interpreter education*. Oxford University Press. https://doi.org/10.1093/

acprof/9780195176940.001.0001

Forestal, E. (2014). Deaf interpreters: The dynamics of their interpreting processes. In R. Adam, S. D. Collins, M. Metzger, & C. Stone (Eds.), *Deaf interpreters at work: International insights* (pp. 29–50). Gallaudet University Press.

Hale, S. (2006). Themes and methodological issues in court interpreting research. *Linguistica Antverpiensia, New Series–Themes in Translation Studies, 5*, 205–228. https://lans-tts.uantwerpen.be/index.php/LANS-TTS/article/download/161/98

Hale, S. (2007). The challenges of court interpreting: Intricacies, responsibilities and ramifications. *Alternative Law Journal, 32*(4), 198–202. https://doi.org/10.1177/1037969X0703200402

Hewitt, W. E. (1995). Court interpretation: Model guide for policy and practice in the state courts. In *Model code of professional responsibility for interpreters in the judiciary* (pp. 197–211). National Center for State Courts. http://cdm16501.contentdm.oclc.org/cdm/ref/collection/accessfair/id/118

Howard, N. (2014). *Deaf and hearing worlds: Enculturation and acculturation* [Presentation]. Conference of Interpreter Trainers. https://streetleverage.com/cit-2014-plenary-deaf-hearing-worlds-enculturation-and-acculturation/

Jacobsen, B. (2012). The significance of interpreting modes for question–answer dialogues in court interpreting. *Interpreting, 14*(2), 217–241. https://doi.org/10.1075/intp.14.2.05jac

Judicial Council of California/Administrative Office of the Courts (CAAOC). (2010). *Recommended guidelines for the use of deaf intermediary interpreters.* https://www.courts.ca.gov/documents/CIP_GID.pdf

Kift, S., Israel, M., & Field, R. (2010). *Learning and teaching academic standards project: Bachelor of laws learning & teaching academic standards statement.* Australian Learning and Teaching Council. https://cald.asn.au/wp-content/uploads/2017/11/KiftetalLTASStandardsStatement2010.pdf

LaVigne, M., & Vernon, M. (2003). An interpreter isn't enough: Deafness, language, and due process. *Wisconsin Law Review* 884, 844–936. https://ssrn.com/abstract=1744291

Mathers, C. (2006). *Sign language interpreters in court: Understanding best practices.* AuthorHouse.

Mathers, C. (2009). *The deaf interpreter in court: An accommodation that is more than reasonable.* National Consortium of Interpreter Education Centers. http://www.interpretereducation.org/wp-content/uploads/2011/06/Deaf-Interpreter-in-Court_NCIEC2009.pdf

Mathers, C. (2016, March 19). *Thinking and talking like an attorney: Issue, rule, application, and conclusion* [Presentation]. Gallaudet University.

Mathers, C., & Witter-Merithew, A. (2014). The contribution of Deaf interpreters to GATEKEEPING within the interpreting profession. In D. I. J. Hunt & S. Hafer (Eds.), *Our roots: The essence of our future conference proceedings Reconnecting with our roots* (pp. 159–173). CIT. https://www.unco.edu/cebs/asl-interpreting/pdf/osep-project/2014-cit-proceedings.pdf

NCIEC Deaf Interpreter Work Team. (2010). *Towards effective practice: Competencies of the deaf interpreter.* http://www.diinstitute.org/wp-content/uploads/2012/07/DC_Final_Final.pdf

NCIEC Deaf Interpreter Work Team. (2016). *Deaf interpreter curriculum.* http://www.diinstitute.org/wp-content/uploads/2016/03/NCIEC_DIC_Digital_Edition_2016.pdf

NCSC. (1995). *Model code of professional responsibility for interpreters in the judiciary.* Author. https://cdm16501.contentdm.oclc.org/digital/collection/accessfair/id/118

Neumann, R. K., Margolis, E., & Stanchi, K. M. (2017). *Legal reasoning and legal writing* (8th ed.). Wolters Kluwer.

Roberson, L., Russell, D., & Shaw, R. (2011). American Sign Language/English interpreting in legal settings: Current practices in North America. *Journal of Interpretation, 21*(1), 6. http://digitalcommons.unf.edu/joi/vol21/iss1/6

Russell, D. (2005). Consecutive and simultaneous interpreting. In T. Janzen (Ed.), *Topics in signed language interpreting and practice* (p. 30). John Benjamins.

Russell, D., & Shaw, R. (2016). Power and privilege: An exploration of decision-making of interpreters. *Journal of Interpretation, 25*(1), article 7. https://digitalcommons.unf.edu/joi/vol25/iss1/7/

Stewart, K. (Ed.) (2012). *Toward effective practice: Specialist competencies of the interpreter practicing within court and legal settings* [Working paper]. National Consortium of Interpreter Education Centers. http://www.interpretereducation.org/wp-content/uploads/2012/10/FINAL_Legal_Competencies_Document_2012.pdf

Stewart, K., Witter-Merithew, A., & Cobb, M. (2009). *Best practices: American Sign Language and English interpretation within legal settings* [Working paper]. National Consortium of Interpreter Education Centers. http://www.interpretereducation.org/wp-content/uploads/2011/06/

LegalBestPractices_NCIEC2009.pdf

Stone, C. (2009). *Toward a deaf translation norm*. Gallaudet University Press.

Tester, C. (2018). How American Sign Language-English interpreters who can hear determine need for a deaf interpreter for court proceedings. *Journal of Interpretation, 26*(1), 28. https://digitalcommons.unf.edu/joi/vol26/iss1/3

Tester, C. (2019). *Scoping study: What is the deaf interpreter's perception of their interpreting process in the courts* [Unpublished manuscript]. Heriot-Watt University.

Tester, C. (2021). *Intralingual interpreting in the courtroom: An ethnographic study of Deaf interpreters' perceptions of their role and positioning* [Unpublished doctoral dissertation]. Heriot-Watt University.

Tuck, B. (2010). Preserving facts, form, and function when a deaf witness with minimal language skills testifies in court. *University of Pennsylvania Law Review, 158*(1998), 905–957. https://scholarship.law.upenn.edu/penn_law_review/vol158/iss3/6

Turner, T. L. (2015). *Flexible IRAC: A best practices guide*. Southwestern Law School Research Paper No. 2015-16. SSRN Electronic Journal. https://doi.org/10.2139/ssrn.2633667

Wilcox, P. (1995). Dual interpretation and discourse effectiveness in legal settings. *Journal of Interpretation, 7*(1), 89–98.

Part Two

Best Practices

4 INTERPRETERS AS WITNESSES AND THE EXPERTS WHO EXAMINE THEM: THE PRAGMATICS BEHIND THE POLITICS

Carla M. Mathers

EDITOR'S INTRODUCTION

> *Interpreting is only one aspect of legal interpreting. Interpreters who want to work in legal settings must be cognizant of every aspect of this type of work. One such aspect of legal interpreting is the potential to interpret for or be called as an expert witness and have to provide testimony. The legal system, particularly in the United States, is an adversarial one. It is the responsibility of defense attorneys to point out potential flaws in the system. When an interpreter's practice or product is called into question, they (or another interpreter) may have to provide testimony as to the quality of the interpretation or explain best practices. Here Mathers provides an insightful legal analysis of the interpreter as a witness. This contribution provides a myriad of resources for legal interpreters to add to their toolbox.*

WHEN INTERPRETING PRACTITIONERS or educators consider the idea of interpreters being subpoenaed to testify, they often think that the issue is limited to legal interpreting specialists. While the risk is highest for interpreters working in law enforcement settings, any interpreter working in a nonprivileged setting can be subpoenaed and should be prepared to respond accordingly. In fact, the bulk of generalist work is nonprivileged and susceptible to being subpoenaed. Interpreting in any setting can draw the ire of someone challenging the accuracy of the interpretation and result in serving the interpreter with a subpoena. Only in a privileged setting can the interpreter assert a defense of the privilege on behalf of the deaf consumer to try to avoid testifying about a prior assignment.[1]

As a result, the possibility of being subpoenaed to testify about interpreting in settings such as community interpreting, educational interpreting, and some medical interpreting settings is quite real. It befits educators and students alike to understand the issues and be prepared to respond professionally to a subpoena. The chapter will provide content and context for a variety of educational activities to supplement learning. The educator could create an activity for students to practice testifying about decisions made in prior work to ensure consistent role explanations. In the testimony, students could be tasked with incorporating the language used by experts in reviewing an interpreter's work. By using language from the legal standards of accurate interpretation, students will be in a position to explain their work under pressure more defensibly. Students can be assigned interpretations to review and to assess using the expert witness lens and prepare a short expert report explaining their opinions regarding the interpretation. Finally, for more advanced coursework or projects, students could review and interpret, create an expert report, and submit to mock testimony to defend the opinions in the report.

To accomplish these ends, this chapter will discuss the legal basis for interpreters being called to testify, the role of an expert witness who will examine the quality of the interpretation in order to render an opinion, and the measures interpreters can take to prepare to give testimony in a legal matter regarding the prior provision of interpreting services. Once interpreters understand the risk of being called to testify, they can modify their practices to ensure they are prepared. Understanding the work of experts will permit interpreters to defend their work and assist counsel in defending their client. Finally, this chapter will assist educators prepare students in conducting their general interpreting practice in order to be prepared when subpoenaed to testify.

---

1. Note that the privilege belongs to the consumer involved in a relationship with the professional. The interpreter can assert the privilege on behalf of the deaf consumer. At the same time, the consumer can waive the privilege in effect requiring the interpreter to testify.

THE ISSUE FOR INTERPRETERS AND THE COMMUNITY: CONFIDENTIALITY

Interpreters are regularly thrust into some of the most sensitive matters in a deaf person's life, becoming privy to delicate information of the utmost importance to consumers. The profession's requirement to be part of the community and, at the same time, not share information, inadvertently or otherwise, learned about the community on the job requires care, skill, tact, and thoughtfulness. Interpreters are thoroughly schooled in the interpreting profession's Code of Professional Conduct. An interpreter's commitment to keep assignment-related information confidential and maintain the deaf consumer's privacy is inviolable. A code of conduct is necessary because it engenders responsibility, accountability, and trust in and between the provider and the service recipient. These principles would be meaningless if the interpreter were not bound to secrecy. Hence, the Registry of Interpreter's for the Deaf's (RID) Code of Professional Conduct's first ethical tenet sets forth the charge that "[i]nterpreters adhere to standards of confidentiality." (Registry of Interpreters for the Deaf, 2005, p. 2). It is useful to examine the guiding principles illuminating the tenet.

> Interpreters hold a position of trust in their role as linguistic and cultural facilitators of communication. Confidentiality is highly valued by consumers and is essential to protecting all involved.
>
> Each interpreting situation (e.g., elementary, secondary, and post-secondary education, legal, medical, mental health) has a standard of confidentiality. Under the reasonable interpreter standard, professional interpreters are expected to know the general requirements and applicability of various levels of confidentiality. Exceptions to confidentiality include, for example, federal and state laws requiring mandatory reporting of abuse or threats of suicide, or responding to subpoenas.[2]

---

2. This chapter will revisit the reasonable interpreter standard in the discussion of an expert witness' review of a challenged interpretation.

Little doubt exists that if confidentiality mandates were disregarded, the profession would be significantly negatively impacted. The sometimes-fragile web of trust that exists between the deaf community and the interpreting profession would be severely compromised if not eradicated entirely. The very idea of a court of law requiring an interpreter to take an oath to tell the truth in open court and to breach confidentiality by disclosing the contents of a prior interpreting assignment threatens to tear the fabric of the relationship with the deaf community. Yet, as noted in the guiding principles above, the professional interpreter is required to understand and apply the various levels of confidentiality required in a variety of settings, including a legal setting. Likewise, the interpreter must understand the issue of why confidentiality must be subordinated to the power of a court subpoena. To the legal reasons for requiring an interpreter to violate their oath to the community, we turn next.

THE LEGAL BASIS UNDERGIRDING THE REQUIREMENT THAT INTERPRETERS TESTIFY

In trial practice, the rules of evidence govern the admissibility of testimony and other evidence. Federal practice is governed by the Federal Rules of Evidence (FRE) in conducting trials and most evidentiary hearings. Many state courts model their state rules of evidence on the federal rules with several important exceptions in application of those rules. Below, we examine those evidentiary rules governing the admission of interpreted testimony that require the interpreter to testify.

Personal Knowledge and Hearsay

The legal system has spent generations developing a complex set of rules to protect the integrity of evidence used by the jury and the judge to determine the facts of a lawsuit or criminal action. The rules of evidence dictate which testimony and physical evidence will guide the jury in its determination of whether facts or conduct amount to a crime or a compensable legal injury. In order to ensure facts admitted are untainted, several bedrock principles guide courts. When considering evidence in the form of witness testimony, the notions of reliability and trustworthiness are paramount. FRE, Rule 602 states, among other things, "a witness may testify to a matter only if evidence is introduced sufficient to support a finding that the witness has personal knowledge of the matter." Only actual personal knowledge of a fact provides a sufficient guarantee of reliability to be admitted into evidence and introduced to the jury.[3] The person who perceived the event is the only one trusted to answer questions on cross-examination about the conditions surrounding the event.

If one is speaking from personal knowledge, the system can trust the veracity of the statement. If a witness has personal knowledge of an event, the opponent can test the integrity of the witness's recollection through cross-examination. Cross-examination is the attorney's greatest tool for ascertaining truth. The cross-examiner can inquire as to whether the witness has a motive to distort, skew, or outright lie. The attorney can test whether the witness has a bias or prejudice in favor of or against one side or the other. Moreover, the attorney can inquire into any physical, mental, or emotional conditions that might affect the person's ability to remember and recite events. For example, in a sexual assault trial, the attorney can ask whether the witness themselves is a survivor of sexual assault; whether they have a prior romantic relationship with the defendant; or even, whether they have ever posted under the #metoo or #timesup hashtags. Affirmative answers can be used in argument to imply the witness's version should or should not be believed. Or, if an automobile accident were at issue, the attorney might inquire on cross-examination whether the witness wears eye glasses or hearing aids or if there are any other physical issues that might distort the person's ability to observe, recall, or relate the incident accurately. During argument, the attorney can suggest that the person did not have the physical abilities necessary to recall the incident without distortion. If the witness's story has changed over time, the attorney can challenge the accuracy of the witness's memory regarding the

---

3. Rule 601 specifically excludes expert witnesses from this requirement.

events or suggest a fabrication. The attorney is hampered in these important impeachment methods if they do not have a witness with personal knowledge on the stand.

When the witness is not testifying from personal knowledge, the attorney has no ability to examine these critical factors to determine whether the witness is skewing the facts intentionally or otherwise. If a witness derived their knowledge of the event only because someone else related it to them, then the cross-examiner has been deprived of an important mechanism to ascertain truth. Evidence relayed through secondhand knowledge impedes proper cross-examination, lacks the required indicia of reliability and trustworthiness demanded by the rules of evidence, and sometimes runs afoul of the Sixth Amendment's Confrontation Clause. Hence, secondhand testimony or repeated testimony is aptly named *hearsay*.

While hearsay is generally inadmissible, it is subject to many exceptions, including several typically used for admitting interpreted testimony, the rules of evidence define hearsay as:

> Hearsay means a statement that (1) the declarant does not make while testifying at the current trial or hearing; (2) a party offers in evidence to prove the truth of the matter asserted in the statement.

In other words, this means that the witness is repeating a prior statement and the party introducing the statement wants the jury to believe the statement is true. Because this runs afoul of the personal knowledge requirement, hearsay is inadmissible in court unless it satisfies one of the carefully crafted and well-supported exceptions.

Repetitions: The Second-Hand Nature of Interpreted Renditions

By their very nature, interpreted conversations are repeated conversations, and, as we have seen, repeated conversations comprise hearsay. A look at how interpreter's view their task vis-à-vis how interpretation is viewed by the legal system illustrates the problem.

Interpreters conceive of their task as the act of conveying linguistic and cultural information between two or more interlocutors, though newer lines of thought agree that the interpreter is, to some extent, a participant in a triadic exchange (see Roy, 2000; Wadensjö, 1998). The law, however, conceives of interpretation as an interpreter repeating statements between two people involved in an interaction who do not share the same language. In *Taylor v. State* the deaf individual creates an utterance in a sign language, and the interpreter repeats that utterance in a spoken language. The individual who can hear utters a statement in a spoken language and the interpreter repeats the utterance in a sign language.

> Two declarants made testimonial assertions: Taylor made a declaration in sign language; and then Smith, in his interpretation of Taylor's sign-language declaration, declared that Taylor had said that he (Taylor) had hugged the female students. Taylor is the declarant of his sign-language responses (recorded on the video), and Smith is the declarant of his English interpretations of Taylor's responses. (recorded on the audio; *Taylor* at 350, citing *State v. Montoya-Franco*)

Taylor had personal knowledge of the purported hugging. Smith did not. However, Smith was the only one with personal knowledge of Taylor's statement, and, as between the officer and Smith, Smith was the only one who could repeat it. Officers naturally do not have personal knowledge of the events in question, but they would typically, absent an interpreter, have personal knowledge of the confession or adverse statement.

The fundamental nature of the task of interpreting is the repetition. The recipient of the interpreter's repetition does not have personal knowledge of the utterance because they do not know the source language. Only the interpreter has personal knowledge of the original source language utterance whether it is signed or spoken. Hence, a hearsay issue would arise if the recipient of the interpretation were asked to testify as to what the interpreter told them.

Interpretation, then, involves two separate repetitions, both of which are considered hearsay under the rules of evidence. The first repetition occurs when the interpreter repeats the source language utterance to the hearing person involved in the interaction. The second repetition occurs when the hearing person repeats the interpreted message to the court in the form of witness testimony. The court held in *State v. Rodriguez-Castillo* (2008) that interpreted statements are assertions and are an additional layer of hearsay, that is, double hearsay within this context. The rules of evidence anticipate instances in which an utterance, whether spoken or more commonly in writings, contains multiple instances of hearsay.

Double Hearsay Rule

Hearsay within hearsay is not excluded by the rule against hearsay if each part of the combined statements conforms with an exception to the rule (FRE, 2011, Rule 805).

Hence, the hearing individual's (typically the officer) repetition of the deaf person's statement may be admitted if both of the statements are either not hearsay or satisfy an exception. Many cases have considered how to admit interpreted utterances under the hearsay rules. While no consensus exists, there are trends that will be examined shortly to permit the recipient of an interpreted message to testify as to the contents of the message.

Interpreters generally attribute the repeated utterances to the source language speakers and consider their work to be simply a mechanism to allow individuals who do not share a language to communicate. Nevertheless, in the eyes of the law, the repetition of a statement from someone with personal knowledge is the exact evil the hearsay rules are designed to eliminate. Interpreted statements constitute hearsay and must be dealt with in order to try cases involving individuals from differing language backgrounds.

How the Rules Deal With Interpreted Evidence?

Obviously, much evidence would be lost if the personal knowledge rule and the hearsay ban were to be strictly enforced. Many situations involve "he-say-she-say" evidence that necessarily requires the repetition of statements. Some crimes and civil actions penalize the very act of making a statement. The charges of making threats, bribery, extortion, conspiracy, perjury, racial harassment, hostile work environment, slander, hate speech, and terroristic threats typically involve the making of statements, and proof of the charge involves repeating those statements and attributing them to the speaker (Tiersma et al., 2012). In a criminal context, when the speaker is a defendant, the state cannot simply put the defendant on the stand and ask whether the defendant admitted to making the statements to establish liability. The Fifth Amendment to the Constitution protects a defendant from being forced to testify against themselves in a court of law. Hence, some exception to the hearsay rule must be devised to permit repetitions of a defendant's statement to establish liability.

Hearsay exceptions are created if they satisfy a two-pronged test. As mentioned, at times important testimony would be lost without an exception because no other way exists to introduce the evidence from someone with personal knowledge (e.g., the statement of a decedent about the cause of their death). In other words, the need for the evidence is high and the declarant is unavailable. The rules set forth a host of exceptions all premised on the defendant being unavailable to satisfy this "necessity prong." For purposes of the rules, unavailability includes the declarant being outside the jurisdiction of the court, not being able to remember, being subject to an evidentiary privilege such as the Fifth Amendment's privilege against self-incrimination, or simply by refusing to testify regardless of a court order directing them to do so (FRE, 2011, Rule 804(a)).

The other prong of the test for creating hearsay exceptions is termed the "reliability prong." To meet this test, there must be some indicia of reliability surrounding the event in which the statement is made to indicate that it was not fabricated at the time of its making. Described as "circumstantial guarantees of trustworthiness," these include situations such as the dying declaration exception just mentioned. The person dying had to make the statement under the impression of impending death, the person had to die, and the statement made had to concern the nature and the cause of death. If these conditions were met, the person who overheard the statement could, without personal knowledge, repeat the statement in court. Because the circumstances surrounding a mortal wounding and subsequent death likely did not provide the speaker much time to fabricate, the statement was considered reliable. The statement would be considered hearsay; however, it would be admitted under the exception for dying declarations.

Likewise, confessions or statements against interest are considered under an exception to the hearsay rule because of the high likelihood that the statement can be trusted to be true. The thinking goes that, except on television, one does not make an incriminating statement lightly. Hence, the statement is reliable, trustworthy, and likely true.[4] Furthermore, the declarant is unavailable because the Fifth Amendment's privilege against self-incrimination prohibits the state from calling the defendant to the stand and querying about the prior statement. As a result, one who overhears a confession or a statement against interest may repeat it in court without running afoul of the hearsay rule.

Statement of a Party-Opponent

An opposing party's statement is not considered hearsay in several instances. If it is offered against that party and "was made by a person whom the party authorized to make a statement on the subject" or "was made by the party's agent or employee on a matter within the scope of that relationship and while it existed" (FRE, 2011, Rule 801(d)(2)(C-D). Many civil employment discrimination cases involve accusations of mistreatment at the workplace by employers and could not be litigated if the plaintiff were not permitted to repeat what the employer said or did that demonstrated discriminatory intent. Likewise, many business or contract disputes would not be able to be successfully litigated without introducing repeated statements. Hence, if the employer or a person authorized by the employer made discriminatory statements or statements in breach of an agreement, these are attributed to the defendant and may be repeated by the plaintiff without objection.

---

4. Of course, there are a myriad of instances of proven coerced confessions and wrongful convictions. Much work has been done by legal scholars in this regard. See generally, the Innocence Project at https://www.innocenceproject.org/causes/false-confessions-admissions/ (last accessed 3/6/19).

Under the theory of agency liability, statements may be made directly by the person or adopted by that person either expressly or impliedly and are not hearsay. If one's authorized employee makes an agreement, the employer is held to the agreement. This is true even if the employer was not present when the statements were made. If the employee or agent is acting within the scope of their employment, the statements are attributed to the employer. These statements could be repeated in court without personal knowledge and either impliedly or expressly attributed to the employer. Agency liability is the legal theory by which interpreted statements are typically introduced.

The Interpreter as an Authorized or Joint Agent

Turning to how the rules of evidence consider interpreted statements, take the example of an interpreter at an employment setting in which a supervisor is disciplining a deaf employee. The supervisor makes discriminatory statements about the deaf person. The interpreter hears the statement and has personal knowledge of it. The deaf person is the recipient of the interpretation and does not have personal knowledge of the statement. In the absence of a hearsay exception permitting the deaf person to repeat the supervisor's discriminatory statement, only the interpreter has personal knowledge and can be called to testify directly about the statement. The interpreter's repetition in court of the supervisor's statement would not be considered hearsay under the statement by a party-opponent theory just discussed. The supervisor made the statement within the scope of their employment and was authorized. However, since the deaf plaintiff must necessarily testify, an exception needs to be found that permits the deaf plaintiff to explain to the jury what the supervisor said, how it made them feel, and the other attributes of the interaction.

Most courts use an agency analysis to determine if the interpreted statement is admissible. If the interpreter is an agent of the parties, they implicitly authorize the interpreter to make the statements, and the statements can be attributed to the parties since the interpreter is simply a conduit for their communications. In the case above, if the interpreter were an authorized agent, the interpreted rendition that the deaf person "heard" would be attributed to the supervisor. The deaf person could testify to the interpreted statements without fear of drawing a hearsay objection. If the interpreter were not found to be an authorized agent, the deaf person could not testify. The analysis to determine whether the interpreter is an agent and how that process occurs is key for interpreters to understand.

Federal courts use what they call the language-conduit-agency theory to permit the repetition by the recipient of the interpreted message to be admitted into court, which was first set forth in a case called *Nazemian* decided by the 9th Circuit Court of Appeals years ago (*United States v. Alvarez*, 1985; *United States v. Bel-Iran*, 1985; *United States v. Cordero*, 1994; *United States v. DaSilva*, 1983; *United States v. Lopez*, 1991; *United States v. Martinez-Gaytan*, 2000; *United States v. Nazemian*, 1991; *United States v. Sanchez-Godinez*, 2006; *United States v. Santana*, 1974; *United States v. Ushakow*, 1973; *United States v. Vidacak*, 2009). Some courts put significant thought into the analysis and others put in only a perfunctory effort. In addition, at the state level, some states undertake a more stringent analysis of the factors comprising agency while others follow the federal courts (see *Chao v. State*, 1985; *Correa v. Superior Court*, 2002; *Cruz-Reyes v. State*, 2003; *Durbin v. Hardin*, 1989; *People v. Gutierrez*, 1995; *People v. Hinojas-Mendoza*, 2005; *Saavedra v. State*, 2009; *State v. Felton*, 1992; *State v. Garcia-Trujillo*, 1997; *State v. Patino*, 1993; *State v. Randolph*, 1985; *State v. Spivey*, 1986). In some of the least intellectually rigorous analyses, courts simply declare that because the parties used an interpreter, agency existed. Other more thoughtful state courts require that the interpreter testify to the existence of the agency factors. Whether one was authorized and whether an actual agency relationship existed, under the federal rules, is a preliminary question under Rule 104(a). This means a judge determines whether the interpreter is an agent of the deaf person and the hearing person in determining whether the statement is hearsay or not hearsay. The existence of agency *vel non* is a decision that the judge makes as a preliminary matter prior to admitting the repeated statement.

The federal *Nazemian* factors courts use to determine whether the interpreter was the agent of the deaf party include:

1. Which party supplied the interpreter;
2. Whether the interpreter had any motive to mislead, lie, or distort;
3. The interpreter's qualifications and language skills; and
4. Whether actions taken subsequent to the translated statement were consistent with the statement as translated. (*United States v. Nazemian*, 1991 quoted in *Saavedra v. State*, 2009)

The general rule requiring an interpreter to testify has been stated in *Saavedra v. State* (2009) thusly:

> If a declarant makes a statement in a foreign tongue and A translates the statement to B who does not understand the language in which it was originally spoken, the original declaration may be admissible if proper proof of it is made, as an admission of a party. Is B's evidence as to A's report to him of the declaration admissible: It is clear that it is violative of the hearsay rule and inadmissible. *It is necessary to produce the interpreter himself as a witness and would have him testify to the terms of the declaration.*

In the absence of a finding of agency, the interpreter would have to testify. However, under *Nazemian*, the interpreter doesn't testify *to the terms of the declaration* as stated in the quotation above; rather, the interpreter would be asked about the factors such as who hired them, what their credentials are, whether they have any improper motive to skew the interpretation, and the like. Once the interpreter is deemed the agent, then the other parties to the interaction can testify as to the interpreted message.

The federal courts and the state courts handle proving the existence of agency differently. As mentioned, the federal courts permit the judge to determine under FRE 104(a) if agency exists. Many times, the interpreter will not have to testify in federal courts if there is sufficient information in the record or from the parties to support the factual basis of agency, for example, who supplied the interpreter, if any motive to skew is present, their qualifications, and subsequent conduct. Some states require the proponent of the agency relation to call the interpreter to testify as to these preliminary matters.

One wonders how a judge can make the factual agency determinations in the absence of interpreter testimony. What factual findings can a judge make as to whether the interpreter had a motive to distort or lie if the interpreter is not on the stand answering questions designed to elicit motivation? Furthermore, how can a judge speculate on the interpreter's qualifications, background, and skill without having the interpreter on the stand to explain their credentials? Will the parties always know who supplied the interpreter for the assignment? Or if the interpreter has an improper relationship? Only the interpreter can respond to these inquiries.

Recently, some courts in criminal matters have taken the analysis to the constitutional level and have said that interpreted statements rise to the level of declarations by the interpreter of the intent of the deaf person's message and, as such, the Constitution's Confrontation Clause requires that the interpreter be produced by the proponent of the testimony, and the defendant has the constitutional right to confront the interpreter to test the accuracy of their prior interpretation, their qualifications, bias or prejudice, their motive to skew the interpretation in any manner, and any other traditional cross-examination topics. To this class of cases and the consequences for interpreters and the deaf community at large, we now turn.

TAYLOR V. MARYLAND: A CONSTITUTIONAL CASE ON POINT

Clarence Taylor was charged with and convicted of two counts of sexual abuse of minors in a jury trial in Maryland. On appeal, Taylor argued that the two sign language interpreters who interpreted the 5-hour interrogation should have testified at trial. The trial court overruled the objection and allowed an interpreted recording of the interrogation to be played to the jury. On the recording, the English interpretation rendered by the interpreter was audible. Taylor contended that the interpreter's "statements violated his constitutional right to be confronted with the witnesses against him" (see *Taylor v. State*, 2016a, b). The Court of Special Appeals agreed with Mr. Taylor, and the case was remanded for a new trial.

Mr. Taylor was employed at the state school for the deaf as a dorm counselor and coach. Several teens alleged that he had touched them numerous times on the breasts and buttocks, had kissed them, and had exchanged provocative text messages with them. According to the interpretation of Mr. Taylor's statements to the police, he admitted that he might have accidentally brushed the girls in the hallway and that a typical greeting might involve a hug. During such a hug, according to the interpretation, an accidental brushing of the buttocks or breast of the girls might have happened. Taylor denied any intentional conduct. The interpreter stated that Mr. Taylor admitted touching the girls accidentally and that he had immediately apologized.

At trial, Taylor contended that he never admitted even accidental touching and that he had said to the officer only that *it could have happened*. Mr. Taylor contended on the stand that he had said *if* he had accidentally touched one of them, he *would have* immediately apologized and that the interpreter did not accurately interpret the statement. He testified repeatedly there had been misinterpretations by the interpreting team and that these assertions could not be attributed to him. Because the state did not call the interpreters to testify, Mr. Taylor had no way to confront the interpreters involved in the interpretation (*Taylor v. State*, 2016).

The interpreters hired by the police consisted of a deaf and hearing team. The court erroneously described the deaf interpreter as a certified deaf interpreter.[5] In truth, neither of the interpreters held RID certification.

Interpreters as testimonial hearsay declarants: If it's testimonial, the defendant gets to confront it.

The court in *Taylor* explained the requirements of the Confrontation Clause:

---

5. According to a contemporaneous check of the RID database at the time of Mr. Taylor's trial, neither interpreter was certified. Subsequently, the hearing interpreter attained certification.

The Sixth Amendment to the United States Constitution provides: "[i]n all criminal prosecutions, the accused shall enjoy the right . . . to be confronted with the witnesses against him[.]" (*Taylor v. State*, 2016)

The right of confrontation attaches to testimonial statements by a declarant against a defendant. A statement is testimonial when it can be expected that the statement would be used in a proceeding as evidence to prove a case. This proposition was announced in a seminal 2004 Supreme Court case—*Crawford v. Washington*—which overruled prior Supreme Court precedent, which used a hearsay analysis for whether the defendant had a right to confront the maker of an out-of-court statement (*Crawford v. Washington*, 2004). Post-*Crawford*, without question, out-of-court statements made in a police interview are within the purview of testimonial statements used to prove a matter in court. Hence, the defendant has a right to confront the declarants of those testimonial statements.

The question in the interpreted cases is whether the interpreter's rendition of the deaf person's statements is a testimonial declaration and whether the defendant has the resulting constitutional right to confront the interpreter. Classifying an interpreter as a "declarant" may cause a certain anxiety among interpreters who steadfastly maintain that they are not participants in an interaction. The field of interpretation has historically used conduit-based metaphorical language such as comparing an interpreter to a telephone or other invisible method of language transmission denying any independent volition on the part of the interpreter as participant. To further complicate matters, the trial judge in *Taylor* suggested summarily that the defendant did not have a right to confront the interpreters because "the interpreters are not accusers" (*Taylor v. State*, 2016). To which the appeals court responded that the term "accuser" appears nowhere in the Sixth Amendment's Confrontation Clause or in its Maryland predecessor. As such, the term "accuser" is not an appropriate lens through which to conduct the analysis of declarants of testimonial hearsay. The reasons underlying classifying an interpreter as a declarant of testimonial hearsay for Confrontation

Clause purposes require an examination of several recent Supreme Court cases. Those cases examined other collateral individuals involved in an investigation and determined that as declarants their presence in court as witnesses was required.

SUPREME COURT PRECEDENT REGARDING TESTIMONIAL HEARSAY AND DECLARANTS

After *Crawford* overruled *Ohio v. Roberts* (1980), all agreed that the Supreme Court had dramatically altered the landscape of the Confrontation Clause analysis; however, the Supreme Court did not provide extensive guidance to the lower courts to determine what constituted testimonial hearsay. While announcing the rule that the hearsay balancing tests used in *Roberts* did not satisfy the strict standard of actual confrontation and cross-examination, the Supreme Court left the lower federal courts bereft of a definition of testimonial hearsay. The Supreme Court began to remedy the issue in *Melendez-Diaz v. Massachusetts* (2009), which involved forensic reports that were created by nontestifying experts of the results of a chemical analysis of a quantity of cocaine. Those nontestifying individuals were the chemists who conducted the analysis of evidence using chemistry tests and issued reports on the nature of the drugs. The reports would have been admitted under a traditional hearsay exception without requiring the officials who created the reports to testify. The Supreme Court indicated that the statements within the reports (the results) were testimonial declarations and therefore the state had to produce for cross-examination the maker of those statements. As a result, the individuals who conducted the tests were required to testify, and the defendant must be permitted to confront and crossexamine them. This is true even though they had no personal knowledge of the crime, the crime scene, or the defendants—in other words they were not percipient witnesses to the crimes.

Subsequently, in *Bullcoming v. New Mexico* (2011), the Supreme Court held that an analyst who certified the results of a blood alcohol test for the purpose of using at trial to show the driver exceeded the blood alcohol limits under state law must appear and be subject to cross-examination. The analyst recorded the results from the breathalyzer onto a form that was submitted as evidence. While the analyst was not a percipient witness to the alleged drunken driving, they were a declarant in the sense that the results asserted in the report were used as part of an investigation for the purpose of demonstrating culpability at trial. As such, the analyst's statements in certifying the results were testimonial, and the Confrontation Clause requires the state to produce the analyst for cross-examination. Just as these more remote participants in the prosecution of a criminal case had earlier been excused from testimony due to various hearsay exceptions, interpreters had also been previously excused from testifying due to the language-conduit hearsay reasoning. Just as the forensic participants in *Bullcoming* and *Melendez-Diaz* now were required to testify under the Confrontation Clause, courts are examining whether interpreters fall under this analysis. *United States v. Cuberlo* (2003) is another case challenging the Confrontation Clause. In this case, the court found the interpreter a declarant, but no error presented because the interpreter was present for cross-examination. However, in *State v. Lopez-Ramos* (2018), the Court held the interpreter was not a declarant and declaring *Nazemian*'s language-conduit approach to be consistent with the Confrontation Clause, and, in *Comm. v. AdonSoto* (2016), the court questioned *Nazemian*'s approach and required going forward that all interpreted interrogations be recorded for expert review.

The *Taylor* court examined these cases and determined that while not an exact fit, strong legal reasons existed for classifying the interpreter as a declarant of testimonial hearsay statements in the same manner as *Bullcoming* and *Melendez-Diaz* classified forensic examiners. The interpreter's statements were made to a police investigator. The statements were made in the course of an actual criminal investigation conducted by an arm of the government. The purpose of the statements was to create evidence to be used against Mr. Taylor in a criminal prosecution. By the *Taylor* court's reasoning, the interpretation may have been accurate and reliable under a hearsay analysis (or may not have been as Mr. Taylor asserted), but nonetheless, it was testimonial and must be made available for confrontation, just like the laboratory analyst who recorded an objective fact into a report when he transcribed a machine-produced result (*Taylor v. State*, 2016).

The state of Maryland had argued in *Taylor* that the interpreter was merely relaying Taylor's own statements in a different language. The state suggested that the interpreter's words were simply the words of Taylor and that "Taylor had no right to cross examine himself" (*Taylor v. State*, 2016). The appeals court disagreed stating,

> To the contrary, [the interpreter] made representations each time he translated the statements from one language to another. *See*, e.g., *State v. Rodriguez-Castillo*, 345 Or. 39, 47 (2008) (rejecting state's argument that interpreter makes no independent assertions when interpreter converts statements between languages.). For example, one portion of the interrogation transcript contains this simple exchange:
>
> DET. CAMP: What about when you hug the girls?
>
> [TAYLOR]: Yes. I do, we do hug.
>
> The actual speaker of that answer was not Taylor, a man who literally does not and cannot enunciate spoken words in the English language. Rather, the speaker was the interpreter, Smith, attributing the response to Taylor. In the example above, two declarants made testimonial assertions: Taylor made a declaration in sign language; and then Smith, in his interpretation of Taylor's sign-language declaration, declared that Taylor had said that he (Taylor) had hugged female students. Taylor is the declarant of his sign-language responses (recorded on the video), and Smith is the declarant of his English interpretation of Taylor's responses (recorded on audio). (*Taylor v. State*, 2016)

The court characterized the state's position that the interpreter was simply a mouthpiece as a fallacy that ignored the reality of the interpreter's task.

> An interpreter must listen to what is being said, comprehend the message, abstract the entire message from the words and the word order, store the idea, search his or her memory for the conceptual and semantic matches, and reconstruct the message (keeping the same

register or level of difficulty as in the source language). While doing this, the interpreter is speaking and listening for the next utterance of the language to process, while monitoring his or her own output. (*State v. Montoya-Franco*, 2012, cited in *Taylor v. State*, 2016)

Critically, the court reminded readers "[t]he English words that the jurors ultimately heard in this case were not the words of Taylor, but of Smith, expressing his opinion as to a faithful reproduction of the meaning of Taylor's sign language expressions" (*Taylor v. State*, 2016).

> The Taylor court suggested that cross-examination of the interpreter could bring out not only their language fluency but also touched on factors critical to impeachment of the interpretation. The court stated: "[j]ust as the task of interpretation is not uniquely immune to human error, so too is it not uniquely immune to human suggestion or manipulation." (*Taylor v. State*, 2016)

Consider if the interpreters in *Taylor* had been subject to confrontation on even the hearsay examination of the *Nazemian* factors. Had the interpreters been produced on cross-examination, Taylor's attorney may have learned that the deaf interpreter was referred by and related to an official at the school for the deaf. Taylor's attorney may then have argued that the deaf interpreter might have had a motive to skew the interpretation to favor the school and protect her family member. Had the interpreters been produced on cross-examination, Taylor's attorney may have learned that the deaf interpreter and hearing interpreter were family members. Taylor's attorney them may have argued that both interpreters had reason to skew their responses to make each other appear competent because of the familial relationship. Had the interpreters been produced on cross-examination, Taylor's attorney may have learned that neither interpreter was a practicing legal interpreter and neither had any training or certification. Taylor's attorney may then have argued that the team did not have the skill, training, and knowledge to interpret in high-risk investigatory settings. Had the interpreters been produced on cross-examination, Taylor's attorney may have questioned whether it is standard interpreting practice to interpret a 5-hour interrogation without a team to switch off with and without adequate breaks. As the court indicated, "Over the nearly five-hour course of Taylor's interrogation, the interpreters received only two breaks: a ten-minute break after about two and a half hours of testimony, and a two-minute break another hour later. Most of the more incriminating statements attributed to Taylor occurred during the later portions of the interrogation. Live testimony from the interpreter might have suggested that fatigue or inattention undermined the accuracy of those interpretations" (*Taylor v. State*, 2016). Mr. Taylor's attorney may then have argued that the team may have been fatigued and more prone to make errors particularly in the later parts of the interrogation where the admissions against Mr. Taylor's interest occurred. Even in the less demanding *Nazemian* hearsay analysis, a serious challenge to whether these interpreters constituted Mr. Taylor's agents could have been launched. Because the state did not call the interpreters to the stand, the responses to these and other critical cross-examination questions were never shared with the jury.

IN A CONFRONTATION CLAUSE CHALLENGE, THE CLAUSE TRUMPS THE HEARSAY RULES

In a matter in which the Confrontation Clause is not asserted because it is a civil case or because the interpreted statements were of a witness and not a defendant, under the joint agency analysis, properly done, the interpreter should still be called to testify with respect to the *Nazemian* factors (see *Durbin v. Hardin*, 1989; *People v. Villagomez*, 2000; *State v. Ambriz-Arguello*, 2017; *State v. Montoya-Franco*, 2012; *State v. Rodriguez-Castillo*, 2008; *United States v. Curbelo*, 2003; *United States v. Martinez-Gaytan*, 2000). Once the interpreter testifies about how they came to be involved in the matter, their qualifications, and any motive or indications of bias, then the other person involved in the encounter can testify to the deaf person's interpreted statements. This foundational aspect is still necessary in order to admit interpreted testimony. The Confrontation Clause analysis goes further by requiring the interpreter's presence and not leaving the agency decision to the vagaries of a judge on a preliminary determination with potentially incomplete or inaccurate information.

In *United States v. Charles* (2013), the Haitian defendant was interrogated in the Miami airport for knowingly using a fraudulently altered travel document using a Creole interpreter. The government did not call the interpreter to testify, and the court on appeal determined that Ms. Charles's right to confront the testimonial declarations by the interpreter was violated. The court held that the language-conduit doctrine was found "both inapplicable and inappropriate for analyzing whether the interpreter's statement is testimonial under the Confrontation Clause [because the idea was] premised on the court's assessment of the interpreter's reliability and trustworthiness, principles supporting the admissibility of the interpreter's statements under the [Federal Rules of Evidence], but having no bearing on the Confrontation Clause" (*United States v. Charles*, 2013). Essentially, the court was saying if a person has testimonial evidence, the requirement of confrontation cannot be eluded by a judicial hearsay determination that the evidence is reliable. In other words, the Confrontation Clause means what it says—the defendant has the right to see and examine evidence against him that comes from human witnesses.

Regardless, then, of whether the interpreter's statements would have been admissible previously under a joint or authorized agency theory, this new line of cases clearly confirm the superiority of the Confrontation Clause's requirement that the interpreter be produced and testify about their prior interpretation. In criticizing the federal approach and the *Nazemian* test, the *Taylor* court wrote that it ignores the reality of what interpreters do in real time while interpreting. Taylor faulted the legal fiction of conflating the interpreter with the deaf person, which may be convenient for admitting testimony, but, according to Taylor, does not satisfy the constitutional right to confront witnesses against the defendant. As stated in *Taylor*, "*Nazemian* guides judges to make a threshold determination of the interpreter's honesty, proficiency, and methodology without the testimony from the one witness whose testimony could best prove the accuracy of the interpretations—the interpreter himself or herself" (*Taylor v. State*, 2016).

On a final note, the implications that the Taylor decision has for the deaf community are significant. In the future, if the state of Maryland intends on introducing an interpreted conversation into evidence, it must call the interpreters to testify and be subject to cross-examination on the *Nazemian* factors among other typical cross-examination topics. Critically, the state must ensure that law enforcement hires interpreters whose work is untainted with conflicts, are appropriately credentialed, and who work in teams consistent with standard legal interpreting practice. Better practice suggests, as seen in the Massachusetts case, *Comm. v. AdonSoto* (2016), all interrogations should be videotaped in order that the interpretation is preserved for expert review. Interpreting teams for law enforcement assignments should include properly trained and credentialed deaf and hearing interpreters. Sufficient interpreters should be retained in order for the interpreters to alternate properly to avoid fatigue and misinterpretations. Interpreters should receive enough preparation information in order to examine their relationships for conflicts of interest that might be brought out in a *Nazemian* analysis. Interpreters should also consider adjusting their remuneration since accepting a law enforcement case in Maryland now also requires additional time to be available to work with the government to review the interpretation, to prepare to face an expert witness, and to testify.

Ultimately, law enforcement officials must do far more than they did in *Taylor* to ensure that the interpretation is defensible. In the end, the quality of interpreters in interrogations should improve benefiting not only the deaf community that interacts with officers but also the legal system in ensuring that justice is more aptly dispensed.

For an interpretation to be defensible, law enforcement interpreters must be ready, willing, and able to testify in court regarding their decisions in accepting cases and in rendering interpretations. Law enforcement interpreters and other interpreters in nonprivileged settings must be prepared to respond to expert review of their work. This chapter now looks to the process that experts undergo when reviewing interpretations and then that interpreters should undertake in preparing to testify.

EXPERT REVIEW: ISO THE REASONABLE INTERPRETER STANDARD

Next, this chapter will examine those rules that govern the testimony of experts. Experts are not only governed by the rules of evidence that dictate how they arrive at their opinions and the subject matter they can opine on, but also by case law developed in the courts that sets forth the requirements of a constitutionally acceptable accurate interpretation. Experts also rely on the RID guidelines and other literature within the legal interpreting profession delineating the responsibilities of the interpreter in providing an ethical, accurate, and unbiased interpretation. These provide a baseline for a comparison of the interpreter's actual behavior and interpretation with what is a legal floor below which the interpretation would not be considered competent.

Starting from the professional ethical perspective, the RID sets forth its own standard that governs interpreters and that recognizes various subspecialties will have different requirements placed on interpreters. The Code of Professional Conduct states, "[w]hen applying these principles to their conduct, interpreters remember that their choices are governed by a **"reasonable interpreter"** standard. This standard represents the hypothetical interpreter who is appropriately educated, informed, capable, aware of professional standards, and fair-minded" (Registry of Interpreters for the Deaf, 2005, p. 1). As RID itself states: "[t]he driving force behind the guiding principles is the notion that the interpreter will **do no harm**" (p. 1).

The test set forth by the RID is an objective test. Rather than being concerned with what motivated the interpreter specifically in creating an interpretation or deciding on a course of action, the test looks at what a hypothetical interpreter would likely do when presented with a similar set of circumstances. In other words, what would a reasonably competent interpreter do under this circumstance? Would they accept the assignment and what factors would affect their decision-making? The test set forth by RID mirrors the tort standard of civil liability, which looks at what a reasonable professional in a similar position would do to determine if the interpreter's conduct deviates from the standard of care that would be followed by a reasonable hypothetical interpreter. If the deviation from the standard of care causes injury, financial or otherwise, to someone, a cause of action sounding in tort lies against the interpreter. Standards of care are supplied from case law, standard practices, and other mandates within the profession and are used when experts develop their opinions.

In criminal cases, standards of care typically focus on the accuracy of the interpretation. One Texas court explained the due process standard of review for the adequacy of interpretation as whether "the inadequacy in the interpretation made the trial fundamentally unfair" (*United States v. Huang*, 1992 cited in *West v. State*, 2013). Stated somewhat differently, a federal court suggested "[a] criminal proceeding [*sic*] is denied due process when: (1) what is told him is incomprehensible; (2) the accuracy and scope of a translation at a hearing or trial is subject to grave doubt; (3) the nature of the proceeding is not explained to him in a manner designed to insure his full comprehension; or (4) a credible claim of incapacity to understand due to language difficulty is made and the district court fails to review the evidence and make appropriate findings of fact" (*United States v. Cirrincione*, 1985). Each of these prongs except the final prong goes directly to the ability of the interpreter to craft an accurate and intelligible interpretation. In another case, the court identified three types of evidence tending to prove that the interpretation was incompetent: (1) direct evidence of incorrectly interpreted words, (2) unresponsive answers by the witness, and (3) the witness's expression of difficulty understanding what is said to him (*Perez-Lastor v. INS*, 2000). An expert witness uses these standards to evaluate the interpretation, the decisions made, and whether there was an appropriate fit for the deaf consumer.

Expert Witness Protocol

Expert witnesses are of two varieties—consulting experts and testifying experts. Interpreters can expect to encounter both. A consulting expert is one who reviews an interpretation and provides an opinion to counsel. The consultant may be used throughout the litigation or initially to help the attorney understand a particular issue within the expert's practice. The existence of consulting experts does not have to be disclosed to the opponent during discovery, unlike testifying experts who typically provide deposition testimony in civil cases and trial testimony in criminal cases. Once an expert has communicated with one party to litigation, the expert is conflicted out from speaking to or working with the opposing party.

An expert witness's opinion must be helpful to the trier of fact, must be reliable, and must be relevant to the matter at issue (FRE, 2011, Rule 702). The opinion must be shown to be based on sufficient facts or data, and it must be the product of reliable methods and principles. The opinion does not have to be based upon personal knowledge and can be gained from reviewing materials, interviewing individuals, and even by observations during the trial itself (FRE, 2011, Rule 703). The expert must show, however, that they reliably applied those principles to the facts in arriving at their opinion. These concepts have been the subject of much debate and litigation over the years because of a series of Supreme Court cases in the 1990s requiring scientifically stringent testing of a principle in order to admit an expert's opinion (*Daubert v. Merrell Dow Pharmaceuticals, Inc.*, 1993; *Kumho Tire Co. v. Carmichael*, 1999). Courts struggled with how to apply these scientific expert opinion standards to social science experts. The Supreme Court indicated that these rules also apply to expert social science testimony (*Kumho Tire Co. v. Carmichael*, 1999).

Because interpretation is not an empirical science, it is more difficult to demonstrate that an opinion about an interpretation is based on reliable scientific principles and methods. Research in the field of interpretation typically can be challenged because of small sample sizes and the inability to generalize from small samples.

Furthermore, interpretation research suffers another flaw as most interpretations have never been replicated to demonstrate consistency and achieve consensus over time. Replication of results is one hallmark of the empirical method that courts have come to expect from experts. Many experts in social sciences then base their opinions on their years of experience in the field as an interpreter or as a linguist and a general consensus of standard practices in the field. To some extent, the rules of evidence sanction this as a basis to admit an opinion. If an expert can show that their methods, discussed below, use the same facts and processes that other people in the profession reasonably rely upon in developing an opinion, then their opinions are more likely to be found admissible.

The Basis of the Expert's Opinion

The methods used by experts in interpreting to arrive at an opinion may vary depending on the background and skill of the expert. However, given the subject is usually the accuracy of the interpretation for the particular deaf person or the ethical decisions made by the interpreter, then the methods used will be similar to how interpreter educators review and analyze interpretations of their students.

The process begins initially with an expert conferring with counsel to determine the scope of the assignment and the issues presented. Experts can be expected to interview the deaf person to determine language preferences and linguistic background. If possible, school records or other documentation that provide a social background and criminal background (if relevant) of the deaf person would be examined. The expert will review the interpreter's work and look for a fit between the interpreter's language and the deaf person's language. Furthermore, the expert will examine the interpreter's work to determine if the rendition was accurately interpreted without omissions or alterations.

The expert will typically prepare a transcription and a back-translation of the interpretation. Most experts have an outside verification process of the back-translation. For example, the expert might want a deaf translator to review the interpretation and the back-translation or specific parts of it. The expert will consider statements from the interpreter, if any, that may be in counsel's possession and begin the process of developing opinions for testimony. To inform the opinion, the expert may have evidence of whether the interpreter followed best practices. For example, did the interpreter require a certified deaf interpreter for a police investigation? Did the interpreter insist that the interview was videotaped? If not, why not? Did the interpreter use the appropriate mode of interpreting for the interview? Or, did the interpreter require a team if one was indicated for the assignment? The expert will consider the decisions made collateral to the interpretation and the impact of these decisions on the interpretation.

Finally, the expert will prepare a final report analyzing the interpretation's consistency or effectiveness as compared to the original source language and whether the interpretation was appropriate for the specific background of the deaf person. In the process of developing opinions, the expert will use the legal standard of care and compare the interpretation and the decisions made against it. For example, the expert might opine that the interpretation deviated from the standard of care in that there was direct evidence of incorrectly interpreted words, unresponsive answers by the witness, or that the witnesses expressed difficulty understanding what was interpreted. Submitted with the report are the expert's portfolio of credentials, a bibliography, and a list of prior cases in which the expert has provided testimony.

WHAT TO DO IN CASE OF A SUBPOENA

The final section of this chapter examines how to prepare to testify in a manner that is consistent with the reasonable interpreter standard. Being subpoenaed to testify is a frightening experience. In the past, advice from educators and professional organizations consisted of suggesting that the interpreter tell the requestor that they simply cannot remember what was interpreted. A more defensible approach would be to understand what constitutes a high-risk interpreting environment and to accept assignments with caution and mindfulness. An interpreter should be prepared to testify and justify the decisions they came to in rendering an interpretation in a manner that is professional, respectful to the community, and defensible in court.

Interpreters should assume that their nonprivileged work will be reviewed later by an expert, particularly when the nonprivileged work is legal work. Interpreters should take contemporaneous notes of their decision-making process from the time the assignment is accepted. Notes should be made of the salient decisions that arose in preparing for, staffing, and carrying out the interpretation in the case. They should note any factors they considered in ensuring they followed best practices. They should debrief after the assignment as well and note any unusual or nonstandard events that may have occurred. Because memories do fade and change over time, contemporaneous notes are critical.

Prior to testifying, interpreters should review the interpretation and refresh their memories regarding the decisions made. Interpreters should be prepared to turn over any relevant notes as a part of the discovery process. They should note any deviations from standard practices and justify their decisions or explain the rationale for the deviation. The attorney seeking to subpoena the interpreter can also explain what the challenges to the interpretation are and provide access to the interpreter to review any video, documents, or other evidentiary materials. If the subpoena is from the attorney challenging the interpretation, then the interpreter can ask for these materials from opposing counsel. The interpreter should talk with the attorney who is defending the interpretation and explain their impressions of the accuracy of the interpretation. Interpreters can also provide information and referral to possible experts the attorney may want to consult with or retain in defending the interpretation.

Finally, interpreters should think about how to explain their decisions during their testimony. Attorneys have much advice to witnesses regarding how to respond to questions both on direct examination and cross-examination. Witnesses should listen carefully to the question and think about their answer before giving it. They should remain calm and maintain eye contact with the jury or the judge to whom the interpreter is talking. They should avoid using absolute language, acronyms, jargon, or technical terms specific to the interpreting field. Imagine a jury's impression if the interpreter-witness was talking about having a team "feed" her during an interpretation. Interpreters should not get defensive or upset when the uninformed use terms that are not politically correct in the field, though it is fine for the interpreter to calmly and professionally correct any misapprehensions. For example, if the attorney states that the person is a deaf-mute. The interpreter has the discretion to calmly explain that the term is archaic and supply the proper term for the attorney.

While cross-examination can feel like an attack, interpreters should avoid becoming upset or argumentative with the attorney. If the question contains an incorrect proposition and cannot be answered as phrased, the interpreter should state as much and explain the incorrect proposition. Even when issues occur on cross-examination, the interpreter should keep in mind that the proponent of the interpretation has an opportunity to rehabilitate the interpreter on redirect examination. The interpreter should answer cross-examination questions succinctly and honestly and save the explanations for redirect examination.

CONCLUSION

When adequately prepared, testifying about a prior interpretation is manageable. While the concern regarding confidentiality and trust within the deaf community is real, requiring an interpreter to testify about their prior work serves important purposes in the American system of justice. When an interpreter faces the potential of being a witness, interpreters will be more careful in accepting, preparing for, and adequately staffing assignments. Ultimately, this perceived breach of trust with the deaf community can actually assist in ensuring law enforcement and others hire only interpreters whose work can be successfully defended.

QUESTIONS AND APPLICATION

1. In general terms, consider and explain why the rules of evidence consider an interpretation to be hearsay.
2. Why would an interpreter for law enforcement be considered a testimonial declarant under the Sixth Amendment's Confrontation Clause Analysis under *Crawford*?
3. Discuss the various ways the due process standard for accurate interpretation, the incompetent interpretation standard, and the reasonable interpreter standard for professional malpractice can be applied to specific interpretations or interpreter behavior to determine whether the interpretation meets the constitutional threshold.
4. Consider the terms and conditions you would require prior to accepting a law enforcement assignment, and create a list of items that you would negotiate prior to interpreting an assignment.
5. Consider both direct and cross-examination of the law enforcement interpreter's testimony in a motion to suppress evidence based on an incompetent interpretation—what types of questions would pose the most difficulty for you? Why? How could the interpreter prepare to address direct and cross-examination?

REFERENCES

Brooklyn Law School, Legal Studies Paper No. 263; Loyola-LA Legal Studies Paper No. 2012–14. https://ssrn.com/abstract=2017652
Bullcoming v. New Mexico 564 U.S. 647 (2011).
Chao v. State, 478 So. 2d 30, 32 (Fla. 1985).
Comm. v. AdonSoto, 58 N.E. 3d 305, 314 (Mass. 2016).
Correa v. Superior Court, 27 Cal.4th 444, 453–463, 117 Cal. Rptr.2d 27, 33–41, 40 P.3d 739, 745–7–51 (2002).
Crawford v. Washington, 541 U.S. 36 (2004).
Cruz-Reyes v. State, 74 P.3d 219, 223–224 (Alaska App. 2003).
Daubert v. Merrell Dow Pharmaceuticals, Inc., 509 U.S. 599 (1993).
Durbin v. Hardin, 775 S.W.2d 798 (Tex. App. 1989).
Federal Rules of Evidence. West Pub. (2011).

General Electric v. Joiner, 522 U.S. 136 (1997).
Kumho Tire Co. v. Carmichael, 526 U.S. 137 (1999).
Ohio v. Roberts, U.S. 56 (1980).
Melendez-Diaz v. Massachusetts, 557 U.S. 305 (2009).
People v. Hinojas-Mendoza, 140 P.3d 30, 38–39 (Colo. App. 2005).
People v. Gutierrez, 619 P.2d 598 (Colo. App. 1995).
People v. Villagomez, 730 N.E.2d 1173, 1182 (Ill. 1st Dist. 2000).
Perez-Lastor v. INS, 208 F.3d 773, 778 (9th Cir. 2000).
Registry of Interpreters for the Deaf. (2005). *NAD-RID code of professional conduct.* https://drive.google.com/file/d/0B-_HBAap35D1R1MwYk9h-TUpuc3M/view?resourcekey=0-iOY8FKhinQcukf4Uv8wNjA
Roy, C. (2000). *Interpreting as a discourse process.* Oxford University Press.
Saavedra v. State, 297 S.W.3d 342 (Tex. Crim. App. 2009).
State v. Ambriz-Arguello, 397 P.3d 547 (Or. Ct. App. 2017).
State v. Felton, 330 NC 619, 633–37; 412 S.E.2d 344, 353–355 (1992).
State v. Garcia-Trujillo, 89 Wash. App. 203, 208, 948 P.2d 390, 392 (1997).
State v. Lopez-Ramos, 913 N.W.2d 695 (Minn. Ct. App. 2018).
State v. Montoya-Franco, 282 P.3d 939, 940 (Or. Ct. App. 2012).
State v. Patino, 177 Wis.2d 348, 366–371; 502 N.W.2d 601, 608–610 (1993).
State v. Randolph, 698 S.W.2d 535, 537–539 (Mo. App. 1985).
State v. Rodriguez-Castillo, 188 P.3d 268 (Or. 2008).
State v. Spivey, 710 S.W.2d 295, 297 (Mo. App. 1986).
1A R. Ray, Texas Law of Evidence Civil and Criminal Section.
Taylor v. State, 130 A.3d 509, 528 (Md. Ct. Spec. App. 2016a).
Taylor v. State, 226, Md. App. 317, 324 (Md. Ct. Spec. App. 2016b).
Tiersma, P. M., & Solan, L. M. (March 7, 2012). The language of crime. In P. M. Tiersma & L. M. Solan (Eds.), *The Oxford handbook of language and law.* Oxford University Press.
United States v. Alvarez, 755 F.2d 830, 859–860 (11th Cir. 1985).
United States v. Bel-Iran, 761 F.2d 1, 9–10 (1st Cir. 1985).
United States v. Charles (2013).
United States v. Cirrincione, 780 F.2d 620, 633 (7th Cir. 1985).
United States v. Cordero, 18 F.3d 1248, 1252–1253 (5th Cir. 1994).
United States v. Curbelo, 726 F.3d 1260 (11th Cir. 2003).
United States v. DaSilva, 725 F.2d 828, 832 (2d Cir. 1983).
United States v. Huang, 960 F.2d 1128, 1136 (2d Cir. 1992).
United States v. Lopez, 937 F.2d 716 724 (2d Cir. 1991)
United States v. Martinez-Gaytan, 213 F.3d 890, 892093 (5th Cir. 2000).
United States v. Nazemian, 948 F.2d 522, 526–28 (9th Cir. 1991).
United States v. Santana, 503 F.2d 710, 171 (2d Cir. 1974).
United States v. Sanchez-Godinez, 444 F.3d 957, 960–61 (8th Cir. 2006).

United States v. Vidacak, 553 F.3d 344, 352 (4th Cir. 2009).
United States v. Ushakow, 474 F.2d 1244, 1245 (9th Cir. 1973).
Wadensjö, C. (1998). *Interpreting as interaction*. Routledge.
West v. State, 406 S.W.3d 748, 763 (Tex. App. 2013).

5 MORE THAN LANGUAGE JUGGLING: MEASURES TO BE ADDED TO JUDICIARY INTERPRETER TRAINING IN THE 21ST CENTURY

Scott Robert Loos

EDITOR'S INTRODUCTION

To have any meaning, an assessment must be psychometrically sound. This means that a psychometrician has assessed the validity and reliability of the assessment tool. That is, the assessment yields duplicable results and the assessment tests what it was designed to test—a person's ability to interpret between two languages. In his contribution, Scott points out the elephant in the room: Are we assessing the right domains or enough domains? Where does cultural literacy fit in our assessments of interpreters? Given that language is intertwined with culture and interpreters are working with at least two languages, it makes sense that we also need to be assessing interpreters' ability to understand and communicate effectively in both cultures. Using his 40-plus years of experience of working as a trainer, examiner, and supervisor of English–Spanish interpreters, as well as being one himself, he is able to illustrate the misconceptions held by those with decision-making authority and makes a clear argument for why cultural literacy is a necessary domain in judiciary interpreting training.

As we find ourselves entering the first quarter of the 21st century, the issue of provision of language access professionals in formal public settings across the United States is seen as a challenge. Every provision relating to access to the courts refers quite broadly to "language professionals," an umbrella term for interpreters, translators, bilinguals, and so on and often to "certification," "credentialing," or "licensure" of said individuals. To comply with statute and rule as well as broadly defined law, such as U.S. Title VI, judicial administrators and the bench in general attempt to balance the supply and demand by administering skill-based examinations and overseeing, to a minimum degree, the practice of those individuals qualifying for the work. Interestingly, even in the 1970s, when the California State Interpreter Certification and the U.S. courts interpreter certification laws were enacted, the decision to test without assessing the demography, academic preparation, and development of the pool was never addressed other than via written, multiple-choice exams not unlike those used for college entrance screening.

Because of this omission, immediately following the initial sittings of the first exams, the observation, to the consternation of administrators and the bench, was that so few of the target population (i.e., de facto judiciary interpreters, allegedly bilingual court staff, Spanish-language majors, allegedly bilingual practitioners in other fields, etc.) were successful in their performance on these examinations. This conundrum was of a dual nature: The population group who would be the potential practitioners were apparently not up to the task, and all the work that had been performed to date was now seen as suspect, causing concern about postconviction challenges.

Unfortunately, the presumption reached by practitioners, aspirants, and the consumer population (court officers and managers of the time) was that the examination was too demanding, too difficult, ill-conceived in some way. However, no thought was given to the fact that perhaps the innate skills of the bilingual were not enough to guarantee a viable pass rate on the instrument. In contrast to other professional fields, for example, nursing, medicine, accounting, or law, the professional was not expected to demonstrate abilities in pertinent aspects of the work they would be performing, in most cases as a prerequisite to even the administration of the exam. Usually this included generic academic prerequisites, and the technique "teaching to the test" in preparing the candidate for the challenge.

The concept of testing cultural literacy and the proper mastery of linguistic concepts in order to perform as a liaison in an intense and high-level forum has been neglected over the past 40 years and even today is still often overlooked. The objective here is to posit a more formalized curriculum to be required for professional admission into the field, considering the challenges of the forum in which the individual must perform.

CURRICULUM DEVELOPMENT

The first aspect of the curriculum development is the identification of the skills required to perform the work. In Gonzalez et al. (1991), the authors posit that the level of language sophistication to be held by a person expecting to be employed as a judiciary interpreter is approximately 14 years of education in the American system. This places them at approximately the level of a recipient of an Associate of Arts degree, that is, a community college diploma. Despite this presumption, for decades, no academic level was required either for skills testing or application for employment in the field as a spoken language interpreter. To date, in general there is no mandatory educational requirement for admission to practice. The reasons cited usually include a fear that appropriately skilled candidates would be barred from practice despite the passage of the skills exam, and the continual dearth of potential practitioners would not be remedied.

Considering that judiciary interpreters are expected to maintain the source-language speaker's register, tone, and, of course, semantic value would presume that the interpreter would be of approximately the same education level as that of the most highly educated of their target subjects or at least have been exposed to and instructed in that language reality. Because the majority of interpreters in subject-matter areas, including the law and the courts, have no formal interpreter training outside of online courses or weekend workshops, the presumption that the potential practitioner can grasp and can reproduce the source language in their target language is faulty.

One of the emphases addressed in the training of judiciary interpreters is the production and review of "flashcard glossaries," the two-column word lists offered for the memorization of the target-language item by the interpreter. The presumption that each word used in law (a) has an exact equivalent in the target language and (b) that there is always a one-to-one equivalency between the two, often morphologically similar terms, is woefully ill-conceived. The working lexicons show pairings like *court/corte, law/ley, crime/crimen*, and, as can be seen here, creates an oversimplification of the concept and therefore of its proposed equivalent. There also exists the naïve perception that all alleged users of the two languages can identify equivalencies between the two languages and instantly call them into service while engaged in the phenomenon of interpreting. We can then move to the challenge of finding practitioners who are educated and sophisticated in the social norms of both languages' societies. This then presumes training in, testing in, and oversight of the practice in a wide range of subject areas, not to mention linguistic awareness allowing for an appropriate analysis of lexicon and discourse.

The instruction of the judiciary interpreter in the subject of "law and the courts" is an obvious start. The daily requirement that the judiciary interpreter grasp and process common-law doctrinal concepts into languages not connected to a European, let alone an English, system, is the trainer's first challenge. Although it seems apparent that this would be required, many training programs skip directly to the "how-do-you-say" or "what-do-you-use-for?" method, which ignores the fact that the trainee may not truly understand the semantic value, conceptual basis, or usage of the term in context.

For the purposes of this analysis, we look to the most frequent language combination used in American courts of law, that is, English and Spanish. And then within that pairing, the interpreted directionality of English to Spanish or technical register in Spanish to English.

The trainer's method should always begin with an honest appraisal of their own knowledge and understanding of these concepts and their manifestation, then develop a curriculum designed first to assess that understanding in the student's mind and lay the groundwork for the student's own self-assessment. A great deal is dependent on the practitioner's assessment and prediction of the colloquy awaiting them and ways in which to confront the challenge.

One phenomenon of the preliminary stages of judiciary interpreter development has been the endless coinage of terms presumed to be the equivalent in the target language. Semantic defects have arisen, unfortunately, out of the instructor's own unfamiliarity with the target-language system. This system has bred numerous terms and collocations that would have been incomprehensible to a monolingual legal professional working in the target-language community, not to mention the monolingual lay user of the target language. Often the inappropriateness of the coinage rises to semantic defect, as well. The alternative is to (a) orient the student as to the concept in English law, (b) orient the student as to the existence or lack of same in the target system, and then (c) discuss appropriate parallel semantic units, accepting, modifying, or rejecting terms on an ad hoc basis. This practice should occur for a training program to start with the beginner and move to the more seasoned practitioner within the work environment.

At the initial stages of training, it falls to the trainer to groom the trainee in the cultivation of their own set of skills and techniques but centering on the ability to research terms and concepts in the law and other fields, to learn to accept or reject terms found in bilingual or monolingual dictionaries as to their semantic value and appropriateness. Structural themes in the source-language text would also be considered, but that goes as well to modal skills rather than solely language skills per se. This illustrates one of the reasons why a professional and/or academically prepared translator of the same language combination is not necessarily equipped for the interpreter's task.

Due to the nature of U.S. litigation, the ability of the interpreter to field meaning from, for example, oral argument, jury instruction, and the examination of witnesses at trial is essential. The cultural awareness factor, especially in references used among counsel and between the court and counsel and those directed to a lay audience, is an essential device in the interpreters' toolbox. The lawyer is constantly seeking similes, metaphors, and other analogies to get their point across to the witness or the judicial officer. Such figurative allusions often constitute the most taxing challenges for the interpreter.

The recruitment of practitioners is usually based on the perception of the deciding authorities in a field in which they are essentially laypeople, not experts or practitioners. These authorities, usually court managers, human resource managers, sometimes judges and occasionally lawyers, or even support staff, are unfamiliar with the foreign language interpreting field itself, a field that has yet to evolve into a true profession in regards to prerequisites for the practice: For the most part, there is no licensure; there is no peer oversight. The decision to establish certification exams as the sole determinant of the field in the 1970s essentially stalled the movement in its path toward an academic degree with a follow-up of the passage of a professional exam, without which the individual, no matter what the perception of skill level either among colleagues, or mentors, or their own self-assessment, would not be permitted to work in the field. There are jurisdictions in the United States in which some ongoing training is required, but again there is little follow-up of improvements arising out of such "classes."

Because there is generally no standard academic or professional requirement for practice in the field, it is difficult to choose and/or train the interpreter as an employee. The trainer, often a senior interpreter with little preparation in teaching, training, or orientation, rarely says, "Well, when you were in interpreting school, you may remember the class in common-law doctrinal terminology," because the likelihood of there being such a common experience is practically nil. One of the first challenges faced in the late 1970s in the California State certification process and the U.S. Court certification process was to determine a minimum pretest skill level, since there were so few "interpreting schools" whose degree would stand as a prerequisite for testing. The fear at the time was either that there would be a perceived preferential treatment among candidates (native over nonnative speakers of one language or the other, experiences of an interpreter in another subfield, such as conference interpreting, the practice of law, graduates from the small number of true interpreter schools, etc.) In *Fundamentals*, Gonzalez et al. (1991) address the language competence level as follows:

> The court interpreter must have a superior, unquestionable command of two languages and must be able to manipulate registers from the most formal varieties to the most casual forms, including slang. The interpreter's vocabulary must be of considerable depth and breadth to support the variety of subjects that typically arise in the judicial process. At the same time, the interpreter must have the ability to orchestrate all of these linguistic tasks while interpreting in the simultaneous and consecutive . . . modes for persons speaking at rates of 200 words or more per minute.

Due to the lack of any standardized academic programs to generate a pool of practitioners in 1979, the year the U.S. Interpreter Act was made law, the administration of a skill-based exam instrument without some preparatory screening would have been impractical. At the time, a considerable percentage of practitioners were court employees engaged in other tasks, with no training in the interpreting field and often with no determination of their language competence, let alone their technical interpreting skill. A simple avowal of self-assessment by the employee usually sufficed. Therefore, the Administrative Office of the United States Courts (AOUSC) opted to administer a written-language proficiency exam in a multiple-choice format to determine whether the candidate had the passive language competency of the holder of an associate's degree (2 years of community college) in the two languages, English and Spanish. This was based on Gonzalez's (1977) finding in her doctoral dissertation.

Another neglected aspect of interpreter training for a judiciary setting was the candidate's language identity. Whereas in conference interpreting the interpreter is customarily tagged by the order of proficiency in the two or three languages in which they work, the judiciary interpreter is not. Conference interpreting pragmatics normally has the interpreter placed in a soundproof booth, and the listener is given audio equipment allowing the identification of the language in which they wish to hear the discourse. The interpreter who is channeling the speech delivered in Spanish into an English version is thus assigned to the "English booth" and the English-speaking attendees then listen to the interpreter's interpretation. The presumption is that this interpreter is a native speaker of English and that English is seen as their "first," "native," or "A" language. The theory behind this custom is to ensure the lack of a foreign accent or nonnative usage in the version heard by the attendee and to put the attendee at ease and avoid error or misunderstanding. If there are other official languages to be employed, the interpreters of those languages interpret the English booth's version into their A languages. This can be referred to as "relay interpreting."

This procedure is normally not employed, no matter what the individual's "best" language might be, in courtroom settings. The interpreter is referred to as "the Spanish interpreter," no matter what their personal language identity might be, and the expectation by court and counsel is for the interpreter to interpret everything spoken in English into Spanish and vice versa, no matter what the setting or the pragmatics in which the concepts are delivered. The presumption is that the interpreter's pronunciation of the two languages is at a level of precision and comprehensibility that does not impede communication, including a universally understood accent in both languages or, at the very least, the accents of the interlocutors present. Unfortunately, most interpreter skill exam instruments do not evaluate the accent quality except in a subjective fashion, and the presumption is that the accent remains acceptable only until the rater of the exam finds that the mispronunciation would not allow for the monolingual interpreted subject to grasp the meaning; that is, the interpreter fails in this task.

This phenomenon then extends to cultural identity. Therefore, it is presumed that the Spanish A interpreter has little difficulty comprehending the speech of the monolingual Spanish-speaking subjects. On the other hand, the English A usually has less difficulty fielding the English spoken by monolingual English-speaking Americans, than the English B or C might have. This then brings us to the challenge of assigning a judiciary interpreter to a particular case proceeding based upon the potential issues for them that arise out of language identity. The speech of the layperson in court, whether a civil litigant or a criminal victim, is identified in order to determine the difficulty level for the judiciary interpreter. The decision for the interpreter manager is also to assess skill level vis-à-vis direction of the interpretation. That is, is it more important for the Spanish-only witness to clearly understand the interpreter's version of counsel's questions in English on the witness stand, or is it more important that the English version of that testimony be clear and comprehensible to courts, database, and the jury if there is one? In addition, there is the neverending concern about the record, that is, the preservation of the courtroom language that forms the basis for challenges such as appeals and rulings on motions. Unfortunately for the communication patterns, the monolingual subject appraises skill sets of the interpreter based on the degree of comprehensibility of that interpreter's language, distinct from the interpreter's actual interpreting ability. That is the reasoning behind the attorney's statement that they prefer interpreter X, because, let us say, they are an English A and therefore presumed to be more easily understood by that attorney and the court audience in general.

This writer is unaware of any language identity-related training programs conceived to address this concern. A good deal of this issue arises out of the reality of the courtroom setting for the interpreter. Approximately 75% of all the interpreted discourse in a general jurisdiction court of law in the United States at present is performed in the simultaneous mode. Approximately 95% of that simultaneous interpretation is performed taking English into the foreign language. It is extremely rare for a judiciary interpreter to render a simultaneous version from Spanish, converting it to English, due to physical pragmatics of court interpreting. There is a reluctance to interpret simultaneously into English for the record because the source-language voice and the target-language interpretation are being pronounced at the same time and there is audio overlap, which can affect comprehension by the listeners. The phenomenon of the A or B language arises constantly in the practice of the judiciary interpreter because there is an imbalance in the two languages' use in a court of law. English, being the language of record, is pronounced by, for the most part, native English speakers who are professionals in the field of law, bandying about technical, semantically dense, and detailed terms, at a swifter and swifter rate every day, while the foreign language, for the purposes of this chapter, Spanish, exhibits lay language at a much less detailed and technical register, almost always converted into English, using the consecutive mode. It is rare for a judiciary interpreter in the United States to interpret consecutively into English from Spanish.

Interpreter training programs tend to be based on the interpreting mode, rather than the language combination of the students. The challenges faced by the English A interpreter versus the Spanish A interpreter are somewhat distinct. The errors committed by those language groups are not unlike the errors committed by any language learner in any forum. False cognates, prepositional phrase usage, verb-tense choice, general syntax, and so on, all need to be addressed in assessing the interpreted discourse of the students and, in fact, later on in the practice of the interpreter in an actual court setting. There are some benefits to the mixture of language combination individuals in the classroom or the lab because each subgroup is, to a degree, immersed in the others' language contexts. Unfortunately, many interpreter training programs today use online, individualized remote practice sessions where there is no exchange among or exposure to the fellow students. The classroom setting with a varied demographic allows for commentary among the students. This phenomenon is not unlike the conference team interpreter method, in which two or three interpreters take turns delivering target-language versions, while the other two listen to that person's version and either learn from it or comment on its shortcomings.

The concept of interpreter training is often focused on vocabulary, and many training environments are simply vocabulary expansion workshops. One of the phenomena present in courtroom discourse situations is the use of technical or topic-specific vocabularies relating to the case at hand. The attorneys arguing the matter, the witnesses testifying in the matter, and very often the litigants themselves, have been preparing for months, sometimes years, to present their matter before the court. The interpreter, unfortunately, is often asked to perform with very little preparation and is expected to have a competent command of the terminology to be used at trial, with little or no notice. Unfortunately, the layperson often believes that "if the individual knows" the language, they should be able to yield the technical language and convert it into the target language without any effort. One misunderstanding by court and counsel when the interpreter or the interpreter provider asks for advanced notice regarding the existence of an interpreter need, and any materials relating to that matter, is that the requesters are concerned about scheduling, staffing, or other practical concerns alone. Often, professional interpreters must do research weeks, or even months, in advance, in order to be adequately prepared for the topic to be discussed at trial. This misconception is linked to the presumption that the challenge for the interpreter is solely that of mastering legal and courtroom language. In many instances, if the interpreter is assigned to a fact witness, or more importantly, an expert witness, the specialized terminology used in the event creates the biggest test for the interpreter. So-called law- and courts-related terminology and usage actually may signify less of a challenge for the judiciary interpreter, since most interpreters appear frequently in courts, having heard that language as it applies to most cases.

There are approximately 10 fields or themes that are frequent visitors to courtroom discourse, and which ones present a challenge to the interpreter varies by the individual. Some arise from the nature of the litigation, for example, motor vehicles, human anatomy, business practices, pharmacology, accounting, and so on. Others arise out of the debate of the litigators or pronouncements by the judicial officer, that is, references to Shakespeare, the Bible, classical mythology, film and television, government, social mores, and so on.

All the above topics should be addressed in the interpreter training curriculum. The nature of the equivalency chosen depends largely on the target-language culture. The breadth with which the trainer addresses the subject matter may depend on the area of the law: Family law deals with finances and real estate; criminal law, with sexual conduct and drug traffic; civil law, with contracts and workplace injuries; and so on.

Because English and Spanish are both Indo-European languages with a great deal of common history, the pairing of semantic units across culture and language is relatively practicable. In identifying and analyzing the above subjects, there are specific challenges and characteristics to consider. Taken individually, they are discussed as follows.

SUBJECT-MATTER CHALLENGES

The Sciences

Human anatomy, pharmacology, chemistry, medicine, ballistics, and other forensic sciences are all relatively static. As in all fields generating their own terminologies, one must take into account the broad spectrum of users and usage. Usage that may be correct in Scotland or Uruguay alone are really not applicable in a forum where the English is American, and the Spanish is Mexican. Therefore, a gradual paring down of the terminological ranges is necessary. In lexicography, the identification of the speech sites is usually done before the general opus is begun, or else detailed editorial tags and comments are added to the body of the work.

The next distinction here is that drawn between the scientific reality and the term of art. In forensic medicine and forensic police investigation, the distinction must be made between the true scientific term, for example, *cardiovascular*, and the term of art, for example, *crime scene*.

Technology/Everyday Life

Motor vehicles, as a topic, represent a challenge arising out of the lay connection with the automobile as well as in several other areas to be considered below. The framework of vocabulary in automotive discussions ranges vertically from the lay term to the professional or technical usage and then ranges horizontally from region to region. In Spanish, the distinctions among automotive parts-naming standards are roughly equivalent to those in British versus American English: "lorry/truck," "trunk/boot," "hood/bonnet," "gearbox/transmission," and so on. The judiciary interpreter must either learn the lexicon used by the subject demographic from scratch or discard their own stock in favor of that used by the interpreted subject. This underlines the needs of the judiciary interpreter to inquire about the national origin of the speech subject: Is the person Mexican? Costa Rican? Venezuelan?. Or ask about the region of origin of the person within a nation: If they are Mexican, are they from Chihuahua? Mexico City? Oaxaca? And then followed by an assessment of how that identity impacts the topic and treatment of the same. Another aspect of many of these areas is the familiarity with collocations within the topic: The judiciary interpreter who has never operated a car within the dialectal region in play may be at a loss to interpret descriptive conduct surrounding the factual hardware of the vehicle. For example, "Did you apply the brakes?" "Was the car in neutral?" "The truck skidded and then rear-ended the cab, in the bumper." The inverse is also true, when the foreign language speaker uses a regional or slang term for a feature on the vehicle with which the interpreter is unfamiliar.

Physical Appearance

A parallel exists here when discussing clothing or the physical descriptors of a person. The term "bathing suit" as used by the U.S. English speakers can generate as many as 10 equivalents in the Spanish-speaking world. The exchange between the English speaker and the Spanish-only speaker may require the judiciary interpreter to ask permission to inquire of the Spanish-only subject as to what the reference signifies.

The horizontal and vertical sweeps come into play in other areas as well; the judiciary interpreter may be quite adept at human physiology and anatomy but ignorant of lay usage, including euphemisms and "baby talk," to avoid using the medical term. As with almost all lay jargon, these usages vary within the region. This becomes extremely prevalent in criminal prosecutions for sexual offenses where avoidance of specific usage leads to endless euphemisms in the source language as it is converted to the target: The use of the word "pipi" by the victim of a sexual abuse act should promote the production of the word "wee-wee" by the judiciary interpreter, not an adult slang term for the organ or the choice of a medical professional. Unfortunately for the judiciary interpreter, who is, in the end, the human speaker, some subjective sense of the usage is essential in this area, as opposed to the scientific or technical usage. The management of register usage within a nation is essential for the appropriate rendition, whether in an interview or a witness examination at trial, since the picture painted is often the interpreter's and not the speaker's. This phenomenon then urges the need to create event discussions among the subjects as to the terms to be used and, in a perfect world, some continuity of the individual interpreter in the series of contacts: The probability of the semantic thread being broken is often determined by the number of different individual interpreters who have been involved in the process. Each individual interpreter may choose different usage in either direction of the interpreted discourse, and the English-only subject (the attorney, the judicial officer) may construe that there is a change in meaning produced by the Spanish-only subject and not by the interpreter, leading to allegations of inconsistency on the part of the subject.

At times, a decision must be made as to a stipulated term: When the foreign language subject says X, the interpreters will agree to say Y throughout various exchanges among the subjects, even though Z could arguably be semantically correct. Z may be rejected, if its morphology produces a slightly different subjective or, at times objective, take on the part of the audience member or the interlocutor. Consider the case of the choice of "brush against" to translate the Spanish "*sobar*," rather than "rub." The essential elemental aspect of the offense arises out of the intentional conduct of the alleged offender and so impacts defense counsel's strategic discussions as to proper handling of the client's case. If it is perceived that the perpetrator brushed against the victim's leg, their culpability is questionable based on the offense's code definition and therefore affects both the prosecution's and the defense's strategy at trial.

The broadest range of semantic continuity is dependent on the judiciary interpreter's grasp of legal doctrine, jurisdictionally specific usage, statutory language, and terms of art, all of which must then be confronted with the language of the social and national demographic of the foreign language speaker. The argument made is frequently that the average litigant, criminal defendant, victim, or witness are not familiar enough with technical legal language for the semantic choice to have an impact on them other than to alienate or confuse. However, it must be presumed that the individual has acquired a specific amount of lay knowledge from film, media, or personal exposure ("my cousin got a divorce and she had to ask for alimony . . . "). The experienced judiciary interpreter often asks the English speaker to use the technical term in pretrial interviews in order to sensitize the client, witness, or victim with the term that they will hear in court, through the interpreter, but then, in the interview, to give them a layman's definition or explanation in order to clarify its meaning and usage. Often the English speaker, in addition to the foreign language speaker, will wrongly presume that the interpreter acts as a filter, clarifying, simplifying, or defining the discourse throughout, even though the professional interpreter has been admonished against such practice in their training.

To use the Spanish-only subject as the point of departure, the American English A judiciary interpreter must realize what the semantic or conceptual or doctrinal equivalents in a civil code country would be for the common-law terms used in an American court of law. Currently, Mexico is undergoing a major modification in its criminal process, which has given rise to numerous terms of art to define and qualify procedural and doctrinal differences accompanying those changes. The challenge for the American judiciary interpreter is to have terms at the ready for a new generation of Mexican nationals in order to define the American process for them and mirror, where appropriate, the new Mexican system. The caveat here is the true grasp of the semantic value and practical application of the terms within their own system. This would aid in avoiding the errors made in the 1970s where the practitioner attempted to employ terms or coinages that were simply not up to the task. Often the choice was made based on consultation with a nontechnical bilingual dictionary whose editors were either unaware of the legal usage or opted not to include them because they were seen as technical.

For decades, American judiciary interpreters have used terms as equivalents for common-law and statute-specific usage without considering the actual underlying semantic value in either legal system. Referring to "burglary" using a qualified form of the Spanish word "robo" (denoting either robbery or theft) does not correctly communicate to the foreign language speaker the semantic value (or legal definition) of the term "burglary" in common law. In fact, it often elicits a reaction by the said subject, who denies having committed the offense, since the term used does not carry with it the correct value of the American common-law or state criminal code ("but I didn"t steal anything!"). Such lopsided two-column terms have been used for decades, promoting misunderstanding and ill-conceived decision-making among parties and counsel (e.g., *asesinato* for "manslaughter," *rapto* for "sexual assault," *cómplice* for "accomplice"). *Asesinato* is a broader semantic concept, not addressing intent or recklessness and denoting "murder," *rapto* normally connotes a statutory age range for the victim, and *cómplice* extends to the concept of "accessory."

Because Mexico and various other Latin American systems do not categorize or typify criminal offenses in the same way U.S. codes do, the interpreter's job must be to have at the ready a source of terms that express the semantic value of the offense without colliding with the foreign language term that happens to have a specific semantic value and usage in the home country of the foreign language subjects. If there is an inherent element in the naming of the offense that is not connoted or expressed in the foreign language's term, it must be added adjectivally with a brief prepositional phrase, which of course adds syllables and duration to the pronunciation of the target version. It is, however, an essential element in creating a semantic parallel. Such addition of verbiage is a challenge to the judiciary interpreter, especially in the simultaneous mode, because they may lag excessively behind the source-language delivery when adding those syllables. The classic example again is the common-law term "burglary," which is normally defined in the U.S. common law as an unlawful entry into a private space with the intent to commit another felony or any sort of theft. Because the English word "burglary" is essentially unique to that usage, it does not have an exact twin in Spanish. Lay English–Spanish dictionaries often offer something with the term "*robo*" as the lead, which then creates confusion, since in common law, one can burgle, or burglarize, without stealing anything.

Since the common-law process is based on an oral tradition, there exists a presumption of the existence of parallel procedural and proceeding-specific terms in other systems such as Latin American systems. Mexico has, in the past decade, moved to a rough equivalent of the "oral" trial, creating and naming events to describe the phases of the process. Ironically, the terms utilized and coined by the Mexican legal and judicial fields are not identical to the coinages of the American legal and judicial fields. This triangular semantic flow should actually be a temporary stage in the cross-cultural dance between the systems. Another phenomenon is the coinage of names for functionaries and proceedings that are not actually found in the basic American common-law system and the lack of knowledge about how to interpret them in the foreign target language. Concepts like "trial management judge," "case assignment judge," "trial judge," "pretrial conference commissioner," and so on are hybridized coinages created by court management and implemented by the bench itself. They also vary somewhat across jurisdictional and regional lines in the United States. Unfortunately for the judiciary interpreter interpreting into the foreign language, almost all of these require preconceived explanatory phrases, such as "the judge who oversees the case prior to actually proceeding to trial," "the judge who chooses another judge to preside over the actual evidentiary stage of the trial," "the judge who presides over the actual evidentiary stage of the trial," "the magistrate who receives the case after arraignment but before the assignment of the trial management judge and who hears potential dispositive proceedings," and so on.

To the layperson, no matter what language, most of the phrases sound like basically the same thing in a system in which the parties appear before at least seven or eight different judicial officers. The challenge for the judiciary interpreter is to mark the terms sufficiently in order to allow for comparative distinction when the English-speaking attorney distinguishes for their clients: "After the pretrial conference, we'll move to the trial management judge prior to the trial assignment judge selecting a trial judge. . . . "

Outside of the "technical" language used both in and out of court, the judiciary interpreter must also be ready for discourse aimed at the layperson but pronounced by the bench or the bar in the opening statements and closing arguments, examination of lay witnesses, analogies used to express concepts to the lawyer's client, expressions of emotional impact in family and criminal proceedings, all depending on references to religion, literature, media, popular culture, politics, sports, government, and so on. The judiciary interpreter should have a good command of idioms, similes, proverbs, and other frozen language, whether pulled from Aesop's fables; the tales of the Brothers Grimm; the Bible; Greek, Roman, Norse, or Egyptian mythology; classical literature, Shakespeare; and so on. For the source-language judiciary interpreter at least the cultural and literary realities have some overlap: Centuries of interchange created standardized translations, depending on the degree of interaction among the cultures. The farther apart the sociocultural realities of the language populations, the harder it is for the judiciary interpreter to produce equivalents—and equivalents that produce the same emotional and subjective impact and imagery are often a challenge. Again, we consider the horizontal range and vertical range—making references to biblical heroes with fixed phrasing describing their conduct is near impossible when the interlocutor, or the judiciary interpreter themselves, are from cultures without any reference to such tradition. The presumption is that the judiciary interpreter is at least primed for these references in either direction; even if they do not have a prepared equivalent ready to deliver, at least they can express conceptual equivalence in either direction. The crime victim using the phrase to express the impact of the perpetrator's conduct should expect a solution that conveys a comparable subjective value to their target listener.

A proper tool in teaching language styles are works like Hirsch et al. (1993) and Wilson and Jones (2009). Both of these works, offering a broad overview of knowledge, can be employed by the interpreter trainer with an eye toward assessing the interpreter's global knowledge and, therefore, their ability to field source-language allusions and transform them into target-language solutions.

The curriculum that is generated, therefore, by this rather broad range of topics must have a logical progression from analysis and discussion to actual application within the strictures of the interpreting modes. The instructor should define the most frequently used topics and incorporate their analysis into the curriculum. Here (Table 1) is an example of the phase of the curriculum that addresses the broad topic of "law," it being an essential model for the other subject areas chosen by the instructor. It is counterproductive to present topics within modal exercises that have not been addressed in the classroom; for example, discussing the "burden of proof" and "weight of the evidence" is essential before the interpreter student or trainee can begin interpreting oral arguments in which those two phrases are used. It is often useful to provide some terminology in advance to the students or trainee, solely to ensure recognition when actually discussed in the classroom. It also allows the instructor to evaluate the terminologies on the basis of modal skill rather than vocabulary knowledge.

One aspect of interpreter success that is often discounted is the basic level of recognition on the part of the interpreter, of the usage and discourse in the forum in which they are to perform. If an experienced interpreter is to change jurisdictions within their career, it is likely that the interpreter will spend time in court simply listening and digesting the colloquy as it exists in that jurisdiction. It is also essential that the interpreter be exposed to the rules of procedure and the codes in force within that jurisdiction in which they are to perform, because their mention will be bandied about endlessly by court and counsel, with no concern for the listeners' ability to process them. The interpreter, for example, performing in a criminal change-of-plea proceeding, will be expected to juggle the sentenc-

Table 1. Model Balanced Curricular Structure for English-to-Spanish Interpreters Practicing in the United States.

Common-Law Usage and Lexicon (U.S. English)				Civil Code Usage and Lexicon (Mexico)			
Analysis	Contextual samples	Modal practice	Review by instructor	Analysis	Contextual samples	Modal practice	Review by instructor
History and patterns	Language taken from codes, constitutional text, and pleadings	• Sight translation • Simultaneous	Classroom discussion of performance	History and patterns	Language taken from codes, constitutional text, and pleadings	• Sight translation • Simultaneous	Classroom discussion of performance
Law Enforcement Investigative Instruments (U.S. English)				Law Enforcement Investigative Instruments (Latin America)			
Syntax, lexicon	Actual instruments (police reports, pre-sentence reports, etc.)	• Sight translation • Consecutive of mock explanation and commentary from English-only subject	Classroom discussion of performance	Syntax, lexicon	Actual instruments	• Sight translation • Consecutive of mock explanation and commentary from English-only subject	Classroom discussion of performance
Nonlaw topic usage and lexicon (see body of chapter)				Nonlaw topic usage and lexicon			

ing ranges, stipulations, and the fines to be imposed, not to mention the names of the offenses as employed in that jurisdiction.

In general, the interpreter should be encouraged to prepare for major proceedings, such as trials, by researching and drafting a lexicon to have available during the project. The notion that the interpreter performing at a trial, the broadest and most complex of court proceedings, without these specific tools to support them during its pendency is ill-conceived. Each cause of action is unique in its legal issues, subject-area records, and factual narrative. One of the causes of interpreter challenges is that few interpreter supervisors insist on this sort of preparation for trial work; in addition, it creates a challenge for the interpreter who is assigned ad hoc to a case with no opportunity to prepare. This goes to the identification of the interpreter career as a nonprofessional field of endeavor. Unfortunately for the practicing judiciary interpreter, the final say as to the degree of preparation and level of performance usually falls to someone outside of the field, although seen, structurally, as the overseer of the work. Therefore, it is advisable, in a position in which the interpreter is expected to perform at trial, no matter what the area of the law, to have a preformatted file listing facts and strategies to be offered and records of procedure carried out before trial and case-specific data, such as certain usage by counsel and interpreted subject, nationality of the speakers, and so on. The latter can also be useful if the interpreter who has prepared the file is not the interpreter expected to perform at the time of trial because of staffing pragmatics.

CONCLUSION

Judiciary interpreter practice is a field requiring an extremely broad range of familiarity and knowledge. The aspects of the work noted here must be balanced with the modal skill development throughout the career of the practitioner. Law and the sciences, society, and communication all evolve constantly, and, if the topic is addressed in a court of law, the interpreter must be expected to have at the ready the appropriate equivalents to facilitate communication in that setting. The broadest challenge to the practitioner currently is the resistance of the court and its management to identify these issues and to cooperate with the interpreter community in their handling.

QUESTIONS AND APPLICATION

1. What does cultural literacy mean?
2. How might one demonstrate they are culturally literate in the languages they are working between?
3. What are the tell-tale signs that someone is not culturally literate in a particular language?

REFERENCES

Gonzalez, R. D. (1977). *The design and validation of an evaluative procedure to diagnose the English aural-oral competency of a Spanish-speaking person in the justice system* [Unpublished dissertation]. University of Arizona.

Gonzalez, R. D., Vásquez, V., & Mikkelson, H. (1991). *Fundamentals of court interpretation*. Carolina Academic Press.

Hirsch, E. D., Jr., Kett, J. F., & Trefil, J. (1993). *The dictionary of cultural literacy*. Houghton Mifflin Company.

Wilson, W., & Jones, J. (2009). *An incomplete education*. Random House.

Part Three

Research

6 DEAF WISDOM FOR DEAF ACCESS

Christopher Stone and Gene Mirus

EDITOR'S INTRODUCTION

> *Interpreters are constantly working to appear native in at least two languages. Educators often encourage new interpreters to immerse themselves in the communities for whom they will interpret. This works for everyday conversations about health, life events, school, and so on. However, when the discourse becomes specialized—that is, medical, academic, legal—interpreters must engage language experts. Through their study, Stone and Mirus's discussions with two attorneys show the benefits of learning how deaf attorneys talk about and communicate about the law.*

TECHNICAL/SPECIALIZED LEGAL terminology in American Sign Language (ASL), as with other minority languages, seems to have emerged and evolved due to the need for experts in the legal field to communicate with precision and brevity. This represents a different language pressure than providing access to lay deaf people to the legal process. For deaf professionals this is shaped by two concerns: the initial emergence of a specific discourse type within legal education, via sign language interpretation, and the development of the legal discourse type with deaf–deaf professional interaction. This process is often at odds with, or somewhat different from, the institutionalization of interpreter-led ASL lexical development. These projects tend to be aimed at supporting interpreters when working in the legal system to interpret for deaf nonlawyers in the legal system.

It is our contention that due to this difference, deaf professional ASL language ideology should be part of ASL interpreters' ASL repertoire. The rationale for this is that it can inform interpreters working with sign languages. It should also encourage interpreters to explore the occurrence of this phenomenon within their own Deaf community professional networks so that they can reflect upon their language use and language repertoires within legal settings for different language needs.

When deaf students begin their training as lawyers and require sign language interpreters to access this legal education, they often engage in discussions with their interpreters to craft language that is appropriate to their needs, language sensibilities, and language ideologies. These language resources are often created on a local basis, in situ, and draw upon a variety of translanguaging strategies (ASL sign-compounding co-articulated with English, Latin mouthings, fingerspellings of English, Latin, fingerspelled signs, and so on; see Stone & Mirus, 2018) but are rarely shared as part of a wider community of practice. (We will discuss the layering of resources and repertoires in greater depth below.)

This language use is also professionalized as deaf lawyers engage in legal practice on a daily basis. This practice typically involves the engagement of small teams of preferred interpreters without much interaction with larger language projects/institutions (e.g., the development of legal signs). Often these larger projects are strongly focused on interpreters supporting interpreters rather than drawing upon deaf professional's specialist acumen. Most of the instructional resources created to date are based on the language use by nondeaf signers, with very little incorporated into such resources pertain-ing to Deaf community–generated knowledge and professional dis-course. These projects may therefore miss resources and repertoires in deaf lawyer communities of practice that could be part of a larger community of practice.

Hearing sign language interpreters across the United States are not afforded the opportunity to interact regularly with deaf lawyers whose networks are professionally focused. These networks afford opportunities for deaf lawyers to come together as colleagues without the need for interpreters. As such, interpreters are often not privy to or familiar with ASL legal terminology used by deaf professionals. Furthermore, sign language interpreters bring their own language ideologies that may be at odds with those of deaf professional lawyers, who are bilingual and engaged in multiresource multilingual translanguaging.

This chapter will explore data from interviews with two deaf lawyers identifying the strategies that they describe engaging in when wishing to discuss the law with fellow experts, either during their education via interpreters or with each other. By better understanding how deaf ASL users with legal knowledge engage in legal discourse, we are better able to understand how interpreters can craft an interpretation that suits the needs of deaf ASL users in general and in so doing provide appropriate access to justice.

LANGUAGE IDEOLOGIES

In recent years, deaf peoples have often struggled to maintain and safeguard their traditional in-group languaging because of language policies (and their underpinning ideologies) created and enforced by dominant-language groups. Through time, language ideologies (Kroskrity, 2000) are negotiated at different levels and are constructed and reconstructed (Blackledge, 2000). The examination of power and identity among both minority and dominant "language" groups is a prerequisite to understanding their respective language ideologies (Woolard, 1998).

The majority of sign language users are not raised using sign language and so may have access to mainstream privilege, that is, hearing people with institutionalized power. In this regard, language ideologies can either threaten a minority "language" community, such as by language development being planned and maintained by those who are not primary users of sign languages, or, positively, there could be a concerted effort to support the community with, for example, bilingual policies that ensure traditional linguistic features are respected as sign languages are used in newer domains. Our data speak to these issues.

With respect to the language ideologies found within the community and those taught to sign language interpreters, it can be difficult to ensure that sign language teaching and interpreter education are both sensitively delivered such that educated interpreters draw upon multiple resources appropriately moment by moment and situation by situation. Teaching can essentialize language in line with the language ideology of the sign language teacher. It can also focus on constructions that might be significantly different from majority surround languages but less frequently used in everyday community (Fenlon, 2019). This focus can then mean that educated interpreters overrely on structures and strategies they have been taught rather than being responsive to requests from their service users as we now discuss.

Language Ideologies in Interpreter Training

Within interpreter education, explicit exploration of language ideologies is rarely found and yet the notions of needing to "be more visual" or "use more depiction" (Dudis, 2004) or "fingerspell more/less" are all instances of educators, both deaf and hearing, raised in sign language or acquired later, permeating their teaching with language ideologies. Many of these ideologies rely on intuitions or personal insights rather than being evidence based, such as frequency-based data from sign language corpora (this being a relatively recent phenomenon; Fenlon et al., 2015).

These intuitions may have crystallized during the educators' own training, may be due to exposure to specific local practices, and may not be sensitive to language use of different populations, different geographical regions, or evolving languaging practices. It can be difficult to ensure that students learn strategies that will support their development within the classroom but not stymie their practice when working with language users, when we know that languages change over time.

Often at the forefront of changes in practice are the everyday users of the language; keeping abreast of these changes and developments can be difficult for those who do not socialize with them. In a crowded curriculum, it can be challenging to ensure that interpreters professionalize their languages in ways that are sensitive to languages users, some of whom may fall outside of the smaller community of practice that learners are exposed to (i.e., peers, sign language teachers, local deaf community members, professional interpreters). The practices that become habitual and the ideologies underpinning them may be at odds with deaf communities as we will now discuss.

Language Ideologies in Deaf Communities

Deaf communities often have their own language ideologies that may be categorized as folk linguistics (Stegu et al., 2018, for further discussion), which can include believed etymologies of sign lexicon, the use or nonuse of mouthings (Sutton-Spence, 1999), the use or nonuse of fingerspellings, and so on. Silverstein (1979, p. 193) defines linguistic ideologies as "sets of beliefs about language articulated by users as a rationalization or justification of perceived language structure and use." These ideologies may come from folk linguistic rationalizations or be grounded in some linguistic training (as we will see below); nonetheless, they influence how we think about the "correctness" of the language use we see before us and our reactions to it. Deaf communities and sign language interpreters often have overlapping ideologies, but these ideologies are by no means the same.

There is no monolithic deaf community with a single ideology, and recent work on translanguaging (Kusters et al., 2017), language portraits (Kusters & de Meulder, 2018), and language shaming (Haualand & Holmström, 2019) demonstrate that in different places at different times, notions of language, languaging, and use of different varieties can be seen positively or not. Much is the same with interpreting professionals (which is also not a monolithic "community"), with different interpreters being motivated to produce sign language that conforms to some idealized or essentialized notion of "pure" sign language or providing access to majority spoken language terminology without considering how this may or may not be achieved in a way that reflects local preferences and practices.

We know from our interviews (described below) that there is "intergenerational" transmission of strategies and lexicon within the deaf communities our informants come from. Both interviewees mentioned that they had passed on their experience of working with interpreters at law school to other potential law school students. And more specifically that they had discussed their strategies for creating lexicon for legal concepts and even shared some of the vocabulary that they had used during their law school years with peers.

In many ways, this sharing of wisdom enables the circumvention of the need to invent/translate/problem-solve within the classroom and focus on learning. This can in fact be understood as a form of calculated consumer labor (Brunson, 2008, 2010), where the consumer engages in labor that could be conceived as the labor of others. Interpreters could engage in this labor; however, as the transmission of this ASL linguistic capital appears to be limited, to some extent we feel that an exploration of the strategies used will help us to better understand how linguistic resources can be put into effect. This could in turn reduce the calculated consumer labor deaf lawyers need to engage in.

In our data set, we also see that sign neologisms or new usages must be conceptually accurate and aesthetically presentable; if the *new* sign lexicon breaks either of these rules, it is not deemed fit for the purpose. To this extent, we would expect to see some rapid changes in lexicon, and a corpus of specialized legal discourse would in many ways help us to explore and address the differing strategies that different deaf legal professionals engage in.

Layering of Linguistic Resources

Sign languages comprise a variety of linguistic features that co-occur to form words, sentences, and discourse. Sign phonemes are described by features such as handshape, movement-hand internal, movement-path, place of articulation, and so on (Brentari, 1998). As expected by the duality of patterning, morphemes are comprised of these phonemes, although we also see the co-articulation of a set of mouth gestures (Boyes-Braem & Sutton-Spence, 2001) that have adjectival and adverbial properties. The mouth can engage in mouth gestures or mouthings where mouthing may be considered as an additional language resource.

Mouthing is a language feature enabling the borrowing of words from spoken languages into sign languages, either partially or fully articulated on the lips either during the production of a manual sign element or as a standalone production. The mouthing might spread across several manual signs such as a noun phrase or verb phrase, which might influence the full or partial articulation of the "borrowed" word element. Some of these mouthings may well share different semantic representation to their manual components (Vinson et al., 2010).

Most sign languages also have hand configurations (either one- or two-handed) that represent orthographic systems, known as fingerspelling (see Sutton-Spence, 1994, for a comprehensive review). Fingerspelling is often considered nonnative lexicon in sign languages (Brentari & Padden, 2001) in that their phonological constraints and rules differ from those of the other lexicon (core and noncore). Some of these fingerspellings can become nativized such that they are considered sign language lexicon or fingerspelled signs. Other fingerspellings are representative of borrowing from the written form of the surrounding spoken language or from other written languages such as Latin.

We also need to understand that since humans have two hands, they can articulate two different manual elements that can also have a mouthing and other facial grammar co-articulated simultaneously. This simultaneity is exploited when sign languaging and can also include gestural elements of a nonlinguistic nature, also known as depiction (Liddell, 2003). Co-articulation is ever present in sign translanguaging, as we will describe below, where there are expectations of a variety of "language" features being brought together. These code-blends (Emmorey et al., 2005) are complex and, depending on the individual, may include voiced elements too, although this is beyond the scope of this chapter.

INTERVIEWS WITH DEAF LAWYERS

As part of a research project looking into the practices of deaf lawyers and the emergence of ASL legal discourse, we interviewed two deaf lawyers to understand how they talked about the law, whether there were extant deaf legal communities of practice, and whether there was an emerging ASL legal discourse driven by deaf lawyers. The interviews were semistructured (Spradley, 1979) in nature and were videoed for later analysis. The interviewer was deaf, raised with ASL, as were all of the interviewees. Themes and categories were identified in the videos using ELAN (https://tla.mpi.nl/tools/tla-tools/elan/) and analyzed to explore the issues that were salient for the lawyers.

The lawyers we interviewed attended different law schools and did not discuss with each other their ways of navigating law school prior to enrollment. And yet we see that the deaf lawyers engage in many of the same strategies of legal languaging, using a variety of languaging strategies in their work and in the hiring of interpreters to meet their needs. We will now discuss the two main themes that emerged and consider them in the context of legal interpreter education: languaging strategies and preferred interpreters.

Languaging Strategies and Language Ideology

Sign languages layer resources to create meaning with the linguistic features (as described above). This fine-grained description of sign languages supports interpreters to better understand how they can appropriately "pronounce" signs so that they are articulated or "enunciated" well. Descriptions of translanguaging practices that consider a variety of semiotic resources (Kusters et al., 2017; Stone & Mirus, 2018) also enable us to consider how spoken and written language resources are incorporated into languaging strategies. These elements seem to be clearly at play when deaf lawyers enter law school.

Both of the deaf lawyers understand language and languaging to be an evolving process and work with their interpreters to ensure that initial language strategies do not crystallize when it becomes apparent that changes need to be made. Here we see that the deaf lawyers are conscious of the need to engage in calculated consumer labor. For example, lawyer 1 (whom we shall call Bob) said:

> You need to develop [the language/lexicon] as you go along, some are easy, some require more thinking to develop and establish [the language/lexicon], some of the language took three years to establish, it evolved [throughout my time at law school].

This moves away from the idea that there is one solution or that language used within one moment will therefore be used without reflection and change. This ideology itself can be at odds with interpreter education programs, especially where most if not all of the students are second-language learners of ASL and whose first languages are larger languages with instituted legal lexicon. These students may well ask themselves "What is the sign for xxxx?" without there being a discussion around immediate neologisms that might work well in the moment and evolved forms that evolve and change through usage.

It is also important to note that it was the deaf lawyers who led the process of change rather than the interpreters working within the law school environment. As lawyer 2 says (whom we shall call Bobby):

> Sometimes I would feed a sign to the interpreters, they would accept the sign and use it, I would then say no change the sign it does not fit the concept, mentally it would conflict, then the interpreter would change their sign.[1]

We also see that sometimes the evolution of legal signs deemed appropriate by the deaf lawyers in law school can evolve within the moment and over time as greater understanding is developed (discussed in the section "Languaging as Education and Embodied

---

1. The interviews were conducted in ASL; the translations here are the authors own, with participant validation.

Learning" in this chapter). And that this is deaf-led rather than interpreter-led as a languaging practice.

The signs can also change because deaf knowledge is sought. As Bobby says:

> what other [signs] oh MAKE-MISTAKE[2](tort) -T-O-R-T- MAKE-MISTAKE(tort) I learned that sign from another deaf lawyer "I asked when you went to law school what was your sign for this" and the sign was given to me which was fine and I took it.

Here Bobby asks for the sign and also exercised some judgment over whether the sign was acceptable for their own usage. Here we see that the deaf law school student is engaged in invisible calculated consumer labor; that is, interpreters do not see this labor but it contributes to the deaf law school students having a better service. Bobby said that:

> -t-o-r-t- is MAKE-MISTAKE because Tort is a civil action when someone is vexed by someone thinking "you did me wrong."

The root meaning of the legal term falls well within the semantic range of an ASL sign and so this is used. However, the additional semiotic resource of English is also co-articulated with the English mouthing "tort" during the production of the ASL sign MAKE-MISTAKE. The final reason for lexicon changing is because as Bob says:

> Sometimes you have to go back and tweak sign usage because later on you realize that the sign better fits a different legal term that pops up later, so you tweak a previous sign you modify as you go along.

Again, this appears to be motivated by ensuring that the ASL sign chosen for the legal term falls within the semantic range of the sign. And then in Bob's case further reflections enable a finer-grained disambiguation driven by the ASL lexicon and its differentiation between different concepts.

Not only must the concept be right but both Bob and Bobby agree that it needs to be a sign or sign compound that follows the linguistic rules of ASL. Here we see a difference in background;

---

2. ASL signs follow the ID glosses found in aslsignbank.haskins.yale.edu if present.

Bobby has some formal sign language linguistics education at the undergraduate level, saying, "The sign needs to follow the rules and not be made up." Bob relies on a more folk linguistic approach, saying, "Sometimes interpreters have awkward signs the sign must be natural and flow." We can understand that this means the signs need to follow the phonotactic rules of ASL.

Co-Occurrence of Linguistic Features

We will now look at the occurrence of specific linguistic features used by deaf lawyers in the United States to discuss the law. There are several strategies that are adopted and different language features that are used to express these concepts. We will look at fingerspelling, then compounding, and then look at the role of mouthing (English and Latin) in sign translanguaging.

Fingerspelling

Within many sign languages fingerspelling is often articulated in two different ways; the first is often referred to as fingerspelled signs where the orthographic pattern is phonologically reduced. For example, the fingerspelled sign #bus in ASL is not produced as -B- -U- -S- but with the partial articulation of the -U-, which could be represented thus -B-u-S-. This reduced form has a corresponding reduction in the time taken to produce the sign. The second form of articulation is a full orthographic pattern with the full production of each hand configuration for each letter. This can still be produced at speed, but each letter is enunciated.

Fingerspelling is a common way that some lexis enters sign languaging. This strategy can be common within educational contexts, especially if education is being accessed via an interpreter, such as when students are mainstreamed, but is used more broadly as a translanguaging strategy. Fingerspelling is used to a greater or lesser extent by different communities across the United States (and in sign languages across the world). This usage can differ across age, profession, and region. For the deaf lawyers, fingerspelling is used to quote and use both English and Latin legal terms. In our data, we

Table 1. Fingerspelled Legal Terms.

Full Form	Reduced From	FS Sign
	estoppel	
rea judicata		
		-s-j- (summary judgment)
weapon		

see legal terms being quoted and then compounds given (see below), but we also see some legal terms being fingerspelled (see Table 1).

For example, *estoppel* is fingerspelled in a reduced phonological form, and we see *rea judicata* fingerspelled but in a fully enunciated form. The first example "borrows" from "English" and the second from "Latin." Generally, we see that "Latin" legal terms are fully enunciated whereas "English" legal terms are reduced. This difference does not appear to be due to a lack of knowledge or frequency of use per se, but it could be due to the less frequent articulatory pattern of fingerspelled "Latin" words—the phonotactics of the words differ. What is clear is that both types of fingerspelling are used by deaf lawyers for in-group talk among lawyers and with interpreters within education settings.

Compounding

In looking at and documenting signs used by deaf lawyers, it is useful to see what signs are used and to see whether this follows similar patterns observed in historic language change; that is, although these appear to be in-group talk, the compounding process itself is not altogether novel. In looking at the literature with regards to historical change in spoken languages and in ASL (e.g., Frishberg, 1975), change often happens in response to the need for efficiency of production, that is, phonological reduction. For example, historically, the ASL sign GOLD was a compound of the signs EAR and YELLOW, but now that compound has phonologically reduced to a single sign in response to pressures for smoother and quicker movement.

For the deaf lawyers, we see similar compounding occurring, but we also see that part of this compounding is in situ language planning, as Bob explains:

> Most of the time when establishing a new sign for a legal concept, so if I established a new sign or developed a new sign, I felt that it had to have a logical relationship to the meaning, it had to be easy to remember and repeat, that it should not require an exclamation when it was being signed . . . this meant that along the way some signs were tweaked and so it continually evolved.

These neologisms are clearly meaning-driven compounding, but from a position of understanding the law, the terms that are used, and the different language resources that can be co-articulated. It is not clear whether the use of all the resources and their co-articulation are planned, or are spontaneously produced, especially when we consider mouthings, be they partial or full; this will however be considered below. It is possible that the mouthings contribute to pragmatic narrowing by further specifying which aspect of the semantic range the lexicon is representing. What is clear is that it does not violate the innate phonological rules for ASL of the deaf lawyers.

There are several examples of compounds that we can see in our data. When each of these examples were produced during the interviews the metalinguistic and legal knowledge was given by fingerspelling, explanation, and then compound. For example, we see one of our informants saying:

> Injunction—it means you need to file something to stop or put something on hold . . . I try to think how to compound signs, for example FILE+STOP that's easy to remember and to reproduce so that when an interpreter heard the word injunction they could reproduce that compound, and when I signed FILE+STOP they could say the word injunction. This strategy did not require the addition of fingerspelling or an explanation.

Here we use the + to denote removal of the terminal hold for each sign (FILE and STOP) such that the production of each sign is phonologically reduced to produce the compound seen in the English words *black bird* and *blackbird*. The motivation for the neologism stems from wishing to express the notion of *injunction* in something that is more "ASL like."

We also see the same informant giving further examples of compounds, such as *estoppel*, which is produced as the compound TALK+STUCK, and subpoena, which is produced as:

> REQUIREMENT+SUMMON again a compound it means a judge has filed a demand for you to attend court and you are required to show up so the compound could be either REQUIREMENT+APPEAR REQUIREMENT+SUMMON but the sign APPEAR doesn't make sense because the person subpoenaed hasn't come to court yet.

Here we see that the informant is making clear meaning distinctions between the verb APPEAR and SUMMON, demonstrating that the compound has clear rules in its formation.

Thus far, the descriptions we see appear to be examples of traditional language contact rather than examples of translanguaging. Historically it could be said that in ASL the role of mouthing is dis-preferred, with fingerspelling often being articulated with no co-articulation of mouthings. In our data, however, what is emerging is not only the use of fingerspelling (nonnative lexicon) and compounding (of core lexicon) but also the co-articulation of mouthing as a linguistic resource, which we shall now go on to describe.

Mouthing

Mouthings are the partial or full borrowing of spoken languages into sign language, although their articulation is principally unvoiced, and often the orthographic shape is mouthed; for example, the word "doubt" might have mouthed articulation of the silent "b." We can see from one of our informants that different language resources have the co-articulation of mouthings and occur both on fingerspellings and compounds (see Table 2 for examples).

We see that if a fingerspelling is fully enunciated then the mouthing moves toward being closer to fully mouthed. Even so, it is worth reiterating that the mouthing component follows the prosodic rhythm of the fingerspelling—it is a hybrid form that is not part of

Table 2. Signs and Compound Signs.

Signs	Mouthing (Full or Partial)	ID Gloss ASL Signbank (yes = √, no = X)
FILE+STOP	injunction	X + √
SPEAK+STUCK	estoppel	X + X
REQUIREMENT+SUMMON	subpoena	√ +√
REQUIREMENT+APPEAR	subpoena	√ +√
HAMMER +WISE	jurisprudence	√ +√
WISE	jurisprudence	√
SET-UP+BEFORE	precedent	√ +√
SETUP	precedent	√
HAMMER+FINISH	res judicata	√ +√
HAMMER+DECIDEnoix+FINISH	res judicata	√ +√
IF+MANAGE	jurisdiction	√ +√
IF+AREA	jurisdiction	√ +√
AREA	jurisdiction	√ +√
AGAINST	sue	√ +√
AGAINST+	litigation	√ +√
MAKE-MISTAKE	tort	√ +√
COMPLAIN	objection	
COMPLAIN+CONNECT	relevance	X +√
COMPLAIN+OFF-THE-POINT	astray	X +√
COMPLAIN+ OFF-THE-POINT NOT POINT	astray	X +√ X √
PICK-ON+++	badgering	X
SITUATION	case	√

an English speaker's repertoire. In this translanguaging, we see the fingerspelled words that

> historically might have not had any mouthings at all now have mouthings and these include: injunction, estoppel, subpoena, jurisprudence, precedent, tort, res judicata, and jurisdiction.

The compound words also have mouthings that delineate the compounds' noun–phrase prosodic word "boundary." Here we will show the COMPOUND (mouthings), for example, SET-UP+BEFORE (precedent), IF-AREA (jurisdiction) where the words in SMALL CAPITALS are glosses for the ASL manual lexicon (using the ID glosses of the ASL signbank where one exists), and the word in (brackets) represents the mouthing that might be partially or fully mouthed. We also begin to see the disambiguation of signs such as the traditional sign of IF (court/judge) with the use of mouthings: HAMMER (judge), HAMMER+DECISION (jurisprudence), IF (court), IF+ROOM (courtroom). And one of our informants noted that "more and more people use the sign HAMMER (judge)" for "judge" rather than the traditional sign. This could be seen as the lexicalization of a depicted action but with a clear co-articulation of the mouthing of English.

Again one of the important things to note here is that although the coding system we are using, that is, COMPOUND (mouthings), reads as if these elements occur consecutively, instead they are co-articulated. This co-articulation allows for a code-blend of an ASL manual element and an English or Latin mouthing element to be expressed and complement each other.

Languaging as Education and Embodied Learning

The deaf lawyers engage in languaging as a way of being educated and then reflect upon the information represented within their own language, which is itself a repository of knowledge. This self-development is shared not only with their interpreters but also with other deaf people (as seen above). This raises the issue of several lexical items for some concepts, such as "subpoena" where we see two compounds, each of which might represent a different part of the process. ASL could arguably have two signs for this depending on whether the subpoena is being issued or the person subpoenaed is now appearing in court, as described by Bob. This would represent an interesting lexical specificity in ASL. Other alternatives such as jurisdiction or jurisprudence appear to demonstrate phonological reduction as might be expected with typical sign language diachronic change.

The deaf lawyers have clear notions of what the lexicon should and should not be; both say that the signs should not be initialized (unless they are abbreviations), should draw from the ASL lexicon, can be single or compounded signs, and should be conceptually accurate. This also embodies the notion that the lexicon needs to be aesthetically presentable.

Bob feels that "if you need to explain the sign then that defeats the purpose." The sign/sign compounds need to stand alone and be conceptually accurate to the English meaning but drawing upon the semantic range of the ASL lexicon so that it is also faithful to ASL.

The descriptions that we have of lexical development, either of signs or sign compounds co-articulated with English or Latin words, demonstrate an understanding of the English terms with the semantic range of single signs. The signs or sign compounds also represent a fine-grained understanding of productive compounding that conceptually represents legal ideas but is also true to the phonotactics of ASL. They also tell us about deaf wisdom and sign language thinking with respect to terms and concepts within the legal domain that enable deaf lawyers to engage in the multiple co-articulation of their semiotic repertoire.

Close observation of this should be encouraged within the classroom such that interpreters better understand the lived experience of understanding the law, be that as a deaf lawyer in law school or as is more prevalent, a deaf person's experience of the legal system as they navigate through it. There are some comments from the lawyers regarding fingerspelling, such as -w-e-a-p-o-n-, which would satisfy the needs of a deaf lawyer but probably not that of a deaf layperson within the legal system. And in fact it is noted that deaf laypeople within the legal system have different needs from those of deaf lawyers, as Bob says:

> Some would say "I'm a certified interpreter" I would reply "This is different I'm not a deaf client here I'm a deaf lawyer here I want word for word what the judge said what words he used, exactly what my opposing counsel says, exactly what I say even if they appear different."

Here we see that needs not only drive lexical choice but also the style of interpreting required. This also leads us to the discussion of the interaction between the deaf lawyers and interpreters more generally.

Preferred Interpreters

One of the themes that emerged from the interviews was the choice of interpreters, the deaf law students' desires to work with interpreters leading the process for team creation, and the tailoring of the interpreting service to their needs. Both Bobby and Bob discussed the need to inform their preferred agency or law school of the need to choose appropriate interpreters. One of the issues is that even interpreters with a legal interpreting qualification may not have had experience interpreting in law school and that this is a different demand to other types of legal interpreting. Bob said:

> The agency said they would send someone with legal certification but I said this is a different situation as I want all the details interpreted too … not a translation but more of a transliteration.

In many ways this is ensuring that interpreters are sensitive to the needs of different clients. As we know from Kusters (2017), deaf people's interactions often include multiple semiotic resources that may be used at any moment. Different situations might require different varieties and of course a different style of interpreting.

Both deaf lawyers also talked of the need to establish vocabulary for legal terms as detailed above; of interest were their discussions around the reactions of the interpreters to this process. Bob said that for law school he had a team of 8 to 10 interpreters, 3 of whom worked throughout the 3 years of the program. This consistency, as we often find in other work, was important for him. It enabled a consistency of lexical use and of knowledge of the expectations of the type of interpreting that was required.

Bobby also discussed the need for collaboration that is deaf-led. She said:

> One interpreter was very experience, she had worked with another

deaf lawyer before, she feed me some signs for terms, I gave her feedback some of the lexicon was fine others not.

This collaboration worked well and is still around, tailoring one's interpreting service for the needs of the client. This is deaf-led even if the interpreter comes from a place of experience. These decisions were further supported by the positioning of the interpreters. Rather than working side by side, one interpreter sat next to Bobby. This meant that clarification of the sign choice against specific English terms could be given with the interpreter seated next to Bobby writing the English terminology. This process enabled further feedback to be given or for further learning on Bobby's part as a law student. Here again we see that opportunities to learn for the deaf law students happen bilingually and can be facilitated by cooperative interpreters.

CONCLUSIONS

The deaf lawyers were highly engaged with their learning and with the interpreting service that was delivered to them. It can be seen that the lawyers participated in an appreciable amount of calculated consumer labor. For interpreters being educated to work in legal domains, it is important to understand the amount of interaction that they may experience with a deaf lawyer. It is also important to reflect that this may not be a privilege afforded lay deaf people within the legal system, and yet it is something they might very well benefit from.

The deaf lawyers were also sensitive to the fact that they might represent a legally knowledgeable client, which may well be outside the experience of the interpreters that they worked with. As bilinguals who were learning law, the deaf lawyers actively engaged in lexical creation and were keen for that lexicon to evolve as their understanding of law did too. Again, this process is something that we can raise in education. While this is the experience of the deaf lawyer, it is conceivable that this is also the experience of a layperson experiencing the legal system for the first time and gradually gaining a better understanding of different aspects of the process, the different role of different actors, the consequences of legal charges, and so on. This evolving understanding could well be portrayed in the language used by a deaf layperson with incrementally changing understanding. As such, it is also important for interpreters to be sensitive to these moments of understanding and modify their language use accordingly.

The deaf lawyers engaged in the complex use of multiple semiotic repertoire to represent the language of the classroom and to facilitate their learning. This engagement in languaging was fundamental to their learning process, and they worked with interpreters to ensure that was understood and facilitated for them. This flexibility is a useful approach for interpreters in the legal field more generally when working with a diverse range of legally qualified professionals and laypeople as noted above. When educating interpreters to work with the "super" diversity of deaf people in the legal system, from lawyer to layperson, educated to drop-out, we need to ensure that they are given tools, such as the layering of linguistic resources, that enable them to tailor their labor to the peoples they serve.

QUESTIONS AND APPLICATION

1. Develop a plan to work with professionals (deaf and non-deaf) so that you might learn how they discuss their areas of specialization.
2. What do the authors mean by "language ideologies"?
3. The authors suggest that all interpreters have language ideologies, and those can be at odds with the language ideologies of deaf people with whom they work. Discuss your own language ideologies. How do you negotiate language ideologies with consumers, explicitly or implicitly?

REFERENCES

Blackledge, A. (2000). Power relations in the social construction of "literacy" and "illiteracy": The experience of Bangladeshi women in Birmingham. In M. Martin-Jones & K. Jones (Eds.), *Multilingual literacies* (vol. 10, pp. 55–70). John Benjamins.

Boyes-Braem, P., & Sutton-Spence, R. (2001). *The hands are the head of the mouth: The mouth as articulator in sign language*. Signum Press

Brentari, D. (1998). *A prosodic model of sign language phonology*. MIT Press.

Brentari, D., & Padden, C. (2001). Native and foreign vocabulary in American Sign Language: A lexicon with multiple origins. In D. Brentari, (Ed.), *Foreign vocabulary in sign languages*. Lawrence Erlbaum Associates.

Brunson, J. (2008). The practice and organization of sign language interpreting in video relay service: An institutional ethnography of access [Unpublished doctoral dissertation]. Syracuse University.

Brunson, J. (2010). Visually experiencing a phone call: The calculated consumer labor Deaf people perform to gain access through video relay service. *Disability Studies Quarterly, 30*(2). https://dsq-sds.org/article/view/1245/1273

Dudis, P. (2004). *Depiction of events in ASL: Conceptual integration of temporal component* [Unpublished PhD dissertation]. Univresity of California, Berkeley.

Emmorey, K., Borinstein, H. B., & Thompson, R. (2005). Bimodal bilingualism: Code-blending between spoken English and American Sign Language. In J. Cohen, K. T. McAlister, K. Rolstad, & J. MacSwan (Eds.), *ISB4: Proceedings of the 4th International Symposium on Bilingualism* (pp. 663–673). Cascadilla Press.

Fenlon, J. (2019, September 26–28). *Sign language linguistics and sign language reaching: Re-aligning the two fields* [Keynote presentation]. Theoretical Issues in Sign Language Research (TISLR) 13, Hamburg, Germany.

Fenlon, J., Cormier, K., & Schembri, A. (2015). Building BSL SignBank: The lemma dilemma revisited. *International Journal of Lexicography, 28*(2), 169–206. http://discovery.ucl.ac.uk/1437532/7/FenlonCormier-Schembri_BuildingBSLSignBank_IJL_inpress_compressed.pdf

Frishberg, N. (1975). Arbitrariness and iconicity: Historical change in American Sign Language. *Language, 51*(3), 696–719. https://doi.org/10.2307/412894

Haualand, H., & Holmström, I. (2019). When language recognition and language shaming go hand in hand—Sign language ideologies in Sweden and Norway, *Deafness & Education International, 21*(2–3). https://doi.org/10.1080/14643154.2018.1562636

Kroskrity. P. V. (2000). Language ideologies in the expression and representation of Arizona Tewa ethnic identity. In P. Kroskity (Ed.),

Regimes of language: Ideologies, polities and identities (pp. 329–359). James Curray.

Kusters, A. (2017). "Our hands must be connected": visible gestures, tactile gestures and objects in interactions featuring a deafblind customer in Mumbai. *Social Semiotics, 27*(4), 394–410. https://doi.org/10.1080/10350330.2017.1334386

Kusters, A., & De Meulder, M. (2018). Language portraits: Investigating embodied multilingual and multimodal repertoires. *Forum: Qualitative Social Research, 20*(3). http://www.qualitative-research.net/index.php/fqs/article/view/3239/4452. http://dx.doi.org/10.17169/fqs-20.3.3239

Kusters, A., Spotti, M., Swanwick, R., & Tapio, E. (2017). *Beyond languages, beyond modalities: Transforming the study of semiotic repertoires* (pp. 219–232). http://eprints.whiterose.ac.uk/116337/3/IJM%20intro.pdf

Liddell, S. (2003). *Grammar, gesture, and meaning in American Sign Language.* Cambridge University Press.

Robinson, K. (2017). *Looking to listen: Individual "turns" in Deaf space and the worlds they conjure* [Unpublished doctoral dissertation]. University College London.

Silverstein, M. (1979). Language structure and linguistic ideology. In P. R. Clyne, W. F. Hanks, & C. L. Hofbauer (Eds.), *The elements: A parasession on linguistic units and levels* (pp. 193–247). Chicago Linguistic Society.

Spradley, J. P. (1979). *The ethnographic interview.* Harcourt Brace Jovanovich.

Stegu, M., Preston, D. R., Wilton, A., & Finkbeiner, C. (2018). Panel discussion: Language awareness vs. folk linguistics vs. applied linguistics. *Language Awareness, 27*(1–2), 186–196. https://doi.org/10.1080/09658416.2018.1434821

Stone, C., & Mirus, G. (2018). The development of Deaf legal discourse. In A. Blackledge & A. Creese (Eds.), *The Routledge handbook on language and superdiversity* (pp. 442–455). Routledge.

Sutton-Spence, R. (1994). *The role of the manual alphabet and fingerspelling in British Sign Language.* [Unpublished doctoral dissertation]. University of Bristol.

Sutton-Spence, R. (1999). The influence of English on British Sign Language. *International Journal of Bilingualism, 3*(4), 363–394. https://doi.org/10.1177/13670069990030040401

Vinson, D. P., Thompson, R. L., Skinner, R., Fox, N., & Vigliocco, G. (2010). The hands and mouth do not always slip together in British Sign Language: Dissociating articulatory channels in the lexicon. *Psychological Science, 21*(8), 1158–1167. https://doi.

org/10.1177/0956797610377340

Woolard, K. (1998). Introduction: Language ideology as a field of inquiry. In B. Schieffelin, K. Woolard, & P. Kroskrity (Eds.), *Language ideologies: Practice and theory* (pp. 3–49). Oxford University Press.

7 JUSTISIGNS: DEVELOPING RESEARCH-BASED TRAINING RESOURCES ON SIGN LANGUAGE INTERPRETING IN POLICE SETTINGS IN EUROPE

Jemina Napier, Robert Skinner, Graham H. Turner, Lorraine Leeson, Teresa Lynch, Haaris Sheikh, Myriam Vermeerbergen, Heidi Salaets, Carolien Doggen, Tobias Haug, Barbara Bucher, Barbara Rossier, Michèle Berger, and Flurina Krähenbühl

EDITOR'S INTRODUCTION

> *Legal interpreter educators must recognize the unique challenges of working in police settings. The effectiveness of interpreting with the police has a ripple effect for the rest of the case. The authors use a mixed-methods approach and identify potential barriers to access in police settings. Among these barriers are the inconsistent application of and adherence to laws requiring qualified interpreters, the lack of awareness of police officers, and lack of understanding by deaf people. They used this information to develop a training "masterclass" for police, interpreters, and deaf persons.*

THERE IS A GROWING BODY of literature that examines sign language interpreting provisions and practices in legal contexts in various countries, and the common theme in the results of all these studies is the limitations faced by deaf sign language users in gaining access to justice, either through inadequate interpreting provision, poor-quality interpreting services, or lack of training, accreditation, and standards for legal sign language interpreters and translators.

The *Justisigns* project was an action research project funded by the European Commission Lifelong Learning program.[1] It represents a ground-breaking initiative that focused on providing qualified and qualifying sign language interpreters with new competencies in interpreting within *police settings*. The remit of the project was to develop evidence-based training courses to be made available to sign language interpreters, police officers, and deaf sign language users in Scotland, Ireland, Belgium (Flanders), and Switzerland as well as to any other interested stakeholders. In addition, the project developed various other resources to support sign language interpreters, police officers, and deaf sign language users in navigating interactions in police settings.

A mixed-methods study that involved surveying deaf people, interpreters, and police officers through questionnaires, focus groups, and interviews, as well as conducting a qualitative linguistic case study analysis of an authentic sign language interpreter-mediated police interview, was conducted with a view to informing the development of the training courses and other deliverables in the project.

Justisigns was a timely project given the passing of a number of European Union (EU) directives in recent years that relate to the position of those who come in contact with legal systems in the EU as accused persons, witnesses, or victims. There are two relevant EU directives to consider in relation to legal interpreting: (1) Directive 2012/29/EU, establishing minimum standards on the rights, support, and protection of victims of crime, and (2) Directive 2010/64/EU on the right to interpretation and translation in criminal proceedings (Leeson & Phelan, 2016). According to Directive 2010/64/EU, the member states of the European Union are bound to safeguard quality control for all spoken and sign language interpreters in criminal proceedings. In Article 5 of the same directive, it is stated that quality control should be carried out through the establishment of a national register of interpreters, but no definitions or guidance are provided on how this should be conducted. The provision of legal interpreting even *within* many countries in Europe is incon-

---

1. See http://justisigns.eu.

sistent, as, for example, Leung (2003) has reported in the United Kingdom.

There have been various projects that have focused on promoting access to quality and standards in legal interpreting across the EU (e.g., Hertog, 2001, 2003, 2010), and a comprehensive survey of legal (spoken language) interpreting in Europe was commissioned by the European Commission Directorate General (DG) for Interpretation (Hertog & Van Gucht, 2008). The survey found that more than half of the EU member states do not have any specific training in legal interpreting, and any training provision tends to be organized at a local level, which is not accessible to interpreters in the rest of the country. It was also found that there is great disparity in the level and quality of legal interpreter training throughout the EU. A follow-up report (European Commission, 2009) gave an overview of recommendations for best practice for legal interpreting in the EU and stressed that appropriate and consistent training, both for new and already practicing legal interpreters, should be provided across the EU along with an EU Code of Conduct for legal interpreters, and assessment of legal interpreter quality through testing and certification should also be a requirement (Giambruno, 2014). The commission also recommended that empirical data should be collected as a basis for evidence-based, nationally coordinated and informed planning of legal interpreting.

Although it can be seen that there are clear recommendations for standards and best practice of legal (spoken language) interpreting across Europe, according to Gallai (2012, p. 144) there is still an "incoherent kaleidoscope of regulations, guidelines and provisions" for legal interpreters in the EU and until the *Justisigns* project, a pan-European survey of legal sign language interpreting provision, standards, and training had not been conducted.

This chapter provides an overview of some of the key themes that emerged from the *Justisigns* project, with respect to the barriers faced in providing access to justice, and will describe the delivery of two of the key training courses that were developed based on the research findings: (1) a masterclass for deaf people, interpreters, and police officers together, and (2) an online curriculum for credit-based courses for police officers and interpreters.

We will begin by giving an overview of the methodology of the *Justisigns* project and then a review of police interpreting research. We then describe the different stages of the mixed-methods study, with a brief summary of findings, before we detail the examples of two of the evidence-based training courses that were developed and delivered. We discuss the merits of the different training opportunities that were offered, concluding with acknowledgment of the benefits of using an evidence-based approach to training police interpreters. Although we focus specifically on the training of sign language interpreters in Europe, we are confident that the various training courses that we share are applicable to the training of sign language interpreters worldwide.

THE *JUSTISIGNS* PROJECT

The *Justisigns* project was an action research project conducted by a consortium of hearing and deaf researchers and sign language interpreter practitioners from across Europe, who all brought their own experiences to the examination of deaf signers' access to police settings.[2] There were several key challenges that arose throughout the project, in relation to the securing of funding, gaining research ethics approval, collection of data, and dissemination of findings to a diverse group of stakeholders; so it was imperative that the team included deaf researchers who could shape and inform the process in culturally appropriate ways and hearing researchers who are fluent signers. We also gave great consideration to our positionality and responsibilities as a team to ensure the research was carried out to align with deaf-ethical values and to translate into real impact for signing deaf communities (see Leeson et al., 2017, for more discussion).

The ground-breaking initiative focused on providing qualified and qualifying sign language interpreters new competencies in

---

2. In collaboration with the European Forum of Sign Language Interpreters and Interesource Group (Ireland) Ltd.

interpreting within a legal setting and specifically with a focus on *police settings*. The remit of the 36-month project was to develop evidence-based training courses and resources for sign language interpreters, legal professionals, and deaf sign language users in Ireland, Belgium (Flanders), Switzerland, and the United Kingdom, but such resources could also be used more widely by stakeholders across other European countries and internationally. In addition to the training courses, we also developed other resources, including a guidebook and poster for police officers; leaflets and guidelines for deaf sign language users and interpreters; executive summaries in sign language; and translations of police cautions in the project's different written and sign languages.

The mixed-methods project involved the collection of various data across Europe, including the following: desk-research review of relevant police interpreting studies; an online survey to collect empirical evidence of legal sign language interpreting provision across Europe (Napier & Haug, 2016); focus groups and interviews with police officers, interpreters, and deaf sign language users who have been in contact with the police (Doggen, 2016; Leeson et al., 2021; Skinner & Napier, in press); and analysis of an authentic sign language–interpreted police interview (Napier et al., forthcoming). Results of the project have been disseminated in various ways, including written/signed blog posts;[3] academic, community, and professional interpreter conferences; community information events; and critically, ongoing engagement with national/regional/local police forces. Importantly, the findings of the project have been used as an evidence base for the development of training materials, which is the focus of this chapter.

---

3. See, for example: https://lifeinlincs.wordpress.com/tag/interpreting/page/2/, https://lifeinlincs.wordpress.com/2015/05/19/justisigns-promoting-access-to-legal-settings-for-deaf-sign-language-users/, https://lifeinlincs.wordpress.com/2016/08/16/when-dealing-with-the-police-deaf-people-are-at-a-major-disadvantage/.

WHAT DOES RESEARCH TELL US ABOUT POLICE INTERPRETING?

In the 1990s, the seminal "Access to Justice" project was conducted in the United Kingdom, which involved a UK-wide investigation of the experiences of deaf British Sign Language (BSL) users in accessing the British legal system. Findings highlighted a range of issues that prevented equal access to justice, including a lack of deaf awareness on the part of legal personnel, misunderstandings about BSL as a language, issues connected to deaf people's varying levels of literacy skills, and varying standards of interpreting provision (qualified and nonqualified). Various linguistic issues were also identified, in relation to lack of legal terminology in BSL by contrast to the highly formalized and technical discourse of legal English, challenges of bimodal interpreting in legal contexts, modality difference, and misunderstandings of the interpreter's role (Brennan, 1999; Brennan & Brown, 1997; Turner, 1995; Turner & Brown, 2001). Although the Access to Justice project did not focus only on police interpreting, it did highlight some key issues for deaf people when being interviewed by police. The project noted that (at that time) few deaf people understood their own legal rights; interviews with deaf suspects/witnesses/victims were not videotaped so there was no way to corroborate the original sign language source text; police officers did not make the necessary adjustments to enable the interpreter to do their job; there was a need to develop internal policies that promote the use of good practice, such as only booking qualified interpreters and filming interviews; and there was a lack of training opportunities to prepare interpreters to effectively work in police interviews.

More than 20 years on, the sign language interpreting profession still has no official status in Europe or globally (de Wit, 2012), and worldwide we still witness difficulties in obtaining or ensuring the quality of sign language interpreters in legal settings (Brunson, 2008; Kermit et al., 2011). In fact, it had been found that sign language interpreters in the United States choose *not* to specialize in legal interpreting due to a lack of training (Roberson et al., 2012a). This is not only an issue for sign language interpreters; Berk-Seligson

(2009) has found that there are often appeals in legal proceedings due to the use of unqualified spoken language interpreters in police interviews (including relatives or friends of the person interviewed or police interviewers or other police personnel), and there is often evidence of coercive language and abuse of minority language users' vulnerable situation during police interviews with gaps in police knowledge about the process of interpreter mediation (Tipton, 2017).

Thus, the right to a professional interpreter is probably more important during the police interview than later in court, as it is the first stage of the legal process when evidence is collected, and interpreters have a critical role in drafting written records of interviews (Defrancq & Verliefde, 2018). Nevertheless, there are risks and benefits to having an interpreter present in a police interview (Goodman-Delahunty & Martschuk, 2016) as it adds a layer of complexity to the communication (Filipoviç, 2019). Interviews have an evidentiary role; they are essentially an information-gathering act, and that determines the way language is used. The police interview is "a highly regulated form of discourse that is structured around legislative requirements, its 'institutionality' is constructed through the participants' interaction as they negotiate the organisational goals" (Heydon, 2005, p. 4), the primary aim of which is "the collection and synthesis of evidence into a written statement for use in any subsequent court hearing" (Coulthard & Johnson, 2007, p. 80). Monolingual interviews and interpreted interviews are two different entities as the presence of the interpreter impacts on the nature of the co-constructed discourse (Russell, 2001).

In addition to the scripted structure of police interviews, police officers are also trained to employ specific discourse techniques to build rapport, using specific questioning techniques, managing turn-taking, and using silence strategically. Thus, language is a communicative device, a tool to achieve the interview goals. One of the distinctive features of language in investigative police interviewing is the combined use of "ordinary" language with legal language in some parts (Gibbons, 2003). So, it is imperative that interpreters understand the goals of a police interview in order to ensure that the communication is mediated successfully. For example, delivery of the caution[4] and the adjacent stages in a police interview can present particular problems for interpreters and the accurate delivery of the caution (Russell, 2000). The delivery of the caution follows a script and is often accompanied by an explanation of its meaning or simplification of its formulation by police officers. The challenge for interpreters is not only related to legal terminology but also to how language is used in that context. There is a risk that if interpreters use too free an interpretation approach, then the important legal aspects of the caution may not be included, and if too literal an interpretation approach is used, the minority language user might not understand (Russell, 2001), as legal language is particularly challenging for people from language minorities to access (Shuy, 2003).

Although there is now an emerging body of research in spoken language interpreters working in police settings, there is still a dearth of research on sign language interpreting in this context. Nevertheless, much can be learned from the research with spoken language police interpreters. Kruglov (1999) was the first to examine spoken language interpreting in this context and noted that interpreters do not always convey politeness strategies as intended by police officers and that cultural interpretation choices can significantly affect the understanding of the intent of the speaker. More recent linguistic analyses of police–suspect interviews have revealed that if interpreters do not understand the deliberate questioning techniques used by police officers (e.g., use of silence), the techniques can be obfuscated in the interpretation, so it is important that interpreters utilize appropriate linguistic choices and interpreting strategies to match the intent of the police interviewer (Hale et al., 2020; Lai & Mulayim, 2014; Lee, 2017; Määttä, 2015; Mulayim et al., 2015; Nakane, 2007, 2011, 2014). If an interpreter has a lack of "discursive expertise" (Böser, 2013), it can affect the integrity of the interviewing technique. It has been found that interpreters can have a disruptive effect on the conduct of a police-suspect interview in how they handle turn-taking, interruptions, and overlapping talk,

---

4. In the United States, this is known as the Miranda rights.

and police officers can lose control of their ability to build rapport with the suspect through the interview (Gallai, 2013, 2016; Hale et al., 2019, 2020). Power issues are evident since the police interviewer depends on the interpreter to elicit information from the suspect (Nakane, 2014). Furthermore, detainee incomprehension may go unnoticed if police officers rely solely on interpreters to manage the communication (Komter, 2005; Monteoliva, 2020).

All of these sociolinguistic spoken language interpreting studies highlight the intercultural communication challenges faced in interpreted police interviews and, thus, the need for training that is dedicated to specifically exploring the policing context. These studies also reveal the importance of having equivalent research on sign language interpreting in police interviews, in order to identify parallel challenges. A recent study of policing and deaf BSL users in the United Kingdom (Race & Hogue, 2018) surveyed police officers and police crime commissioners through a questionnaire instrument to evaluate their attitudes toward deafness, and deaf community members were surveyed with an adapted version of the questionnaire about their experiences of contact with the police and their perceptions of the level of deaf awareness among police officers. Race and Hogue (2018) found that despite some progress, much more work is needed with training and promoting awareness of the needs of sign language users in police settings. One of the recognized limitations of their study was the limited response from deaf community members due to the questionnaire format, with a recommendation for use of focus groups to elicit a richer data set. Furthermore, Race and Hogue's (2018) study did not focus specifically on deaf users' and police officers' experiences of working with interpreters; also, they did not survey interpreters about their experiences. This was later rectified with research by Skinner et al. (2021), which included focus groups with deaf BSL users, but the focus was solely on deaf BSL users' contact with the police through video remote interpreting. Thus, this is where the *Justisigns* project contributes to a gap in the literature.

WHAT DID THE *JUSTISIGNS* DATA TELL US?

The *Justisigns* project took an interdisciplinary approach, exploring police interpreting from geographic, sociological, and linguistic points of view: (i) geographically, a questionnaire was administered to key stakeholder organizations across Europe to ascertain the level of provision of legal interpreting to deaf sign language users (Napier & Haug, 2016); (ii) sociologically, focus groups and interviews were conducted with interpreters, deaf people, and police officers to explore their experiences of interpreted police interviews (Doggen, 2016; Skinner & Napier, in press); and (iii) linguistically, an authentic sign language interpreter-mediated police interview was analyzed to identify salient communicative features during the interview (Napier et al., forthcoming). In this chapter, we give a brief summary of the method and findings from each stage of data collection in order to contextualize the evidence base that was used to develop and deliver the training. More details of the research findings are discussed elsewhere.

Questionnaire

A questionnaire was developed based on the survey of the literature and input from the *Justisigns* partners and presented in plain English in the online survey tool Survey Monkey. The questionnaire included a range of questions with single-choice answers, multiple-choice answers, and open-ended questions. Target organizations were identified using network and snowball sampling (Hale & Napier, 2013), and the questionnaire link was distributed via the mailing lists of the European Forum of Sign Language Interpreters (efsli), the European Union of the Deaf (EUD), the Sign Language Linguistics Society (SLLS), and also through social media and the personal and professional networks of the research team. The survey was online for one month in 2014.

A total of 87 responses were received. After incomplete and non-European responses were removed, the final number of returned questionnaires considered for the purposes of analysis was

45, from 21 different countries. The respondents included 4 deaf associations, 18 sign language interpreter associations, 10 educational/research institutions (providing interpreter training), 10 interpreting service providers, and 1 translators association.

The results revealed that sign language interpreters are not consistently provided in legal settings across Europe. Where provision is in place, sign language interpreting agencies are primarily responsible for organizing sign language interpreters in legal settings, but the government, courts, or police typically pay for them. The most common legal setting where sign language interpreters work is court, closely followed by police settings. The qualifications required of sign language interpreters in legal settings vary from country to country, ranging from none to general sign language interpreting qualifications; but none require a specific legal interpreting qualification. Some countries offered some form of legal interpreting modules as part of sign language or general interpreter education programs, but none had any formal specific legal interpreter training programs for the purposes of specialization. Continuing professional development (CPD) training is available for professional interpreters on working in legal settings in many of the countries, but the provision is ad hoc. There is no specific legal interpreter certification available for sign language interpreters anywhere in the European countries surveyed, so sign language interpreters cannot currently specialize in legal interpreting in Europe.

Focus Groups and Interviews

In order to drill down into the experiences of stakeholders in police interviews, focus groups or one-to-one semistructured interviews were conducted with a range of deaf people with experience of police interviews, deaf and hearing interpreters with experience of working in police interviews, police officers with experience of working with (nonsign language) interpreters, police officers with experience of interviewing deaf people, and two police officers in the United Kingdom who have a specific remit to work as advisors.

when a deaf sign language user comes into contact with the police[5] (see Table 1).

Prompt questions were tailored for each participant group and probed on experiences across a range of issues in working as, or with, sign language interpreters in police interview contexts, including the following: steps that would normally be taken to ensure an effective police interview, ethical codes for interpreters in police settings, the role of the interpreter in police settings, sign language interpreter qualifications and experience needed to work in police settings, the challenges of interpreting in police interviews, the process of booking and selecting sign language interpreters for police interviews, training requirements for police officers and interpreters on working together, and rights of deaf sign language users in police settings. Each focus group or interview was conducted in the relevant sign or spoken language of the country, depending on the participant group, and was recorded using video- or audio-recording devices as appropriate. The video or audio files were then fully transcribed for analysis. Thematic analysis was used to identify key themes in the discussions, following Braun and Clarke's (2006) proposed six-stage process: (1) familiarization with data, (2) generating initial codes, (3) searching for themes among codes, (4) reviewing themes, (5) defining and naming themes, and (6) producing the final report.

In summary, the findings reveal that despite the fact that there is legislation in place that insists on equality before the law across Europe and that there are clear directives that only qualified interpreters should be used in the legal system, there is an inconsistent approach to the provision of sign language interpreting in police interviews: The use of video-recording of interviews is not consistent, and there are still some instances where a sign language interpreter is not used at all in police interviews.

---

5. Police Link Officers for the Deaf are now deployed in several police forces in the United Kingdom, whereby police officers learn BSL and are trained specifically to provide accessible services to deaf BSL users. The police force that led the way in this initiative was the Hampshire Constabulary. See: http://slfirst.co.uk/community/help-advice/hampshire-police-plod-reaching-into-deaf-community.

Nevertheless, it was perceived that attitudes toward interpreters on the part of police officers are improving, and there is a growing awareness that ideally a qualified, professional interpreter should be used in police interviews, even though interpreters are not always vetted. However, there were mixed views on whether the police have sufficient deaf awareness and understanding of the needs of deaf sign language users in police interview contexts. Deaf participants reported various ongoing barriers and challenges in interacting with the police and how they have developed different strategies to "bypass" these challenges, such as bringing in their own interpreter, adopting other communicative strategies to deal with a police officer if they do not know how to communicate with a signing deaf person, or contacting an interpreter via video communication link if immediate interaction with a police officer is needed (e.g., if they turn up on the doorstep at home), which cannot be foreseen (Doggen, 2016).

A clear picture emerged from the data that interpreters often have a gatekeeping role: signposting officers as to who to appoint as an interpreter, how to maintain ongoing contact with someone who is deaf, how to communicate via an interpreter, and how to communicate with someone who is deaf. This is because the interpreters had a higher level of experience in dealing with deaf people in police settings, whereas officers had low-level experience of deaf people and sign language. Thus, police officers were comfortable in deferring to interpreters and welcomed the interpreter's guidance (Skinner & Napier, in press). Interpreters felt uneasy about this but deemed it a necessary a duty to offer guidance.

It was widely agreed that there is not sufficient formal legal interpreter training for working in police contexts and not a clear enough understanding across the stakeholder groups of the role of the interpreter (e.g., whether they should coordinate turn-taking in interviews).

One big improvement noted by participants is that some police forces have policies in place to guide officers when it comes to interviewing deaf suspects/witnesses/victims, and a few police forces in the United Kingdom in particular have begun to develop online

Table 1. *Justisigns* Focus Group/Interview Participants.

Country	Participant Group	Format
UK	5 police officers with no prior experience of working with sign language interpreters	Focus groups
	4 police officers with experience of working with sign language interpreters	Focus groups
	4 police officers with experience of working with sign language interpreters and with assistance from Police Link Officers for the Deaf	Focus groups
	2 Police Link Officers for the Deaf	1:1 interviews
	4 experienced legal hearing sign language interpreters	1:1 interviews
	9 deaf sign language users	6 in focus group, 3 × 1:1 interviews
Belgium (Flanders)	1 police officer	1:1 interview
	9 deaf sign language users	1:1 interview
Ireland	10 interpreters (5 deaf, 5 hearing, all with experience working in the legal domain)	1:1 interviews
	2 lawyers	1:1 interviews
	2 other stakeholders	1:1 interviews
	32 police officers with experience of working with spoken language interpreters, but very few had experience of working with sign language interpreters	Training programs discussion
	c. 20 judges*	Conference discussion

Country	Participant Group	Format
Switzerland	1 representative of the State Court of the Canton of Zurich	1:1 interview
	1 representative from the Cantonale police force of Lucerne	1:1 interview

* In Ireland, due to protocols in place, it was not possible to formally interview police officers as part of the research project. However, the team was invited to deliver training in a number of venues across Ireland to police officers via our project liaison with GRIDO (Garda Racial and Intercultural Diversity Office). We had the opportunity to draw generally from the participants' comments and discussion. Similarly, at the invitation of the president of the district courts, a presentation was made to the conference of district court judges, with time set aside for discussion of judges' experience (Leeson & Phelan, 2016).

videos, recognizing the specific linguistic and cultural needs of deaf sign language users. Another positive development is that there is now an increased number of deaf professionals working within the legal system, either as lawyers or in other legal capacities. There are not, as yet, any deaf police officers. From the police perspective, experiences of working with interpreters are generally positive, but there is a "training-to-practice gap" as found in the UK survey of police officers with respect to deaf BSL users (Race & Hogue, 2018). This training gap is also identified with respect to working with spoken language interpreters (Howes, 2019; Wakefield et al., 2015).

Authentic Interpreter-Mediated Police Interview

The *Justisigns* team was fortunate to be able to access authentic data provided by Police Scotland of an audiovisual video-recorded sign language interpreter-mediated police interview, which we could examine as a case study of a sign language interpreter-mediated police interview. The participants in the interview were two police officers, a BSL/English interpreter, and a young deaf BSL-using suspect. The interview was led by one police officer accompanied by a second police officer. The interpreter worked in simultaneous mode. The duration of the interview was 36 minutes. The goal of the interview was to collect the deaf suspect's statement related to an incident of assault and burglary. The video footage was transcribed/translated and analyzed in ELAN, a computer program that allows the precise alignment of transcription with video data and which is increasingly used in studies and teaching of sign language interpreter–mediated interaction (e.g., Goswell, 2011, 2012; Major & Napier, 2012).

In line with the work of other sign language interpreter researchers (such as Marks, 2012, 2015; Metzger, 1999; Roy, 2000), the interaction was analyzed through the lens of sociolinguistics and how the interpreter functioned as a participant, identifying examples of rapport-building and politeness strategies, turn-taking, role-taking, and footing shifts. We have also drawn upon the work of spoken language interpreting researchers to consider the examination of the embodied, multimodal nature of the interaction (cf. Davitti, 2016; Davitti & Pasquandrea, 2017) as interpreting between a sign and spoken language is inherently multimodal (Major & Napier, 2019); hence, we considered how the interpreter managed the communication through nonlinguistic means (e.g., eye gaze, body gestures). We also analyzed the interpreted utterances using Wadensjö's (1998) rendition taxonomy to identify any marked utterances that were expanded or reduced or nonrenditions where the interpreter inserted their presence through their own interjection or zero renditions when the source text was not interpreted at all.

Our preliminary analysis has identified the following issues:

- The bimodal BSL/English regime has an effect on the assessment of credibility and cooperativeness of suspects.
- Gestural parameters are significant, for example, a shrug from the suspect—should this be interpreted as a statement or just left as a shrug?
- Frequent side sequences between the suspect and interpreter (nonrenditions on the part of the interpreter) could put the role of the interpreter in jeopardy and damage the integrity of the witness statement. However, the accessibility of the police officers to these sequences due to the interpreter working in simultaneous mode seems to make these asides more acceptable to the police officers than would be acceptable with consecutive/spoken language interpretation (i.e., periods of silence are shorter). But this could still have an impact on the suspect's understanding of the participation framework.
- Frequent nonrenditions produced by the interpreter, often to clarify (e.g., spelling of a name), which is typical practice when working with two languages that have different types of specificity (see Crawley, 2018) and, in this case, can lead into further information gathering.
- Change of footing from third to first person with striking patterns, which is also evident in other sign language–interpreted contexts (see Marks, 2012, 2015).
- Frequent explicitation (expanded renditions) used by the interpreter, which is a typical practice of sign language interpreters (see Lawrence, 1995).

- Frequent reduced renditions produced by the interpreter, with details omitted.
- Interpreter occasionally using hedging, which introduces a level of uncertainty into the discourse.

Here we present two extracts using the horizontal transcription format as employed by Gallez (2010), Metzger and Roy (2011), and Monteoliva (2020) to demonstrate and visualize the turn-taking between participants in the police interview interaction. The first extract shows an example of an accurate rendition by the interpreter (with one episode that has reduced information), but because of hedging introduced into the interpretation, the suspect sounds uncertain but that uncertainty was not present in the original BSL source text (Extract 1).

Extract 1. Uncertainty

Deaf Suspect (BSL)	Interpreter (BSL/English)	Police Officer 1 (English)
		What I've just said to you, that you said you understood. What does it mean to you? What do you mean "you understand that you're not bound to answer?"
	Can you explain to me what I have just explained to you. (BSL)	
You said I don't have to say anything to you, but I can keep quiet or I can tell you and you will use it as evidence in [location implies court].		
	You said that I don't have to say anything er but I can—I can keep quiet or I can tell you and you'll use it for evidence maybe. (English)	

Extract 2 shows an example of a reduced rendition, where the interpreter omitted some details from the description of what happened on the night in question, as well as introducing some hedging into the interpretation.

In addition to the review of relevant policies, legislation, and literature, the three empirical data sets enabled us to collect an evidence base for where police interpreting is systematically provided across Europe; to examine the perspectives of police officers, deaf sign language users, and sign language interpreters on their experiences of interpreter-mediated police interviews; and to interrogate sign language interpreting "in action" (Napier & Leeson, 2016) in

Extract 2. Uncertainty

Deaf Suspect (BSL)	Interpreter (BSL/English)	Police Officer 1 (English)
I started losing everyone from the group, they were going off in different directions, going in different directions. I was left on my own....		
	Erm, I lost my friends and we kind of went off in different directions and there was just me.... (English)	
Eventually I found [bumped into] one of them, this man, tall guy, I don't know him that well. I don't know him well. I've only met him once or twice.		
	...and I found one-one guy. I don't know who he is very well. Er, I've met him once or twice that's all. (English)	

a police interview context. The findings of these three connected studies were used as further data in the development of the *Justisigns* training courses, so we were able to provide examples from lived experiences. One of the clear issues that emerged from the data was the importance of training for police officers and interpreters on how best to work together. This is also acknowledged by Perez and Wilson (2007), who suggest that any training of legal interpreters should be "interlinked" with training of legal personnel in order to maximize the knowledge and experience of both professional groups and promote cross-cultural awareness.

JUSTISIGNS TRAINING COURSES

During the course of the project, the *Justisigns* team engaged in dissemination and knowledge transfer through 59 different events, including a research methods symposium, deaf community information events, roundtable discussions with service providers, and academic and professional conferences, as well as blog/vlog posts. Various CPD training workshops were delivered by the consortium partners to deaf and hearing interpreters, police officers, and deaf sign language users. For the purposes of this chapter, however, we focus on two forms of training that were developed, which we feel were the most significant and innovative outputs.

Masterclass

Two of the project partners—the United Kingdom and Switzerland—were tasked with offering a "masterclass," the goal of which was to deliver training to a combined group of participants, rather than as separate, standalone workshops to the different stakeholder groups. Here we present the model of the masterclass training.

In the United Kingdom, in collaboration with Police Scotland, the Association of Sign Language Interpreters UK (ASLI), the Scottish Association of Sign Language Interpreters (SASLI),[6] and the British Deaf Association (BDA), a one-day masterclass was de-

---

6. Now separated into two organizations: The Scottish Register for Language Professionals With the Deaf Community and the Scottish Collaborative of Sign Language Interpreters.

veloped by the Heriot-Watt University team in Edinburgh to provide a training opportunity for sign language interpreters, police investigative interview trainers, and deaf sign language users together at the Police Scotland campus in Gartcosh.

The structure of the masterclass was carefully designed so that the participant groups had information and practical sessions together, as well as bespoke, tailored, information sessions separately for each group. Vignettes and role-plays were used so that theoretical discussions could be applied in practice and evaluated. After being given an overview of the project, participants had an initial discussion about the challenges of interpreter-mediated police interviews, and then were divided into three groups for bespoke sessions for each stakeholder group. The deaf participants learned about their rights in police interviews and the role of the interpreter; police officers learned about sign language, deaf culture, and the importance of using professional interpreters; and the interpreters learned about legal discourse, the goal of investigative police interviews, challenges in interpreting police interviews, and police interpreting research. The three groups then came together to discuss what they had learned and then participated in role-plays to apply their learning in practice. The role-play scenarios were developed in discussion with Police Scotland based on real cases. The structure of the day can be seen in Table 2.

Following this format enabled us to draw on the evidence base from the research in the information sessions and then apply that knowledge immediately into practice so that we could discuss examples of best practice with all participants. The experimental approach to bringing all the participants together was effective, so that the training was not just "interlinked" but *integrated*. Evaluations at the end of the day from participants confirmed that it was an effective format, as seen in the sample of comments in Table 3. The overarching negative feedback was that participants would have liked more time for discussion.

The Swiss team offered a masterclass that followed a similar format, but the target groups were different. Instead, they integrated two groups together—deaf migrants and police officers. The

Table 2. Structure of the Masterclass.

Time	Session	Details	Participants
15 minutes	Overview of the day	Brief overview of the *Justisigns* project. Goal and purpose of training to pilot structure and get feedback. Developed in collaboration with HWU and Police Scotland and also through process of research and consultation with deaf people, interpreters, and police officers throughout the UK. Overview of structure of the day—using vignettes/scenarios to examine practice and discuss challenges and identify best practice	All
45 minutes	Interviewing deaf people (exemplars)	5 minutes: setting the scene: focus on one scenario as an exemplar. Using volunteer from the audience (inexperienced interpreter). 15–20 minutes: role-play. 20 minutes: debrief—What were the challenges? What did the role-play participants find difficult and why? Was there anything you would do typically that you found you couldn't do?	All
90 minutes	Working with deaf people and interpreters	Focus on giving information about deaf sign language users, the deaf community, and what assumptions not to make about English literacy. Qualifications of interpreters and how interpreters work. Communication tips.	Police
	Your rights to interpreting and translation in police interviews	Focus on rights deaf people have to request an interpreter, protocols for booking interpreters. The role of the interpreter. How an interpreter should manage the communication. Qualifications of interpreters.	Deaf people
	Police interview protocol	Focus on what interpreters need to know about; the key issues for police in conducting investigations. The structure of police interviews, process, and protocol. Their rights in terms of working conditions. Suggestions for managing the communication.	Interpreters

Time	Session	Details	Participants
45 minutes	BREAK		
120 minutes	Joint session: interpreted police interviews (role-plays)	15 minutes: refresh. So what are key points that you learned in last session? Brainstorm. 15 minutes: now reflect back on morning role-play session. What could have been done differently? 90 minutes: 3 × role-plays of 20 minutes each + 10 minutes debrief—different participants. One with very experienced legal interpreter. Make it clear that not everyone has to participate, but you'll get more out of the experience. No judgments being made. We are all here to learn together. Pointers to be considered up on screen.	All
60 minutes	Wrap up and Evaluations	Recap of the day. Cover key learning points—modeling best practice. Summary of key recommendations. Evaluation of the course content and structure.	All

Table 3. Masterclass Participant Evaluations.

Participant	Comment
Police officer	"A good way to learn. Important to break into specific groups to talk about the roles of the police officer/ interpreter/deaf person."
Police officer	"One of the most informative courses/seminars I have attended in a long time."
Police officer	"I found the content excellent and informative. Eighteen years in the police and this was the first real input into this important area of Police Scotland [work]. . . . Great mixture of people brought together. Plenty experience across the room."
Interpreter	"Excellent . . . Gave me more confidence to advise the police officers what I require in order to do my job effectively. The split role-play using an inexperienced interpreter and the afternoon with an experienced shows that some form of formal training is required."
Interpreter	"I enjoyed the role-plays and the interaction with interpreters and police gave me a better insight into both our roles."
Deaf BSL user	"Brilliant to see three different groups working together. I enjoyed learning [about] the police. I also learned that conscience is important in this area of police work. . . . Thank you for the great event!"
Deaf BSL user	"Interesting day with police, interpreters and deaf in one room focusing on rights issues, positions, how to use interpreters, jargon used . . ."

research team from the University of Applied Sciences of Special Needs Education in Zurich developed a Swiss version of the masterclass that focused on best practices for cooperation with sign language interpreters and was delivered in collaboration with "DIMA language school" and the city police of Zurich. Following a similar structure, members of the Zurich deaf community were trained in working with sign language interpreters, the role of interpreter, different situations at the police station (before, during, and after an interrogation or interview as a witness), including role-plays with a police officer and an interpreter. Simultaneously, police officers received deaf awareness training and provided very useful feedback to the poster design on tips for deaf people, which were implemented afterward in the creation of the poster.

Online Curriculum

One of the remits of the *Justisigns* project was to develop an online course curriculum that would be equivalent to 200 hours of student time, using a modular structure so that content could be delivered either as a full course, one-off contained workshops based on one module, or embedded within other courses (e.g., undergraduate generic sign language interpreter training program) and could be utilized by trainers for police, interpreter, or deaf audiences.

The course focuses on the introduction of key concepts and the development of practical skills for stakeholders in police settings that involve deaf sign language users and sign language interpreters. The course is built around what constitutes successful communication in an interpreted event that involves at least three participants (a "triadic exchange"), namely, a police officer, a deaf person (e.g., the accused/offender), and an appropriately qualified interpreter. The content is multimodal in nature: We developed PowerPoint slides and written documents in a number of languages, alongside video clips from a range of community and professional perspectives that offer insights or contain challenges with respect to "'normative'" responses to deaf service users. The course includes 14 modules that cover a range of topics, as detailed in Table 4. The learning outcomes for the course are as follows:

On successful completion of this course, participants should expect to be able to:

- Describe the key provisions of the European Directive 2010/64/EU of the European Parliament and of the Council on the Right to Interpretation and Translation in Criminal Proceedings.
- Describe the key provisions of the European Directive 2012/29/EU of the European Parliament and of the Council establishing minimum standards on the rights, support, and protections of victims of crime.
- Evaluate the local legislation in your region/country with regard to European requirements for equity of access.
- Discuss the recognition of sign languages as "real" languages at national/regional and pan-European level.
- Describe police procedures in your jurisdiction.

Table 4. *Justisigns* Course Curriculum.

Session 1: Legal Basis and Glossary of Terms.

This session outlines the European and International legal basis ensuring access to police proceedings. National laws are also presented. We consider specific instruments such as the European Arrest Warrant, the United Nations Convention on the Rights of Persons With Disabilities (UNCRPD) and consider what significance these have for legal professionals and justice and equality policymakers. We pay specific attention to what this legislation means for police officers.

Session 2: Benchmarking Current Provisions and Practices.

This session reports on a study of interpreting provision in legal settings across the European Union. We consider what the current levels of training, awareness, and provision may mean in terms of quality of access and consequential delivery of justice.

Session 3: Idealized Outcomes?

In this session, we contemplate what a successful outcome would "look like" in terms of a police interaction with a deaf sign language user from the point of view of deaf people, interpreters, interpreter educators, and police officers. We consider the range of standards that impact on provision of services, for example, ISO Standards on Community Interpreting, UNCRPD, European Directives, and local legal requirements. We also consider issues of number of interpreters, mode of interpreting, the inclusion of deaf/hearing interpreting teams, and consider how this maps against practice.

Session 4: Police Protocols.

We outline the protocols that govern police practice vis-à-vis arrest, reading of rights, making a charge, holding and interviewing of suspects, taking of statements, as well as wider engagement with individuals reporting crimes, providing witness statements.

Session 5: Deaf Community Members.

We explore how society views deafness, deaf individuals/communities from a range of perspectives—medical, sociocultural, and from a human rights perspective. We discuss the recognition of signed languages as "real" languages at national and pan-European levels. We critically evaluate other recognitions of sign languages within the framework of a human rights agenda and evaluate what this means for deaf communities, especially with regard to access to the law. These are essential steps to understanding how deaf communities view themselves as linguistic minorities and considering what this means for members of deaf communities who come in contact with police forces and the broader justice system.

Table 4 (*continued*)

Session 6: Sign Languages and Spoken Languages.

This session briefly outlines some of the considerations that those working in police settings need to be aware of when working between spoken and sign languages (i.e., in a bilingual, bimodal setting).

Session 7: Interpreting: A special case of co-constructing meaning.

This session focuses on how meaning is constructed when we communicate, presenting a cognitively driven perspective on the co-construction of meaning in interactive settings such as occur in police interviews/witness statement taking. Specifically, we consider key principles of cognitive linguistics that underpin our view of language and communication. We describe the concept of "frames" and compare and contrast the conduit model and the cognitive model of interpreting. We discuss the "fund of knowledge" that may impede on shared conceptual understanding between deaf witness, interpreter, and police officer/representative of the legal system and outline the challenges arising for interpreters working in healthcare settings as a result of the lack of shared "frames" coupled with the "fund of knowledge" challenge.

Session 8: Sign Language Interpreters.

This session introduces the work of sign language interpreters and explores the scope of practice of sign language interpreters in police settings.

Session 9: Demand-Control Schema.

This session introduces Dean and Pollard's (2013) demand-control schema. We outline the demands that interpreters and police officers deal with in their work and describe the categories of control that interpreters and police officers can apply in managing their work, pre-, during, and postassignment. We pay particular attention to the range of demands that arise in police settings.

Session 10: Putting It All Together: Communicating Within Triadic Exchanges I—Preparation.

This session considers what kind of preparation is needed in order to ensure successful interaction. We consider the recruitment of interpreters, the checking of credentials, and ensuring that there are no conflicts of interests arising from prior relationships with a deaf client. We look at the kinds of questions that may arise pre-arrest, preraid, preinterview, prestatement taking and suggest a list of considerations that will help to facilitate best practice.

Continued

Table 4 (continued)

Session 11: Putting It All Together: Communicating Within Triadic Exchanges Ii—During an Event.

This session looks at the issues that may arise within an interpreted communicative exchange. Here we consider issues relating to the kind of event that is being discussed and how this will impact on questions police officers might put to a suspect/witness; we consider issues of handling complex notions in an interpretation; we look at the modes of interpreting that may be used and why; and we consider how a team of interpreters might be included in a linguistically complex setting. Finally, we discuss the importance of recording the signed content in addition to the written record of an interview.

Session 12: Putting It All Together: Communicating Within Triadic Exchanges Iii—Post Hoc.

In this session, we look at what needs to happen postassignment: debriefings, consideration of vicarious trauma, taking interpreter statements, and so on.

Session 13: Working With Vulnerable Groups.

This session considers additional concerns that arise with regard to ensuring appropriate accommodations for suspects/witnesses who might be considered "vulnerable." Such individuals include minors, deaf people with disabilities, deafblind individuals, elderly deaf people, and other deaf individuals who meet the definition of "vulnerable subject" as per the International Red Cross's definition (2014).

Session 14: Deaf Interpreters.

This session describes the work of deaf interpreters (DIs) and provides a rationale for their involvement as specialists who provide interpretation and translation services, most commonly between a sign language and other visual/tactile communication forms used by individuals who are deaf/hard of hearing/deafblind; translation between a sign language and a written text; and interpretation between two sign languages.

- Outline the key challenges in ensuring equitable access to police settings for deaf community members.
- Describe the key concepts in demand-control schema and how they relate to the work of police officers and interpreters working in police settings.
- Compare and contrast the thought worlds of deaf civilians and police officers.
- Describe the process of "semantic bridging."
- Apply best practice principles to maximize successful communication when operating in triadic exchanges that involve interpreters.
- Utilize terminology regarding hearing status that will not offend deaf or hard of hearing people.
- Define a "vulnerable subject" as per the International Red Cross definition (ICRC, 2014) and outline appropriate strategies for supporting such individuals in police settings.
- Evaluate a police-based interpreted event with respect to the International Standards Organisation Guidelines for Community Interpreting (ISO, 2014).

The content of these modules were trialed through the various workshops and masterclasses that were delivered throughout the life of the project and consolidated into this one curriculum. The curriculum and resources are freely available to anyone through the *Justisigns* website.

CONCLUSION

In conclusion, this chapter has highlighted the importance of specialized training for sign language interpreters who work specifically in police interviews, as also recommended for spoken language interpreters (Hale et al., 2019; Howes, 2018; Mulayim et al., 2015) and builds on the recommendation for general legal specialization training for sign language interpreters (Roberson et al., 2012b). It has also confirmed that there are innovative ways to train interpreters alongside police officers and deaf sign language users. Trainers can give consideration to research findings as an evidence base for the foundation of training courses, and students can access examples from authentic interpreted interactions to identify potential issues, as is also done with court interpreter training (e.g., Burn & Creeze, 2017), or from simulated police interviews (Hale et al., 2020). Students can also have insight into the lived experiences of key stakeholders in order to reflect on consequences of their decisions and behaviors in the police interview context.

Using role-play activities has previously been identified as an effective way to provide experiential learning opportunities for interpreting students by simulating interpreter-mediated interactions (Major et al., 2012; Metzger, 2000; Wadensjö, 2014), and it can be seen that it is also an effective method for bringing together the different stakeholder participants in the triadic exchange to gain insight into the experiences of each participant. Role-plays are also an effective way to bridge the gap between the classroom and what happens in the real world and interpreter-mediated communication (Wang, 2015).

Based on our experience from the *Justisigns* project, we encourage sign language interpreter trainers to actively engage in "evidence-based pedagogy" (Napier, 2013) and also to seek out potential collaborative training opportunities with police officers. By working together, it is possible not only to integrate training of police officers, sign language interpreters, and deaf sign language users together but also to map a curriculum with content so that it can be delivered to all three stakeholder groups in different formats. We recommend that the masterclass training activity and the mapped curriculum can be applied in a variety of contexts, as well as in police settings.

QUESTIONS AND APPLICATION

1. What components would you recommend be included in a "masterclass"?
2. What are the requirements in your area for a person wanting to interpret in legal settings? How do they compare with the countries the authors mention here?

3. What do the authors mean by "evidenced-based pedagogy"? How can that improve practice?

REFERENCES

Berk-Seligson, S. (2009). *Coerced confessions: The discourse of bilingual police interrogations*. Mouton de Gruyter.

Böser, U. (2013). "So tell me what happened!": Interpreting the free recall segment of the investigative interview. *Translation & Interpreting Studies: The Journal of the American Translation & Interpreting Studies Association*, 8(1), 112–116. http://doi.org/10.1075/tis.8.1.06bos

Braun, V. & Clarke, V. (2006). Using thematic analysis in psychology. *Qualitative Research in Psychology*, 3(2), 77–101.

Brennan, M. (1999). Signs of injustice. *The Translator*, 5(2), 221–246. http://doi.org/10.1080/13556509.1999.10799042

Brennan, M., & Brown, R. (1997). *Equality before the law: Deaf people's access to justice*. Deaf Studies Research Unit, University of Durham.

Brunson, J. (2008). Your case will now be heard: Sign language interpreters as problematic accommodations in legal interactions. *Journal of Deaf Studies & Deaf Education*, 13(1), 77–91. https://doi.org/10.1093/deafed/enm032

Burn, J. A., & Creeze, I. (2017). "That is not the question I put to you, officer": An analysis of student legal interpreting errors. *International Journal of Interpreter Education*, 9(1), 40–56. http://www.cit-asl.org/new/an-analysis-of-student-legal-interpreting-errors/

Coulthard, M., & Johnson, A. (2007). *An introduction to forensic linguistics: Language in evidence*. Routledge.

Crawley, V. (2018). Interpreting between modes: Navigating between signed and spoken language. *International Journal of Interpreter Education*, 10(1), 5–17. https://www.cit-asl.org/new/interpreting-between-modes/

Davitti, E. (2016). Dialogue interpreting as a multimodal activity in community settings. In V. Bonsignori & B. C. Camiciottoli (Eds.), *Multimodality across communicative settings, discourse domains and genres* (pp. 116–143). Cambridge Scholars Publishing.

Davitti, E., & Pasquandrea, S. (2017). Embodied participation: What multimodal analysis can tell us about interpreter-mediated encounters in pedagogical settings. *Journal of Pragmatics, 107*, 105–128. https://doi.org/10.1016/j.pragma.2016.04.008

Defrancq, B., & Verliefde, S. (2018). Interpreter-mediated drafting of written records in police interviews: A case study. *Target, 30*(2), 212–239. http://doi.org/10.1075/target.16141.def

de Wit, M. (2012). *Sign language interpreting in Europe*. CreateSpace.

Doggen, C. (2016). *Sign language interpreting in legal settings in Flanders: An exploratory study into the experiences of Flemish deaf people in their contact with the justice system* [Unpublished master's dissertation]. Humak University of Applied Sciences.

European Commission. (2009). *Reflection forum on multilingualism and interpreter training final report*. DG Interpretation.

Filipovic, L. (2019). Evidence-gathering in police interviews: Communication problems and possible solutions. *Pragmatics and Society, 10*(1), 9–31. http://doi.org/10.1075/ps.00013.fil

Gallai, F. (2012). Legalising EU legal interpreters: A case for the NRPSI. *The Interpreters" Newsletter, 17*, 139–156. https://www.openstarts.units.it/handle/10077/8619

Gallai, F. (2013). "I'll just intervene whenever he finds it a bit difficult to answer": Exploding the myth of literalism in interpreted interviews. *Investigative Interviewing: Research and Practice (II-RP), 5*(1), 57–78. https://iiirg.org/wp-content/uploads/2021/02/II-RP-Volume-5-Issue-1-Gallai.pdf

Gallai, F. (2016). Point of view in free indirect thought and in community interpreting. *Lingua, 175–176*, 97–121. http://doi.org/10.1016/j.lingua.2015.08.012

Gallez, E. (2010, July 26–30). *Advantages of a horizontal transcription format for interpreter-mediated interactions* [Paper presentation]. Critical Link 6 Conference, Aston University, Birmingham.

Giambruno, C. (Ed.). (2014). *Assessing legal interpreter quality through testing and certification: The Qualitras project*. University of Alicante/Alicante Publications.

Gibbons, J. (2003). *Forensic linguistics*. Blackwell.

Goodman-Delahunty, J., & Martschuk, N. (2016). Risks and benefits of interpreter-mediated police interviews. *ARSTVOSLOVJE, Journal of Criminal Justice and Security, 18*(4), 451–471. https://www.fvv.um.si/rV/arhiv/2016-4/05_Goodman-Delahunty%20_Martschuk_rV_2016-4.pdf

Goswell, D. (2011). Being there: Role shift in English to Auslan interpreting. In L. Leeson, S. Wurm, & M. Vermeerbergen (Eds.), *Signed language interpreting: Preparation, practice and performance* (pp. 61–86). Routledge.

Goswell, D. (2012). Do you see what I see? Using ELAN for self-analysis and reflection. *International Journal of Interpreter Education, 4*(1), 72–81. https://www.cit-asl.org/new/ijie/volume-4-1/#toggle-id-6

Hale, S., Goodman-Delahunty, J., & Martschuk, N. (2019). Interpreter performance in police interviews. Differences between trained interpreters and untrained bilinguals. *The Interpreter and Translator Trainer, 13*(2), 107–131. https://doi.org/10.1080/1750399X.2018.1541649

Hale, S., Goodman-Delahunty, J., & Martschuk, N. (2020). Interactional management in a simulated police interview: Interpreters' strategies. In M. Mason & F. Rock (Eds.), *The discourse of police investigation* (pp. 200–226). University of Chicago Press.

Hertog, E. (Ed.). (2001). *Aequitas: Access to justice across language and culture in the EU* [Research report]. Lessius Hogeschool.

Hertog, E. (Ed.). (2003) *Aequalitas: Access to justice across language and culture in the EU* [Research report]. Lessius Hogeschool.

Hertog, E. (2010). *Legal interpreting and translation in the EU: Justice, freedom and security through language.* http://www.eulita.eu/sites/default/files/Salamanca%20LIT%20in%20EU_0.pdf

Hertog, E., & van Gucht, J. (Eds.). (2008). *Status quaestionis. Questionnaire on the provision of legal interpreting and translation in the EU.* Intersentia.

Heydon, G. (2005). *The language of police interviewing: A critical analysis.* Palgrave Macmillan.

Howes, L. M. (2018). Community interpreters' experiences of police investigative interviews: How might interpreters' insights contribute to enhanced procedural justice? *Policing and Society*, 1–19. https://doi.org/10.1080/10439463.2018.1447572

Howes, L. M. (2019). Interpreted investigative interviews under the PEACE interview model: Police interviewers' perceptions of challenges and suggested solutions. *Police Practice and Research.* http://doi.org/10.1080/15614263.2019.1617145

ICRC. (2014). *International humanitarian law.* International Committee of the Red Cross. https://www.icrc.org/en/doc/assets/files/other/icrc_002_0703.pdf

ISO. (2014). *Guidelines for community interpreting.* International Standards Organisation. https://www.iso.org/standard/54082.html

Kermit, P., Mjøen, O. M., & Olsen, T. (2011). Safe in the hands of the interpreter? A qualitative study investigating the legal protection of Deaf people facing the criminal justice system in Norway. *Disability Studies Quarterly, 31*(4). http://dx.doi.org/10.18061/dsq.v31i4.1714

Komter, M. (2005). Understanding problems in an interpreter-mediated police interrogation. In S. L. Burns (Ed.), *Ethnographies of law and social control* (pp. 203–224). Emerald Group.

Kruglov, A. (1999). Police interpreting: Politeness and sociocultural context. *The Translator, 5*, 285–303. https://doi.org/10.1080/13556509.1999.10799045

Lai, M., & Mulayim, S. (2014). Interpreter linguistic intervention in the strategies employed by police in investigative interviews. *Police Practice and Research, 15*(4), 307–321. http://doi.org/10.1080/15614263.2013.809929

Lawrence, S. (1995). Interpreter discourse: English to ASL expansion. In E. A. Winston (Ed.), *Mapping our course: A collaborative venture, Proceedings of the Tenth National Convention* (p. 15). Conference of Interpreter Trainers.

Lee, J. (2017). A case study of interpreter-mediated witness statement: Police interpreting in South Korea. *Police Practice and Research, 18*(2), 194–205. http://doi.org/10.1080/15614263.2016.1248840

Leeson, L., Napier, J., Skinner, R., Lynch, T., Venturi, L., & Sheikh, H. (2017). Conducting research with deaf sign language users. In J. McKinley & H. Rose (Eds.), *Doing research in applied linguistics: Realities, dilemmas, and solutions* (pp. 134–145). Routledge.

Leeson, L., Napier, J., Haug, T., Lynch, T., & Sheikh, H. (2021). Access to justice for deaf signers. In G. De Clerck (Ed.), *UNCRPD Implementation in Europe—A deaf perspective: Article 9: Access to information and communication* (pp. 161–175). European Union of the Deaf.

Leeson, L., & Phelan, M. (2016, May 13–14). *Interpreters and intermediaries in the wake of Directive 2010/64/EU and SI No. 565/2013* [Paper presentation]. Annual District Court Conference 2016, Tullow, Ireland.

Leung, M. (2003). Rights to be heard and the rights to be interpreted. *Babel, 49*(4), 289–301. https://doi.org/10.1075/babel.49.4.02leu

Määttä, S. K. (2015). Interpreting the discourse of reporting: The case of screening interviews with asylum seekers and police interviews in Finland. *International Journal of Translation & Interpreting Research, 7*(3), 21–35. http://doi.org/10.12807/ti.107203.2015.a02

Major, G., & Napier, J. (2012). Interpreting and knowledge mediation in the healthcare setting: What do we really mean by "accuracy"? In V. Montalt & M. Shuttleworth (Eds.), *Linguistica Antiverpiesa: Translation and knowledge mediation in medical and health settings* (pp. 207–226). Artesius University College.

Major, G., & Napier, J. (2019). "I'm there sometimes as a just in case": Examining role fluidity in healthcare interpreting. In M. Ji, M. Taibi, & I. Creeze (Eds.), *Multicultural health translation, interpreting and communication* (pp. 183–204). Routledge.

Major, G., Napier, J., & Stubbe, M. (2012). "What happens truly, not text book!": Using authentic interactions in discourse training for healthcare interpreters. In K. Malcolm & L. Swabey (Eds.), *In our hands: Educating healthcare interpreters* (pp. 27–53). Gallaudet University Press.

Marks, A. R. (2012). Participation framework and footing shifts in an interpreted academic meeting. *Journal of Interpretation, 22*(1), 4. https://digitalcommons.unf.edu/joi/vol22/iss1/4/

Marks, A. R. (2015). Investigating footing shifts in video relay service interpreted interaction. In B. Nicodemus & K. Cagle (Eds.), *Signed language interpretation and translation research: Selected papers from the First International Symposium* (pp. 71–96). Gallaudet University Press.

Metzger, M. (1999). *Sign language interpreting: Deconstructing the myth of neutrality*. Gallaudet University Press.

Metzger, M. (2000). Interactive role-plays as a teaching strategy. In C. Roy (Ed.), *Innovative practices for teaching sign language interpreters* (pp. 83–107). Gallaudet University Press.

Metzger, M., & Roy, C. (2011). The first three years of a three year grant: When a research plan doesn't go as planned. In B. Nicodemus & L. Swabey (Eds.), *Advances in interpreting research* (pp. 59–84). John Benjamins.

Monteoliva, E. (2020). The collaborative and selective nature of interpreting in police interviews with stand-by interpreting. *Interpreting, 22*(2), 262–287. http://doi.org/10.1075/intp.00046.mon

Mulayim, S., Lai, M., & Norma, C. (2015). *Police investigative interviews and interpreting: Context, challenges, and strategies*. CRC Press.

Nakane, I. (2007). Problems in communicating the suspect's rights in interpreted police interviews. *Applied Linguistics, 28*(1), 87–112. https://doi.org/10.1093/applin/aml050

Nakane, I. (2011). The role of silence in interpreted police interviews. *Journal of Pragmatics, 43*(9), 2317–2330. https://doi.org/10.1016/j.pragma.2010.11.013

Nakane, I. (2014). *Interpreter-mediated police interviews: A discourse-pragmatic approach*. Palgrave Macmillan.

Napier, J. (2013). Evidence-based pedagogy. *International Journal of Interpreter Education, 5*(2), 1–3. https://www.cit-asl.org/new/ijie/

volume-5-2/#toggle-id-1

Napier, J., & Haug, T. (2016). *Justisigns*: A European overview of sign language interpreting provision in legal settings. *Law, Social Justice & Global Development: An Interdisciplinary Journal*, 2. http://www2.warwick.ac.uk/fac/soc/law/elj/lgd/lgd_issue_2016_2

Napier, J., & Leeson, L. (2016). *Sign language in action*. Palgrave.

Napier, J., Skinner, R., & Böser, U. (Forthcoming). "He said I will ask you questions . . . " Shifts of footing and rapport building in sign language interpretation of a police suspect interview.

Perez, I. A., & Wilson, C. W. (2007). Interpreter-mediated police interviews: Working as a professional team. In C. Wadensjö & B. E. Dimitrova (Eds.), *Benjamins translation library* (Vol. 70, p. 79). John Benjamins.

Race, L., & Hogue, T. (2018). "You have the right to remain silent": Current provisions for Deaf people within regional police forces in England and Wales. *The Police Journal: Theory, Practice & Principles*, 91(1), 64–88. http://doi.org/10.1177/0032258X16689689

Roberson, L., Russell, D., & Shaw, R. (2012a). American Sign Language/English interpreting in legal settings: Current practices in North America. *Journal of Interpretation*, 21(1), 6. https://digitalcommons.unf.edu/joi/vol21/iss1/6/

Roberson, L., Russell, D., & Shaw, R. (2012b). A case for training signed language interpreters for legal specialisation. *International Journal of Interpreter Education*, 4(2), 52–73. https://www.cit-asl.org/new/a-case-for-training-signed-language-interpreters-for-legal-specialization/

Roy, C. B. (2000). *Interpreting as a discourse process*. Oxford: Oxford University Press.

Russell, S. (2000). "Let me put it simply . . ." The case for a standard translation of the police caution and its explanation. *International Journal of Speech Language and the Law*, 7(1), 26–48. http://doi.org/10.1558/ijsll.v7i1.26

Russell, S. (2001). *Guilty as charged? The effect of interpreting on interviews with suspects* [Unpublished doctoral dissertation]. University of Aston in Birmingham.

Shuy, R. (2003). The language problems of minorities in the legal setting. In C. Lucas (Ed.), *Language and the law in Deaf communities* (pp. 1–20). Gallaudet University Press.

Skinner, R., & Napier, J. (In press). Police settings as an (in)accessible institution through sign language interpreting. *Translation & Interpreting Studies: Special Issue on Sign Language Interpreting*.

Skinner, R., Napier, J., & Fyfe, N. (2021). The social construction of 101 non-emergency video relay services for deaf sign language users. *International Journal of Police Science & Management*, http://doi.org/10.1177/1461355720974703

Tipton, R. (2017). "You are foreign, you are nothing in this country": Managing risk in interpreter-mediated police interviews with victims of domestic abuse. *Revista Canaria de Estudios Ingleses*, 75, 119–138.

Turner, G. H. (1995). The bilingual, bimodal courtroom: A first glance. *Journal of Interpretation*, 7(1), 3–34.

Turner, G. H., & Brown, R. (2001). Interaction and the role of the interpreter in court. In F. J. Harrington & G. H. Turner (Eds.), *Interpreting interpreting: Studies and reflections on sign language interpreting* (pp. 152–167). Douglas McLean.

Wadensjö, C. (1998). *Interpreting as interaction*. London: Longman.

Wadensjö, C. (2014). Perspectives on role-play: Analysis, training and assessments. *The Interpreter and Translator Trainer*, 8(3), 437–451. https://doi.org/10.1080/1750399X.2014.971486

Wakefield, S., Kebbell, M., Moston, S., & Westera, N. (2015). Perceptions and profiles of interviews with interpreters: A police survey. *Australian & New Zealand Journal of Criminology*, 48(1), 53–72. https://doi.org/10.1177/0004865814524583

Wang, B. (2015). Bridging the gap between interpreting classrooms and real-world interpreting. *International Journal of Interpreter Education*, 7(1), 65–73.

8 TRAINING INTERPRETERS IN LEGAL SETTINGS: APPLYING ROLE-SPACE THEORY IN THE CLASSROOM

Jérôme Devaux and Robert G. Lee

EDITOR'S INTRODUCTION

Jérôme Devaux and Robert G. Lee demonstrate the way role-space as an analytic framework can be used to train interpreters for legal settings. They suggest that this paradigm provides opportunities for students to anticipate which axes may require more attention during the assignments. Equipping interpreting students with tools that bolster their ability to address challenges preemptively can only improve the quality of the interpreting product. As they work through a study carried out by Devaux, the authors provide ample support for this proposition.

INTERPRETING IN THE legal domain requires not only excellent linguistic and cognitive processing skills but also a keen awareness of the dynamics of the various settings. Often the focus in training legal interpreters is on interpreting quality and ethics, interpreting skills, legal terminology, and awareness of the various parts of the legal systems (e.g., Chilingaryan et al., 2016; Devaux, 2017b; Liu & Hale, 2018). Although essential to the training of legal interpreters, such an approach usually results in overlooking the interpersonal skills required by interpreters in these settings. The very nature of legal settings involves the attempted understanding and interpretation of not only what is said, but how it is presented by all parties in the interaction. Thus, even with excellent linguistic skills, interpreters could potentially detrimentally affect a legal assignment if they are not aware of the impact of their own presentation of self, alignment with the participants, and how they manage the interaction. Therefore, it is imperative that any training for legal interpreters includes awareness of and practice with the paralinguistic skills necessary to effectively render messages in legal settings.

In this chapter, we will draw upon both empirical studies (e.g., Devaux, 2017a) and theoretical approaches (e.g., Llewellyn-Jones & Lee, 2014) in order to posit that role-space can be used as a new pedagogical framework when training legal interpreters. This approach does not discard the need for trainee interpreters to be *au fait* with the legal terminology but adds another layer by incorporating the paralinguistic features that form part of an interpreter-mediated event (IME).

The chapter will first provide an overview of legal interpreting with a particular focus on its requirement and testing mechanism. The second part will provide an introduction of the role-space model (Llewellyn-Jones & Lee, 2014), explaining the relevance of each of the three axes and their role in effective interpreting. Then, a discussion of Devaux (2017a) will highlight the awareness of the manifestation of role-space as articulated by experienced legal interpreters in both face-to-face and remote legal interpreting situations. The data will show that it is possible to encapsulate, in one model, the paralinguistic factors that can have an impact on a legal interaction. Finally, we will provide a discussion of how what has been learned from experienced interpreters can inform the design of training and testing aspiring legal interpreters.

The discussion will be language- and modality-neutral; it can apply to interpreters working with both sign and spoken languages as the reflections are based on the working languages of the individual.

In broad terms legal interpreting is defined, according to the International Organization for Standardization (2019)'s ISO20228, as "interpreting at communicative settings related to the law" (3.1.3) whereby a "communicative setting" is an "environment where an interaction between interlocutors takes place" (3.1.23). As such, legal interpreting is a broad umbrella in the justice system that not only encompasses police and court interpreting but also paralegal and immigration settings, for instance. Within the justice system, interpreters are key players in multilingual criminal court hearings, in ensuring that a witness or defendant's human rights are upheld. Throughout history, there are numerous cases that illustrate how important legal interpreters are in the fairness of the legal process. The absence of competent interpreters can have devastating effects, as proven in the tragic Iqbal Begum's miscarriage of justice in the 1980s.[1]

It is widely accepted, at least within the field of interpreting studies, that legal interpreting is not an ad hoc hobby for bilingual speakers, but interpreters must receive an adequate level of training and be tested accordingly. However, what is less clear is how they should be trained. In England and Wales, the training provision is offered through a mosaic of training providers (from private companies to university training offering legal interpreting modules embedded within undergraduate and postgraduate courses) and delivery methods (online or face-to-face, weekly or monthly courses). Combined with the absence of a compulsory national curriculum, legal interpreting training is very heterogeneous, with some courses focusing primarily on legal terminology and basic interpreting skills while others also include a wide-ranging set of competences.

Against this backdrop, the significance of this chapter resides in the fact that it aims to provide a framework for legal interpreter trainers and trainees to teach, reflect, and assess the interpreter's interpersonal skills. It is worth noting that this approach can be replicated in other interpreting settings (such as health); it is not language-bound, and it can be applied to spoken and sign languages. This approach is original as it complements the legal terminology-focused training by highlighting how role-space can incorporate, in one model, paralinguistic factors that are also essential to interpreters' training.

Section 1 provides an overview of legal interpreting with a particular focus on its requirement and testing mechanism. Section 2 introduces the role-space model (Llewellyn-Jones & Lee, 2014), explaining the relevance of each of the three axes and their role in

---

[1]. For more information, Morris (1999) offers an overview of the major cases that have helped shape court interpreting.

effective interpreting. Then, a discussion of Devaux (2017a) will highlight the awareness of the manifestation of role-space as articulated by experienced legal interpreters in both face-to-face and remote legal interpreting situations. The data will show that it is possible to encapsulate, in one model, the paralinguistic factors that can have an impact on a legal interaction. Finally, Section 3 discusses how what has been learned from experienced interpreters can inform the design of training and testing aspiring legal interpreters.

OVERVIEW OF LEGAL INTERPRETING REQUIREMENTS

There are various pieces of legal provision, standards, and regulations at international, European, and national levels that attempt to define legal interpreting and its requirements. England and Wales have been implementing them to various degrees, which has led to the creation of a very heterogeneous environment whereby only certain aspects of the international standards and regulations have been implemented into training and practice.

Legal Provisions

According to the Universal Declaration of Human Rights (1948), anyone is entitled to a fair trial, regardless of the language they speak. Although there is no explicit reference made to interpreters, the Declaration was a cornerstone in paving the way to various pieces of international and national legislations.

At the European level, the right to have access to an interpreter during legal proceedings has been clearly anchored with various pieces of legislation. Indeed, according to the European Convention for the Protection of Human Rights and Fundamental Freedom (1950):

> Everyone who is arrested shall be informed promptly, *in a language which he understands*, of the reasons for his arrest and of any charge against him. (Art. 5; our emphasis) [sic]

And:

Everyone charged with a criminal offence has the following minimum rights (...) to have the *free assistance of an interpreter* if he cannot understand or speak the language used in court. (Art. 6 (3) (e); our emphasis) [sic]

Since then various European directives have further defined the Universal Declaration of Human Rights within legislative frameworks such as the 2010/64/EU Directive, which ensures that any suspect or defendant has access to an interpreter and that technologies (such as videoconferencing systems) can be used in multilingual legal proceedings. Other directives extend the right to an interpreter to victims of human trafficking (2010/13/EU) and to victims of crime (2012/29/EU).

Further safeguarding the right of a defendant or a witness to an interpreter, the 2010/64/EU directive refers more specifically to the quality of the interpreter's performance by stating:

Interpretation provided under this Article shall be of a quality sufficient to safeguard the fairness of the proceedings, in particular by ensuring that suspected or accused persons have knowledge of the case against them and are able to exercise their right of defence. (Art. 2 s8)

Although this directive attempts to qualify what quality is, in the sense that it has to "safeguard the fairness of the proceedings," the definition is broad, and it is left to national bodies to interpret it.

At the national level, the use of interpreters in England and Wales is anchored within various pieces of legislation. For instance, Code C Paragraph 13 of the Police and Criminal Evidence Act (1984) regulates the use of interpreters in police settings. Several case laws also legislate on various aspects of interpreting such as the need for a competent and impartial interpreter (e.g., *R [on the application of Gashi] v. Chief Adjudicator,* 2001; Mitchell, 1970).

Despite the various pieces of legislation safeguarding the right to an interpreter, it is interesting to note that legal provisions at international and national levels fall short of defining specific requirements within legal interpreting or how interpreting competency is to be achieved. More importantly, there is no attempt to define the training of legal interpreters in terms of content and assessment.

International Standards

Unlike the above legal provisions, the International Organization for Standardization (2019)'s ISO20228:2019 gives a more comprehensive account as to what one should expect of legal interpreters and legal interpreting training. First, it emphasizes the need to train interpreters by delivering modules in interpreting at degree level and/or a state examination and/or official authorization. Second, budding legal interpreters are expected to demonstrate not only a sound knowledge of the legal sphere and to possess excellent language skills, but also need to show interpreting competences. Third, the ISO acknowledges the role that verbal and nonverbal communication (tone, body languages, facial expression, and [explanatory] gesture) play in interpreting. Fourth, legal interpreters should master their role, which includes introduction, positioning, turn-taking, and when and how to ask for clarification. Interestingly, it is expected that interpreters display interpersonal skills so that they "should be able *to build rapport* and to exhibit self-control and impartial behaviour in all legal settings" (Clause 5.6., our emphasis).

The requirements put forward by this ISO emphasize the pluri-dimensional aspect of legal interpreting that goes far beyond linguistic skills, which, to a great extent, aligns with scholarly research. They form the basis of legal interpreting courses, and the necessity to train interpreters, the role that nonverbal communication plays in an IME, and the role of the interpreter as a fully fledged participant in interaction have been widely examined (see. for instance, Berk-Seligson, 1990; Devaux, 2017b; Llewellyn-Jones & Lee, 2014; Napier, 2004; Salaets & Balogh, 2015; Wadensjö, 1998).

General Overview in England and Wales for Spoken Language Interpreters

Since the outsourcing of the court interpreting contract in England and Wales to private translation and interpreting agencies, complaints regarding interpreters' punctuality, qualifications, and performances, have been widely reported in media outlets[2] and within the interpreters' community.[3] It is currently rather difficult to establish a clear picture of training and assessment in England and Wales. This is partly due to the array of training centers, the lack of a centralized approach to curriculum design that is informed by research, and fit-for-purpose assessment.

Training Situation

When describing their pedagogical model to their university-level legal interpreting course, Hale and González (2017, p. 218) state that:

> A core aspect of this model is the need for students to constantly reflect on and analyse their own behaviour and performance (see Kiraly, 2000) and to be able to justify their choices based on the theory and results of research. The fundamental goal of the course is to equip students with necessary tools to make their own professional informed decisions once they leave the classroom (Mo & Hale, 2014).

An approach to fostering students' reflection and analytical skills that is anchored within theory is a model that is established in many university programs in translation and interpreting studies. Students are not only taught the basic interlingual interpreting skills; they are also encouraged to reflect on how their behavior influences an IME within a legal setting. As a result, many university programs provide students not only with the required linguistic skills but also the reflective tools to assess paralinguistic features such as their own behavior.

The provision of legal interpreting training in England and Wales is not solely delivered by higher education institutions but also is offered by various bodies ranging from private local companies or local colleges to online providers. Currently, it is difficult to find relevant information about the courses, entry criteria, pass rates, their curriculum and course content, and the trainers. Although more

---

2. See, for instance, https://www.bbc.co.uk/news/uk-25824907 and http://news.bbc.co.uk/today/hi/today/newsid_9705000/9705901.stm.
3. See, for instance, http://www.linguistlounge.org/.

empirical data are needed to make a stronger claim, discussions with previous candidates and trainers on the Diploma in Public Service Interpreting (DPSI) courses tend to show that some nonuniversity training courses focus primarily on the linguistics skills one must learn to become an interpreter.

These training courses are not compulsory, but the Chartered Institute of Linguists (CIoL), and its affiliate, the Institute of Linguists Educational Trust (IoLET), which awards national qualification in legal interpreting, strongly recommend that all candidates enroll in this training course. Since it isn't required, some may become interpreters without attending any training courses. In their *Procedures and Topic Area*, the CIoL (n.d.) provides a list of topics to be covered for the three DPSI options[4] as a preparation for the examination. However, the information provided to potential candidates does not refer to other skills, such as those described by Hale and González (2017) and ISO20228:2019. This seems to indicate a potential dichotomy between research-led university courses training legal interpreters and other training bodies that may follow the information provided by CIoL only. It also illustrates the need to promote a pedagogical model that not only allows the teaching of the necessary linguistic skills but also includes any interpersonal and paralinguistic features that shape a legal IME.

Testing Situation

In order to become a legal interpreter in England and Wales, it is expected that the prospective candidate passes the DPSI[5] awarded by IoLET. The examination itself is divided into three parts. In Part 1, students are interpreting two live role-plays in which their liaison and whispered interpreting skills are assessed. In Part 2, students are expected to provide two sight translations (into and out of

---

4. There are three DPSI options: Law, Health, and Local Government. Regardless of the options chosen, a successfully candidate will be able to work as a legal interpreter. In other words, an interpreter who passed the Health DPSI will be able to interpret in any legal setting.
5. A bachelor or master's degree in interpreting may be considered as an equivalent and enable its holder to work as a legal interpreter.

English), and in Part 3 students must translate two texts (into and out of English).⁶

Although students must pass each component, testing interpreting skills accounts for only one part of the examination process. The examination role-plays are all scripted, and students may ask for a repetition or clarification when interpreting in liaison mode. Apart from the terminological aspect of each scenario and the rudiments of liaison and whispered interpreting, the examination does not test students in terms of their understanding of paralinguistic content such as ethical dilemmas or the interpreters' role(s) that are predominant in interpreting studies research. In the same note, it fails to assess most aspects of ISO20228:2019. As a result, the extent to which the examination can be seen as a safeguard ensuring that students are ready to become legal interpreters can be at the very least questioned.⁷

Overview in England and Wales for British Sign Language (BSL) Interpreters

Training for BSL/English interpreters in the UK is based on the National Occupational Standards in Interpreting (NOSI, 2017). One can either train via the academic route, through a university course that is mapped to the National Occupational Standards (NOS) or through a work-based route, such as the National Vocational Qualification (NVQ; in England, Wales, and Northern Ireland). Regardless of the route, BSL/English interpreters must demonstrate advanced levels of language skills in both spoken English and BSL. The National Registers of Communication Professionals Working with Deaf and Deafblind People (NRCPD) is the largest register for BSL/English interpreters in the UK. In Scotland, interpreters can register with the Scottish Association of Sign Language Interpreters.

---

6. Samples of previous past papers are available here: https://www.ciol.org.uk/benefits/exam-resources
7. Compounding the testing provision is that as reported in the Ministry of Justice's (2014) Independent Review of Quality Arrangements under the Ministry of Justice Language Services Framework Agreement; some interpreters practice without holding the relevant qualification.

Currently, registration is voluntary, and one must provide evidence of yearly Continuing Professional Development (CPD) in order to stay on the register.

Unlike spoken language interpreters, there are currently no additional formal requirements or additional qualifications (beyond those mentioned above) for BSL/English interpreters working in legal settings. Currently under the outsourcing mentioned above, the Ministry of Justice subcontracts the provision of BSL/English interpreters to a company called Clarion. Clarion states that all their interpreters are registered (as mentioned above) and must have ". . . at least 2 years post-qualifying experience" (Clarion, n.d.). While the NRCPD Code of Conduct (NRCPD, 2015) tells interpreters, "You must work within the limits of your training, skills and experience," beyond this, there are no provisions in law that require additional qualifications/training for BSL/English interpreters working in legal settings.

ROLE-SPACE AS A GENERAL CONCEPT IN INTERPRETING

The concept of role-space was developed by Peter Llewellyn-Jones and Robert G. Lee (Lee & Llewellyn-Jones, 2011; Llewellyn-Jones & Lee, 2013, 2014) in response to the problematic way interpreters were defining their role (as outlined, for example, by Roy, 1993). The core premise of role-space is rooted in the concept of role as outlined by sociologists (e.g., Linton, 1936; Turner, 1956, 1962 inter alia), specifically that individuals *enact* roles, we do not have roles. The manifestation of an interpreter's role in a given interaction is delineated by three interrelated axes—Interaction Management, Participant Alignment, and Presentation of Self (see Figure 1). Interpreters make decisions along each of these axes in order to most effectively interpret in a given situation. Below is a description of each of the axes with illustrative examples.

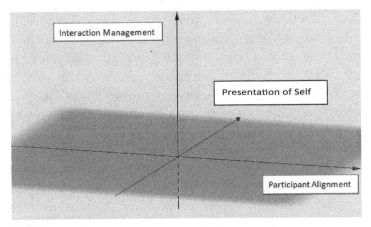

Figure 1. Role-space axes.

Interaction Management

The vertical axis (y-axis) in the role-space model is interaction management; how much (or how little) an interpreter is managing the flow of communication between and among the principal participants. Examples of high interaction management include the following: interpreting consecutively (controlling the pauses of speakers), asking for clarification, paraphrasing or repetition, or reminding participants to address each other in the first person ("Please address her directly and I will interpret what you say.").

Low interaction management examples include the following: not asking for clarification (for a variety of reasons, the setting prohibits it—for example, conference interpreting, or for reasons of status or culture, for example, that a high-status speaker should not be interrupted but lower-status speakers could be in the same situation). It is sometimes the setting that drives the lack of the use of specific strategies, and at other times it is a choice made (either by the interpreter solely or in negotiation with one or more participants) to minimize intrusions to the flow of communication. One example might be a meeting where the overarching communicative goal is to have as many ideas as possible presented by participants without filtering to allow more freethinking. If an interpreter would stop for clarification or repetition, this would thwart the core goal of the interaction.

Interaction management can either be overt or covert. Overt management strategies include the following: stopping the interaction to ask for clarification from one or more participants, asking speakers to pause while either consecutively or simultaneously interpreting, or overtly asking participants if the interpretation has been understood. Covert interaction management strategies include the following: pausing and whispering (or in the case of sign languages, signing in a smaller space) to clarify a minor point (e.g., "Did you say 15 or 50?") while continuing to interpret, nodding to a participant who wants to take the floor to signal that they can speak soon (since the rendition of the interpretation will soon be finished), or using a gesture (instead of saying something out loud) to signal the need for a slight pause in the flow of communication. Bélanger (2004, pp. 10–11) refers to those covert interactions between the interpreter and a single participant as either "parallel" or "embedded" exchanges. These can be very effective in that they allow the interpreter to get information needed for accuracy of the interpretation without halting the entire interaction.

Participant Alignment

The horizontal (x-axis) in the model is participant alignment; those strategies used by the interpreter to build trust and rapport with the principal participants in the interaction. Participants must trust that the interpreter is rendering their message faithfully and that the messages they are receiving are accurate renditions of the other participant(s). The interpreter must therefore appropriately align with the participants enough to engender such trust. In addition, if the interpreter does not align with the individual participants, it will be very difficult for them to then align with each other.

Examples of high alignment include physical proximity to participants, eye gaze with the participants, and/or reacting appropriately to what is being said by the participant before or as an interpretation is being delivered (smiling, nodding, etc.). Also, providing backchanneling (e.g., through the use of phatic utterances, "umm, uh-uh, yes") which signals both attention to the message and also alignment with the speaker. A more overt alignment strategy is when such backchannel information is presented as full lexical items (e.g., "Oh, yes. I understand"). Covert strategies include those that are more subtle, like head-nodding, as well as the use of verbalized nonlexical items such as "Uh-huh" and "mmmm").

Behaviors that are on the low end of the alignment axis: actively avoiding eye contact with participants, having a very closed body posture (e.g., folded arms, crossed legs), or locating oneself physically in the situation that is counter to the locations of the other participants (e.g., an interpreter placing themselves behind a participant). Alignment can and most likely will shift during the course of an interpreted interaction. It is also possible that an interpreter (purposefully or not) can be perceived as highly aligning with one participant while aligning in a low way with another participant. Such an asymmetry could have a significant impact on the perception of the interpreter's impartiality and this on the trust given to the interpreter.

Presentation of Self

The final axis (z-axis) refers to the presentation of self by the interpreter. Contrary to preconceived stereotypes of interpreters as mere "conduits" for meaning (see Roy, 1993, for a discussion of these issues), interpreters are human beings who are a part of the interaction albeit in ways different than the principal participants (following Roy, 1993, 2000; Wadensjö, 1992 for instance). The older stereotyped view is that interpreters can only, to use Goffman's (1981) terms, be animators of the meaning of others; interpreters cannot and should not be authors or be principals, that is, they should not have responsibility for utterances. As mentioned previously, it is vital that participants trust the interpreter and therefore the interpretation. By engaging in an appropriate presentation of self (e.g., introducing themselves by name, instead of just as "The Interpreter"), trust will be more readily developed. Failure to present oneself appropriately can have a negative impact on the participants' trust of the interpreter and, by extension, the interpretation itself.

Examples of high presentation of self include introducing oneself to the participants (either individually or in a group using the expected interaction norms for the languages and cultures involved), directly accepting (or rejecting) offer of food and/or beverages, and responding to (or deferring) direct questions as appropriate.

Examples of low presentation of self include the following: ignoring direct questions (the assumption being that the interpreter is not allowed to author statements; thus, even questions to the interpreter should be interpreted and then answered, potentially, by another participant), referring to oneself in third person rather than first person (e.g., "The Interpreter would like a break" or "The Interpreter did not hear that last statement"). Such low presentation of self behaviors can make participants feel uncomfortable, as the social norms for interaction seem to be different for the interpreter in the room (and seemingly unilaterally decided by them) as opposed to the principal participants. Indeed, ignoring such social norms can be interpreted by the other participants as rudeness and can have a deleterious effect on the communication dynamics and the flow of communication. In addition, such behaviors can be perceived as violations of Grice's Cooperative Principle (Grice, 1975). Even a perceived violation can undermine the confidence/trust in the interpreter and thus be a barrier to effective communication.

The decisions made by interpreters and the resulting strategies employed create the role-space enacted by the interpreter in the interaction. Situational factors, interpersonal factors, and familiarity of the participants in working with an interpreter can all affect how the interpreter enacts their role and the resulting role-space. The next section looks at the application of role-space theory to a specific type of interpreted legal interaction.

ROLE-SPACE THEORY APPLIED TO LEGAL INTERPRETING

This section reports on Devaux (2017a)'s study, with a specific focus on how role-space is operationalized and intrinsically present in a legal IME. The aim is to demonstrate that role-space can be operationalized as a framework that takes into account paralinguistic competencies and skills enshrined within ISO20228:2019 and the existing body of literature in interpreting studies.

Methodological Approach

Devaux (2017a) investigates how videoconference interpreting (VCI) affects the court interpreter's perception of her role in a court hearing. Using Actor-Network Theory as a methodological stance, humans and nonhuman entities (such as videoconferencing equip-ment) are considered actors that can equally affect an interaction.

Overall, 1,150 court interpreters were contacted by email through the National Register of Public Service Interpreters and 18 agreed to take part in the study. The participants all had experience, to various degrees, in VCI A (interpreter physically present in the courtroom) and/or VCI B (interpreter located remotely with the defendant or witness). The participants' profiles are summarized in Table 1.

The data were collected through semi-structured interviews, and Lee and Llewellyn-Jones (2011)'s list of role-space criteria was used as general themes to investigate the participants' presentation of self, participant alignment, and interaction management during the interviews. These criteria were slightly altered based on the results obtained from the pilot study. In line with Lee and Llewellyn-Jones (2011), this thematic approach enabled the researcher to assess each role-space axis and create a role-space model for each participant.

In terms of duration, the shortest interview was conducted with Participant 18 (31 minutes), whereas Participant 6's interviews last-ed the longest (69 minutes), and the time average per interview is 42 minutes.

The data were then transcribed verbatim, which amounted to a corpus of 105,104 words. In order to abide by ANT's tenets of ag-

Table 1. Participants' Profiles

Code	Gender	Qualifications	Years of Experience	VCI A	VCI B
P1	f	BA and MA in Translation and Interpreting	20	defendant	defendant
P2	f	Dip Trans/MA in T/I and DPSI law	15	N/A	defendant and witness
P3	f	DPSI law	12	defendant	defendant
P4	f	DPSI law	9	N/A	witness
P5	f	DPSI law and local government	15	defendant	defendant
P6	f	short course on police interpreting and then DPSI law	8	defendant and witness	defendant
P7	f	Metropolitan Police Test, DPSI law and health, also short courses with the Chartered Institute of Linguists (CIoL)	6	defendant	N/A
P8	f	Metropolitan Police Test	13	defendant and witness	N/A
P9	f	DPSI law	Not specified	defendant	N/A
P10	m	DPSI health	10	witness abroad	N/A
P11	f	DPSI law and health	12	N/A	witness
P12	f	DPSI law	18	defendant	N/A
P13	m	DPSI Law	20	N/A	defendant in prison

Table 1 (*continued*).

Code	Gender	Qualifications	Years of Experience	VCI A	VCI B
P14	f	DPSI law	14	defendant	witness
P15	f	DPSI local government	20	defendant	defendant
P16	f	DPSI local government	5	defendant	witness
P17	f	DPSI local government	20	witness in prison	defendant
P18	f	DPSI health	12	defendant	defendant

nosticism and noncensorship, the verbatim transcriptions included repetitions, hedgers, fillers, and so on. The transcripts were analyzed individually through NVivo in order to ensure analytical consistency, reliability, validity, and consistency (Basit, 2003; Bergin, 2011; Bong, 2002; Robert & Wilson, 2002; Siccama & Penna, 2008; Weitzman, 1999).

Triangulation was achieved through analyst triangulation, whereby other analysts critically reviewed the data findings (Patton, 1999, 2002; Robert Wood Johnson Foundation, 2006). To this end, three scholars in translation and interpreting studies were asked to verify three interviews each. This amounted to half of the data (nine interviews) being verified, which, taking into account their availabilities, was deemed an acceptable number of interviews.

Operationalizing Role-Space

The data analysis is summarized in Table 2 (VCI A) and Table 3 (VCI B).

As argued in Devaux (2018),[8] some interpreters perceived their role differently between the participants in court and the remote

---

8. In this paper, Devaux discusses some of Devaux's (2017a) findings.

defendant/witness. As such they created two sub role-spaces. The findings are summarized in Table 4 (VCI A) and Table 5 (VCI B).

In line with Llewellyn-Jones and Lee's (2014) experience in court, most participants in Devaux's (2017a) study felt that their presentation of self was low. Their presentation of self was often restricted by the court setting and the low-level interaction that took place during court hearings. The participants felt that there was no opportunity, during a court hearing, to be asked any direct questions, and, when needed, they would refer to themselves as "the interpreter" rather than "I." However, the main factor that impacted on the level of presentation of self was the interpreter's ability to introduce themselves, as the court interpreter, to all the parties present in the courtroom and at the remote location. In VCI A and B, this was exacerbated, for some of them, by the perceived physical distance created by the use of VC systems.

Table 2. Role-Space in VCI A

Participant	Presentation of Self	Participant Alignment	Interaction Management
P1	very low	> court	very low
P3	low	> court	low
P5	low	equal	high
P6	low	equal	quite high
P7	low	> court	low
P8	very low	> court	from low to high
P9	low	> court	high
P14	low	equal	from low to high
P15	low	equal	from very low to high
P16	low	> court	from low to quite high
P17	low	> court	low
P18	low	> court	low to quite high

Table 3. Role-Space in VCI B

Participant	Presentation of Self	Participant Alignment	Interaction Management
P1	very low	equal	low
P2	low	equal	low to quite high
P3	low	> defendant	high
P4	low	> witness	quite high
P5	low	equal	high
P6	low	equal	quite high
P11	low	> witness	high
P15	low	equal	low to high
P16	low	> witness	low to quite high
P18	low	equal	low to quite high

In terms of participant alignments, the data analysis reveals that most participants aligned either equally between the different parties or more toward the party with whom they were physically present. Some managed to build trust and rapport by reading the participants' body language and backchanneling accordingly. In VCI A and B and in line with the findings from presentation of self above, it was seen that the physical distance between the participants and the interpreters was one of the main factors affecting the interpreters' participant alignment. Indeed, most interpreters with an unequal participant alignment aligned more towards the parties with whom they were physically present.

Most interpreters overtly managed their interactions. For instance, they asked for clarification or repetition as needed. They also created visual signs to signal when they needed to intervene. Some stated that the use of the VC system did not impair the possibility to manage the interaction, even though they felt that there was no need to do so. However, some felt that the distance impeded on their ability to manage the interaction and, as such, they did not intervene when needed.

Table 4. Split Role-Space in VCI A

Participant	Presentation of Self (Court)	Interaction Management (Court)	Presentation of Self (Defendant)	Interaction Management (Defendant)	Participant Alignment
P10	low	high	very low	quite high	> court
P12	low	low to quite high	very low		equal

The data show that interpreters are aware of a range of interpersonal and paralinguistic factors that can affect their performance. Too often the factors that affect the interpreters' presentation of self, participant alignment, and interaction management tend to be analyzed separately. However, this section highlighted how role-space can be operationalized using different axes to encapsulate, in one model, all the relevant factors.

TRAINING OF LEGAL INTERPRETERS THROUGH ROLE-SPACE

This section will discuss the use of role-space as a course design and testing framework for aspiring legal interpreters.

Role-space can be used as a framework for teaching and assessing competence that complements the terminology-based approach. It builds on various theoretical frameworks (Section 3) that enables one to represent the practice of experienced legal interpreters. Furthermore, it accounts for the ISO20228 paralinguistic factors, namely verbal and nonverbal communications, and role features. Indeed, the use of three axes accounts for the introduction, positioning, turn-taking, and clarification as enacted by interpreters as discussed and demonstrated in Section 3.

It is also important to note that any linguistic errors could potentially affect role-space axes. For instance, not knowing the terminology would certainly affect the interpreter's presentation of self as a professional and potentially the effectiveness of alignment with the participants. As such, the model resolves the perceived dichotomy between knowledge of the terminology and legal systems and the competence required to be a legal interpreter.

For design of teaching, we use the revised Bloom's taxonomy (Krathwohl & Anderson, 2009) in the design of teaching and learning activities to support those training as interpreters in the legal domain. The core idea is that learners go through various stages of dealing with new information, skills, and competencies. Instruction should be designed to guide the learner through the material in a systematic way. According to Krathwohl and Anderson (2009), learners go through the following stages (from more concrete to more abstract): remembering, understanding, applying, analyzing, evaluating, and creating.

First, role-space would be introduced as a concept and as a framework for discussing interpreted interactions. This follows from the work of Hammer and van den Bogaerde (2017), who used role-space in the initial training of Dutch/Sign Language of the Netherlands (Nederlandse Gebarentaal: NGT) interpreters. Knowledge of the theory itself will progress following Dreyfus's model of skill interaction (Dreyfus, 2004, cited in Hammer & van den Bogaerde, 2017).

Before discussion interpreting, it would be helpful to gauge students' knowledge of the specifics of the languages and cultures with which they will work. Therefore, once students have demonstrated an understanding of the concepts of role-space and the definitions of the axes, they can move on to use the model to describe their own linguistic knowledge and competence. Each role-space axis could be used as a lens to allow students to look at their languages and cultures and for them to articulate various features. These can first be done with the individual languages and cultures, and then students could do a contrastive analysis of their similarities and differences and, by extension, determine what issues might arise when interpreting with a specific language pair. It is expected that students will progress through higher levels of Bloom's taxonomy in being able to discuss the features of the languages and cultures with which they work. Below are some guidelines in using the role-space axes as a framework for discussing linguistic and paralinguistic behaviors.

Interaction Management

Students should be able to describe, demonstrate, and discuss the ways in which interaction management is handled by users of their languages. Some indicative questions include the following:

- How do users of this language interrupt one another? Are there differences regarding people's age, gender, family relation, and so on?
- How are requests for clarification and/or repetition handled? Are there

specific grammatical structures used (e.g., echo questions)? Are there culture-specific rules or norms regarding who can ask for clarification/repetition?
- How are shifts in footing (in the sense of Goffman, 1981) signaled by users of the language? Are there cultural expectations depending on the relationships between the participants?
- What are the expectations of interaction management in the majority language used in legal settings? What are similarities/differences in the minority language used in these settings?

Participant Alignment

Students should be able to describe, demonstrate, and discuss the ways in which participants signal alignment in an interaction. Some indicative questions include the following:

- How do users of the languages signal alignment with one another? What are some examples of linguistic as well as paralinguistic features of alignment in the languages?
- Are there culture-specific norms regarding body language, eye gaze, touching, and so on that could affect alignment between and among participants?
- Are there differences in alignment between participants with different relationships (e.g., familial, subcultural, professional)? What are some examples?

Presentation of Self

- What are some examples of introductions in the languages and cultures used? Are there rules concerning age, gender, or in- vs. out-group status?
- Are there rules about introducing one's self as opposed to being introduced by another? Who in an interaction can introduce and who must be introduced by another?
- How are titles and/or honorifics used in the languages? Are there setting-specific rules for using titles and/or honorifics?
- Are there culture-specific norms regarding body language, eye gaze,

touching, and so on that could affect how one presents one's self?
- Are there any culture-specific behaviors (e.g., shaking hands, bowing) that must be observed when presenting one's self?

In addition to students being able to describe and delineate examples, it would be instructive for students to explain these to fellow students unfamiliar with one of their languages. In this way, students can practice metalinguistic skills of explaining linguistic/cultural information to those not from that specific community.

After an understanding of role-space in general, and the ability to analyze and discuss their own linguistic behaviors, students would then be ready to apply role-space in interpreting legal settings. In line with Hale and González's (2017) course design, role-space presents students with the opportunity to not only reflect on their own roles, but to also be used as a tool to discuss strategies they would apply to given interpreting scenarios. Instructors could use the individual axes in the design of situations to highlight manifestations of strategies along each axis.

Based on the authors' experience, role-space can be used to prepare interpreting scenarios, so that students can anticipate, based on the information provided, the shape of their role-space and if they need to pay particular attention to one or more of their axes. As many higher education institutions record students' performances, role-space can be used, at a later stage, by students to analyze and reflect on their own performance and to see how their role-space model evolves throughout the mock interpreted interactions.

In addition to its use in designing the training of interpreters, role-space can also be used in testing. As mentioned in previous sections, much training/testing has focused on linguistic knowledge. However, role-space theory can be used to assess students' reflective and interactional competencies which have not always been examined in testing. Thus, in the UK, there could potentially be a significant change in the DPSI examination. This could be done in different ways, for instance, by asking students to submit portfolios of their understanding of competencies through the application of role-space or asking them to analyze interpreted scenarios through a role-space lens.

Training and assessing legal interpreters must be designed in a way that not only prepares aspiring interpreters to work in a legal context but also equips them with the tools to become reflective practitioners. Although further empirical studies are needed, role-space has already been applied rigorously, as an analytical framework, in scholarly works. These studies provide practicing interpreters with a sound framework to reflect on their own practice in a court. Incorporating role-space and assessment design in the course is significant and original as it encourages course providers to depart from a terminology-focused approach by examining and reflecting on the various paralinguistic factors that form part of an IME, as required in ISO20228. Finally, it is worth noting that as role-space is not context-bound, it can be incorporated in the design of other interpreting courses (such as health).

QUESTIONS AND APPLICATION

1. The authors suggest that the role-space can be used for testing. Design an assessment that incorporates the axes used in role-space.
2. Reflect upon your own practice. Which axis should you focus on first when it comes to working in a legal setting?

REFERENCES

Basit, T. I. (2003). Manual or electronic? The role of coding in qualitative data analysis. *Educational Research, 45*(2), 143–154. https://doi.org/10.1080/0013188032000103235

Bélanger, D-C. (2004). Interactional patterns in dialogue interpreting. *Journal of Interpretation, 17* 1–18.

Bergin, M. (2011). NVivo 8 and consistency in data analysis: Reflecting on the use of a qualitative data analysis program. *Nurse Researcher*

18(3), 6–12. https://doi.org/10.7748/nr2011.04.18.3.6.c8457

Berk-Seligson, S. (1990). *The bilingual courtroom: Court interpreters in the judicial process*. University of Chicago Press.

Bong, S. (2002). Debunking myths in qualitative data analysis. *Forum: Qualitative Social Research, 3*(2). https://doi.org/10.17169/fqs-3.2.849

Chartered Institute of Linguists. (n.d.). *Procedures and topic areas*. https://www.ciol.org.uk/dpsi#quicktabs-dpsi=1

Chilingaryan, K., Gorbatenko, O., & Gorbatenko, R. (2016, October 10–12). Training court interpreters in Germany. In F. Uslu (Ed.), *Proceedings of ADVED 2016 2nd International Conference on Advances in Education and Social Sciences*. OCERINT. http://www.ocerint.org/adved16_e-proceedings/papers/230.pdf

Clarion. (n.d.). *Ministry of justice*. http://www.clarion-uk.com/ministry-of-justice/

Devaux, J. (2017a). *Technologies in interpreter-mediated criminal court hearings: An actor-network theory account of the interpreter's perception of her role-space* [Unpublished doctoral thesis]. University of Salford.

Devaux, J. (2017b). Virtual presence, ethics and videoconference interpreting: Insights from court settings. In C. Valero Garcés & R. Tipton (Eds.), *Ideology, ethics and policy development in public service interpreting and translation* (pp. 131–150). Multilingual Matters.

Devaux, J. (2018). Technologies and role-space: How videoconference interpreting affects the court interpreter's perception of her role. In C. Fantinuoli (Ed.), *Interpreting and technologies* (pp. 91–117). Language Science Press.

Dreyfus, S. E. (2004). The five-stage model of adult skill acquisition. *Bulletin of Science Technology & Society, 24*(3), 177–181. https://doi.org/10.1177/0270467604264992

Goffman, E. (1981). *Forms of talk*. University of Pennsylvania Press.

Grice, H. P. (1975). Logic and conversation. In P. Cole & J. L. Morgan (Eds.), *Syntax and semantics* (pp. 41–58). Academic Press.

Hale, S., & González, E. (2017). Teaching legal interpreting at university level: A research-based approach. In L. Cirillo & N. Niemants (Eds.), *Teaching dialogue interpreting: Research-based proposals for higher education* (pp. 199–216). John Benjamins.

Hammer, A., & van den Bogaerde, B. (2017). Sign language interpreting education reflections on interpersonal skills. In L. Cirillo & N. Niemants (Eds.), *Teaching dialogue interpreting: Research-based proposals for higher education* (pp. 63–81). John Benjamins.

International Organization for Standardization. (2019). *Interpreting services—Legal interpreting—requirements* (ISO 20228:2019). https://www.iso.

org/standard/67327.html

Kiraly, D. (2000). *A social constructivist approach to translator education: Empowerment from theory to practice.* St. Jerome.

Krathwohl, D. R., & Anderson, L. W. (2009). *A taxonomy for learning, teaching, and assessing: A revision of Bloom's taxonomy of educational objectives.* Longman.

Lee, R. G., & Llewellyn-Jones, P. (2011). *Re-visiting role: Arguing for a multi-dimensional analysis of interpreter behaviour.* http://clok.uclan.ac.uk/5031/1/Lee%20and%20L-J%202011.pdf

Linton, R. (1936). *The study of man.* Appleton-Century Crofts.

Liu, X., & Hale, S. (2018). Achieving accuracy in a bilingual courtroom: The effectiveness of specialised legal interpreter training. *The Interpreter and Translator Trainer, 12*(3), 299–321. https://doi.org/10.1080/1750399X.2018.1501649

Llewellyn-Jones, P., & Lee, R. G. (2013). Getting to the core of role: Defining interpreters' role space. *International Journal of Interpreter Education, 5*(2), 54–72.

Llewellyn-Jones, P., & Lee, R. G. (2014). *Redefining the role of the community interpreter: The concept of role-space.* SLI Press.

Metzger, M. (1999). *Sign language interpreting: Deconstructing the myth of neutrality.* Gallaudet University Press.

Ministry of Justice. (2014). *The independent review of quality arrangements under the MoJ language services framework agreement.* https://assets.publishing.service.gov.uk/government/uploads/system/uploads/attachment_data/file/388333/matrix-report.pdf

Mo, Y., & Hale, S. (2014). Translation and interpreting education and training: Student voices. *International Journal of Interpreter Education, 6*(1), 19–34.

Morris, R. (1999). The face of justice: Historical aspects of court interpreting. *Interpreting, 4*(1), 97–124. https://doi.org/10.1075/intp.4.1.10mor

Napier, J. (2004). Sign language interpreter training, testing, and accreditation: An international comparison. *American Annals of the Deaf, 149*(4), 350–359. https://doi.org/10.1353/aad.2005.0007

National Occupational Standards in Interpreting. (2017). https://www.ukstandards.org.uk. Suite: Interpreting.

NRCPD. (2015). *Code of conduct for registrants and regulated trainees.* https://www.nrcpd.org.uk/code-of-conduct

Patton, M. Q. (1999). Enhancing the quality and credibility of qualitative analysis. *HSR: Health Services Research, 34*(5), 1188–1208.

Patton, M. Q. (2002). *Qualitative research & evaluation methods: Integrating theory and practice.* Sage.

Robert, K. A., & Wilson, R. W. (2002). ICT and the research process: Issues around the compatibility of technology with qualitative data analysis. *Forum Qualitative Sozialforschung*, 3(2). https://doi.org/10.17169/fqs-3.2.862

Robert Wood Johnson Foundation. (2006). *Qualitative research guidelines project*. http://www.qualres.org/HomeTria-3692.html

Roy, C. (1993). The problem with definitions, descriptions and the role metaphor of interpreters. *Journal of Interpretation*, 6, 127–153.

Roy, C. (2000). *Interpreting as discourse process*. Oxford University Press.

Salaets, H., & Balogh, K. (2015). Development of reliable evaluation tools in legal interpreting: A test case. *The International Journal for Translation and Interpreting Research*, 7(3), 103–119. https://doi.org/10.12807/ti.107203.2015.a08

Siccama, C. J., & Penna, S. (2008). Enhancing validity of a qualitative dissertation research study by using NVivo. *Qualitative Research Journal*, 8(2), 91–103. https://doi.org/10.3316/QRJ0802091

Turner, R. H. (1956). Role-taking, role standpoint, and reference-group behavior. *American Journal of Sociology*, 61, 316–328.

Turner, R. H. (1962). Role taking: Process versus conformity. In A. M. Rose (Ed.), *Human behavior and social processes: An interactionist approach* (pp. 20–40). Houghton Mifflin.

Wadensjö, C. (1992). *Interpreting as interaction: On dialogue-interpreting in immigration hearings and medical encounters*. Lindköping University.

Wadensjö, C. (1998). *Interpreting as interaction*. Longman.

Weitzman, E. (1999). Analyzing qualitative data with computer software. *Health Services Research*, 34(5), 1241–1263.

Acts of Parliament and Statutes

European Convention for the Protection of Human Rights and Fundamental Freedom (1950).

European Directive (2010/13/EU) on the right to an interpreter to victims of human trafficking.

European Directive (2010/64/EU) on the situation of fundamental rights in the European Union in 2015.

European Directive (2012/29/EU) on establishing minimum standards on the rights, support, and protection of victims of crime, and replacing Council Framework Decision 20001/220/JHA.

Mitchell (1970) 114 S.J. 86.

Police and Criminal Evidence Act (1984).

R (on the application of Gashi) v. Chief Adjudicator (2001).

Universal Declaration of Human Rights (1948).

9 THE INTERACTIVE COURTROOM: THE DEAF DEFENDANT WATCHES HOW THE SPEAKER IS IDENTIFIED FOR EACH TURN-AT-TALK DURING A TEAM-INTERPRETED EVENT

LeWana Clark

EDITOR'S INTRODUCTION

> *Having an interpreter during a court proceeding is commonplace across many industrialized countries. In the United States, it is widely accepted that a team of proceedings interpreters are needed to provide communication access to the dDeaf individual(s) involved in the matter. In this study, Clark explores the effectiveness of speaker identification, marked by the nondeaf certified hearing interpreters (CHIs), at each turn of the conversation in two teaming approaches: one where they rotate in and out of the "on" position and one where they both remain in the "on" position and interpret for assigned speakers. When the single interpreter is in the "on" position, they must mark who is speaking so the dDeaf individual(s) can follow the contributions to the discourse by each speaker. But, for example, when both interpreters remain in the "on" position, they inform the dDeaf individual(s) who is assigned to interpret for the attorney asking questions to an English-speaking witness and who is assigned to interpret for the witness's response. Each time an interpreter begins to sign, the dDeaf person knows who was speaking by virtue of who was signing.*

THE dDEAF[1] DEFENDANT stands before the court, charged with a crime, prepared to go to trial. But because the defendant cannot

---

1. The writing convention in this chapter of "dDeaf" represents those in the Deaf and Hard of Hearing community with varying degrees of hearing loss and social identity.

hear the spoken interactions between the judge, attorneys, and English-speaking witnesses, the court, in the United States, has a legal mandate to provide interpreting services in this venue. The court expects, and the law demands, via the oath, that the American Sign Language[2]-to-English interpreters render a true interpretation (Federal Rules of Evidence, 604; Milenkovski, 2012), which means they must also identify who is speaking as a component of the interpretation (Clark, 2018).

Roger Shuy (2001, 2003) states, "[t]hroughout history, people have been identified, or misidentified, by their voices" (p. 441). He also recognizes when there are multiple speakers, "things get complicated" (Shuy, 2001, p. 442). Listening to a recording of an interaction between two or more people who cannot be seen is analogous to a dDeaf defendant watching an interpretation where the speakers are not identified at each turn of the conversation.

Thus, the problem addressed in this chapter is that sometimes interpreters[3] strategically identify the speaker for each turn-at-talk, but at other times they either do not remember to do so or are not aware that the speaker identification marker is absent or inaccurate (Clark, 2018; Metzger, 1999; van Herreweghe, 2002).

Legal interpreting scholars (Berk-Seligson, 1990; González et al., 1991; Hale, 2001, 2002; Mikkelson, 2010; Roberson et al., 2011; Russell, 2000, 2002; Stewart et al., 2009) have discussed the work of sign language and spoken language interpreters in the courtroom and agree that an accurate interpretation is imperative, given that non–English-speaking defendants have a Constitutional right to be linguistically/meaningfully present (de Jongh, 2008) and readily understand the interpretation (*Arizona v. Natividad*, 1974) so they can aid in their own defense. Although dDeaf defendants cannot hear or track the voices in the courtroom discourse and rely on the American Sign Language–English interpreter to identify who is speaking, according to anecdotal accounts, spoken language in-

---

2. To honor the primary language of the American Deaf community, I use the full name of their language, American Sign Language, in this chapter rather than the acronym.
3. Unless otherwise noted forthwith, the term "interpreter" used in this document refers to the nondeaf certified hearing interpreter (CHI) team members.

terpreters may also at times need to identify the speaker for the non–English-speaking defendant who can hear the voices if the target interpretation lags too far behind the source during a quick exchange of turns. Despite the rich literature on courtroom interpreting, to date, none of it addresses speaker identification as an element of accuracy in the interpretation.

This chapter will discuss the findings of two research questions: (1) How did the interpreters studied identify the speaker at each turn-at-talk during dialogic/two-way discourse of a mock bench trial when two English-speaking witnesses testified? (2) How did the way the interpreters worked together as a team impact their ability to consistently identify the speaker at each turn-at-talk?

THE STUDY

A collective case study bounded by speaker identification consisted of four scripted mock criminal bench trials. I wrote two different mock trial scripts based on two case files purchased from the National Institute of Trial Advocacy (NITA). The first script was a commercial arson case, and the second script was an armed robbery case. Each script was written to last approximately 90 minutes with an average of 560 turns-at-talk containing three types of discourse: monologic (i.e., opening and closing statements), dialogic/two-way (i.e., direct and cross-examination), and dialogic/three-way (i.e., discussion about objections).

The commercial arson script was used for the first and second mock trials, and the armed robbery case was used for the third and fourth mock trials. Each mock trial took place with nine paid participants: judge, prosecutor, defense attorney, dDeaf defendant, two English-speaking witnesses, a table interpreter, and two proceedings interpreters. Each mock trial represents a single case, and the four mock trials together made up the collection. Merriam (2009) infers that a cross-case analysis can guide the researcher to make generalizations, thereby, "enhancing the external validity or generalizability" (p. 50) of the findings.

The mock trials took place in Superior Court Judge Gregerson's courtroom in the Clark County Courthouse in Vancouver, Washington, on January 3 and 4, 2017. The individuals who played the role of the judge and prosecutor were attorneys who each had over 100 hours of trial experience. The defense attorney was an actor. The two dDeaf defendant actors use American Sign Language as their first language although one identified as Deaf and the other as Hard of Hearing. Neither of the dDeaf actors had been involved with the criminal justice system, and both had a minimal understanding of court proceedings and procedures. The two English-speaking witnesses were actors who had no prior experience testifying in court. The scripts and case file were shared with these participants 2 weeks prior to the first day of filming with a warning not to share this information with the interpreters.

However, the case file was shared with the interpreters for preparation purposes prior to the beginning of the mock trial they were scheduled to interpret. None of the interpreters requested preparation information prior to arriving on site. The table interpreter at each trial was present to interpret for the dDeaf defendant and the defense attorney as needed for privileged conversations during the mock trials. The findings of the table interpreters are not discussed here.

The four proceedings interpreters (who gave their explicit permission for their likeness to be used when reporting findings), three female and one male, all CHI, were all SC:L-certified (Specialist Certificate: Legal) with over 500 hours of combined courtroom interpreting experience. Unless otherwise noted forthwith, the term "interpreter" refers to the nondeaf legally certified hearing inter-preter (CHI) who works with another CHI as a pair because it is standard practice for interpreters to work as a team for lengthy and/or complex assignments (Cokely & Hawkins, 2003; RID, 2007; Russell & Hale, 2008).

The boundary of each case was defined as the speaker identification markers representing the change of speaker, at every turn-at-talk in the American Sign Language courtroom interpretation. All other phenomena—including the analysis of the linguistic meaning of the interpretation—are outside the boundaries of the case and were not considered. The data were analyzed through a focused process of pattern identification that resulted in an optimized understanding of the complexities of the phenomenon.

The independent variable (type of teaming model) was manipulated to examine if the inclusion of unambiguous speaker identification markers increased or decreased for the dependent variable (monologic, dialogic/two-way and dialogic/three-way discourse types) used during mock trial proceedings.

The proceedings interpreters worked in pairs. They interpreted only one mock trial per day to reduce the effects of fatigue on their performance. One team of interpreters worked both morning mock trials. They used the Rotate Model for the first trial on the first day and the Remain Model for the first trial on the second day. They had worked together frequently and knew each other well. Next, the other team of interpreters worked the two afternoon trials. They used the Remain Model for the second trial on the first day and the Rotate Model for the second trial on the second day. They met on site and had never worked with each other before this project.

Because the stimulus for this project consisted only of spoken English conversations, not directed to the dDeaf defendant, both teams of proceedings interpreters were instructed to use simultaneous interpreting throughout. They were not told of the specific focus of the study, but they were told that I was exploring how the different teaming models affected their ability to uphold their oath: to render a true interpretation by interpreting accurately, completely, and impartially by using their best skill and judgment in accordance with the standards and ethics of the interpreter profession.

Four cameras were used to videotape the mock trials. Camera 1 was focused on the interpreter(s) in the "on" position. Camera 2 captured the judge and the English-speaking witness. Camera 3 recorded a wide shot of the courtroom. Camera 4 recorded the dDeaf defendant actors at the defense table with the defense attorney, the table interpreter, and the interpreter in the "off" position (when the interpreters worked in the Rotate Model).

After the data were collected, I created a number of ELAN[4] documents that I used to analyze the interpretation from each mock trial. The analysis of the speaker identification marker was not based on whether the interpreter produced a marker or not but on whether the marker was unambiguous or underdetermined. In other words, the examination of each turn-at-talk asked if the dDeaf defendant could presumably follow who was talking at each turn of the conversation as the judge, prosecutor, defense attorney, and witness spoke to each other at different times throughout the trial.

This chapter discusses how the interpreters identified the speakers at each turn-at-talk and how the two teaming approaches, the Rotate Model and the Remain Model, impact the interpreter's consistent ability to identify each speaker throughout the mock trials for different types of discourse.

TYPES OF DISCOURSE DURING MOCK BENCH TRIALS

The discourse used by attorneys, witnesses, and the judge during a trial is classified either as monologic or dialogic. Coulthard and Johnson (2007) define monologic discourse as "one speaker . . . addressing the court, as in opening and closing statements by the lawyers, or the judge instructing the jury" (p. 96). Dialogic/two-way discourse occurs when "two speakers are interacting, as during the examination and cross-examination of witnesses" (Coulthard & Johnson, 2007, p. 96). The distinct definitions of monologic and dialogic discourse by Coulthard and Johnson (2007), which only count the number of speakers, differ from Wadensjö's (1998) inclusion of the number of speaker(s) and listener(s) in the dialogic event. Dialogic/three-way discourse is when the judge and attorneys discuss the admission of exhibits or when an attorney objects to something said during direct or cross-examination, which is ordinarily followed by a discussion regarding procedure between the judge and the attorneys.

---

4. ELAN is professional-grade tier-based software widely used in academia and is well received in the disciplines of sign language and conversation analysis (ELAN, Version 6.2) [computer aoftware]. 2021.

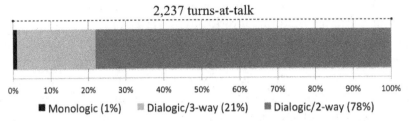

Figure 1. Types of discourse used in courtroom conversations.

As shown in Figure 1, of the 2,237 turns-at-talk in my data set, monologic discourse only counted for 1% of the discourse, while dialogic/three-way made up 21%. Although the percentage of speaker identification was low for both monologic and dialogic/three-way discourses, the dDeaf defendant is not directly affected by these conversations because they are informational and procedural in nature and make up a small portion of the discourse in the mock trials (1% + 21%). Overall, the bulk (78%) of the mock trial conversations consisted of dialogic/two-way discourse. Dialogic/two-way discourse comes primarily from the question-and-answer sequence between an attorney and the witness who is testifying.

For dialogic/two-way discourse, a missing or underdetermined speaker identification marker may negatively impact the defendant's ability to enjoy the Constitutional right to confront the witness. Also from an access perspective, the dDeaf defendant may become frustrated if they cannot follow the conversation between the attorney and witness without consistent speaker identification markers.

Now looking at the first research question: How did the interpreters in my dissertation study identify the speaker at each turn-at-talk during dialogic/two-way discourse of a scripted mock bench trial when two English-speaking witnesses testified?

INTERPRETERS WORKING TOGETHER AS A TEAM

As an American Sign Language–English interpreter, I have worked with colleagues who adhere to the belief that a team of interpreters must divide their work of producing the interpretation by switching in and out of the "on" position regardless of the type of discourse being used by multiple interlocutors. This practice aligns with Metzger's (2005) assertion that "the 20-minute shift has become the de facto practice for interpreters working in teams" (p. 266). Here, one interpreter works in the "on" position, interpreting for everyone making a contribution to the dialogue during their shift, regardless of the number of speakers (one person giving a speech, two people engaged in a dialogue, or multiple parties discussing a topic). Yet, a standard descriptor of this rotating teaming approach does not exist, perhaps because best practices (Stewart et al., 2009) promote it as the only way to team together. So I named this teaming approach the "Rotate Model" (based on Hoza, 2010)—where the interpreters rotate in and out of the "on" position (Figure 2). While in the "on" position, a single interpreter interprets for every interlocutor in the conversation during the shift.

The justification of the Rotate Model is based on two fatigue studies: Babbini Brasel (1976) and Moser-Mercer et al. (1998), who found that cognitive and physical fatigue could negatively impact an interpretation. Thus, a pattern of "work-rest-work-rest" (Cokely & Hawkins, 2003, p. 51) for interpreters is justified. Yet, neither Babbini Brasel nor Moser-Mercer et al. studied interpreters working in teams in interactive settings, and both concurred that switching

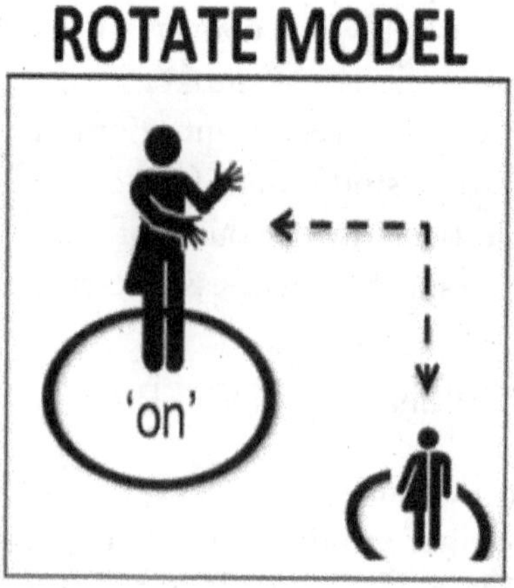

Figure 2. Rotate Model.

interpreters during a presentation "may appear disruptive" (Babbini Brasel, 1976, p. 26 and Moser-Mercer et al., 1998, p. 48). Although the Rotate Model may be the current de facto teaming approach, it is not the only way interpreters work together.

Russell (2008) reports that one team in her study chose to "split the work by language considerations" (p. 127) when they interpreted for a dDeaf witness. While one interpreter worked from spoken English into American Sign Language as the attorney asked a question, the second interpreter worked from American Sign Language into spoken English when the dDeaf witness answered. Neither Russell nor the interpreters named this teaming approach, and I did not study this teaming approach in my dissertation.

Then Mickelson and Gordon (2015) report an "unusual teaming configuration that came out of a spontaneous set of changes that evolved over the course of a presentation" (p. 12). Initially, the interpreters started with one interpreter in the "on" position. The interactions between the two workshop presenters became very dynamic, and the second interpreter joined the first interpreter on the stage. The interpreters quickly decided to reconfigure and split the work, so "each took on the work of one presenter, allowing the presenters the freedom to dialogue and providing the audience with a clear indicator of who was speaking" (Mickelson & Gordon, 2015, p. 12). Both of these interpreters worked from spoken English into American Sign Language. I named this teaming model (based on Mickelson & Gordon, 2015) the "Remain Model" (Figure 3) because both interpreters remain in the "on" position for the interpreted event.

In the Remain Model approach when working from spoken English into American Sign Language for dialogic/two-way discourse during direct and cross-examination, there are two interlocutors and two interpreters. Prior to the beginning of the trial, the interpreters discuss who would interpret for the attorney asking questions and who would interpret for the English-speaking witness's response during the question–answer sequence. Both teams of interpreters assigned the interpreter seated closest to the attorney to interpret for the questions and then the second interpret-

Figure 3. Remain Model.

er would interpret for answers. One team kept these assignments for both English-speaking witnesses questioning series. However, the other team changed their assignments for the second English-speaking witness to mitigate fatigue (although they did not change their physical seating arrangement). Prior to the beginning of the trial and when the assignments changed, the interpreters informed the dDeaf defendant who was assigned to interpret for the attorney asking the questions and who was designated to interpret for the English-speaking witness.

As they work only for their assigned interlocutor, the interpretation flows back and forth between the interpreters so the dDeaf defendant can experience who is talking in a more authentic manner. As reported in the literature, an interpretation becomes considerably more authentic (González et al., 1991) when interpreters consistently identify who is speaking. Thus, the Remain Model approach eliminates the need for an interpreter to incorporate a speaker identification marker for each turn-at-talk in the interpretation during dialogic/two-way discourse such as when an attorney is questioning an English-speaking witness on the stand. Two benefits of this model is that the interpreters do not have to remember to include the speaker identification marker for each turn-at-talk and the

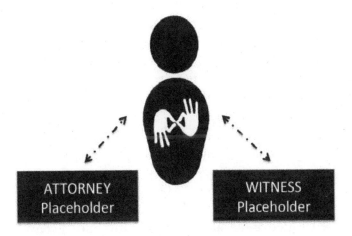

Figure 4. Placeholders.

dDeaf defendant can readily see who is talking during the interactive exchange between the attorney and the witness. It should be noted, however, that speaker identification markers are necessary when a third interlocutor (e.g., the opposing attorney or judge) begins a conversation with the attorneys dealing with an objection (dialogic/three-way discourse) or when one speaker is giving a closing statement (monologic discourse), for example. Neither teaming model (Rotate Model or Remain Model) supported the interpreter's ability to consistently mark who was speaking at each turn-at-talk during dialogic/three-way discourse. Additional study is needed to address this challenge.

Either teaming model, the Rotate Model and the Remain Model, appears to support the unambiguous speaker identification when the interpreters are interpreting monologic discourse during a courtroom trial. The dDeaf defendant likely already knows the information that the prosecutor and defense attorney will share during the opening statement if they have prepared for trial with the defense attorney or has seen the police report. The dDeaf defendant will also likely know what the prosecutor and defense attorney may say in the closing statements as the attorneys recount their view of the evidence collected during testimony. Similarly, the verdict does have a direct impact on the dDeaf defendant. The judge's verdict, at the conclusion of a bench trial, informs the defendant as to the outcome of the court proceeding. If the speaker identification marker is not present, the dDeaf defendant may be able to pick up clues from the environment as to who is speaking as they stand next to the defense attorney looking at the judge.

SPEAKER IDENTIFICATION FOR EACH TURN-AT-TALK

In their studies of American Sign Language, researchers (Baker-Shenk & Cokely, 1980; Liddell & Metzger, 1998; Padden, 1986) have noted ways that dDeaf people take turns during conversations. American Sign Language has nomenclature for referencing who is talking, which focuses on different types of markers: person reference (Friedman, 1975), role shifting (Lentz, 1986; Padden, 1986), and person deixis (Meier, 1990).

"Once a signer has established a person, thing, or place in space, all future references to it will be consistent with that location unless the referent has clearly been moved to another location or the topic has changed" (Baker-Shenk & Cokely, 1980, p. 227). In my research, the interpreters marked their right placeholder position as the attorney who sat/stood to their right and their left placeholder position as the English-speaking witness who sat behind them (Figure 4).

The following eight distinct speaker identification markers were found in the data: Assigned, Body Movement, Directional Question, Indexing, Lexical Marker, Neutral Position, NEXT SPEAKER, and Raised Hand. Each is described and illustrated in Figure 5.

An interesting phenomenon occurred with all of the interpreters when they primarily worked in the Rotate Model. They sometimes used these markers alone and at other times used two or more of them in combination. Overall, there were 191 permutations and combinations of the recognized speaker identification markers across the four mock trials. For example, the judge was identified with both the indexing marker and the lexical marker of "JUDGE." However, my analysis found that adding more than one unambig-

(1) Assigned
An interpreter is assigned to interpret for either the attorney asking questions or the English-speaking witness responding.

(2) Body Movement
One of the most commonly used speaker identification markers was the interpreter's body movement (role-shifting) with varying degrees of twists/leans/shifts/tilts.

(3) Directional Question
The visual representation of the question mark starts with the back of the hand towards the person asking the question moving toward the person being asked and stopping once the question mark has been made.

(4) Indexing
Also a commonly used speaker identification marker. Typically produced with the index finger of either hand, sometimes with directional eye gaze but can be also produced with the thumb.

(5) Lexical Marker
The American Sign Language sign for JUDGE was used as a speaker identification marker.

(6) Neutral Position
The interpreters marked the judge's talk from the neutral position (in between the attorney and witness placeholder positions) but they did not reserve that location for every time the judge spoke.

Judge   Witness   Prosecutor   Defense

(7) NEXT SPEAKER
By pointing to the prosecutor and then pointing to the defense attorney (for example), this sign indicates the next speaker but does not identify the judge as the current speaker.

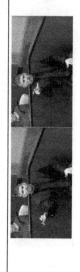

(8) Raised Hand
The interpreter raises her right hand and maintains the HOLD-A-MINUTE sign with her left hand as she speaks to the judge.

Interpreter

Figure 5. Speaker identification markers.

uous speaker identification marker per turn-at-talk was redundant and did not add further clarity.

SPEAKER IDENTIFICATION FOR DIALOGIC/TWO-WAY DISCOURSE

From my data, the interpreter's ability to mark each speaker varied from individual to individual (as seen in Table 1) as they worked in the Rotate Model. Interpreter 1 clearly and consistently marked 94% of the dialogic/two-way turns-at-talk during the shift in the "on: position. In similar fashion, Interpreter 2 marked 89%, Interpreter 3 marked 88%, and Interpreter 4 marked 79%. The ability to mark the speakers of 94% of the turns-at-talk during a conversation is laudable. But remember, the 6% of the unmarked turns-at-talk may still negatively impact the dDeaf defendant's opportunity to confront the witness at some level depending upon where the unmarked turn-at-talk comes in the discourse and how often consecutive unmarked turns-at-talk occur over a period of time. And the impact of missing or underdetermined speaker identification markers for 78% to 85% of the dialogic/two-way discourse by the other three proceedings interpreters from this project has yet to be explored. But we may agree that the difficulties of following the flow of the conversation during the interpreted courtroom event increase for the dDeaf defendant as the percentage of unmarked turns-at-talk grow larger.

In contrast, when the interpreters worked in the Remain Model interpreting for dialogic/two-way discourse, being assigned to either the attorney or English-speaking witness during dialogic/two-way discourse helped the interpreters achieve near-perfect speaker identification for each turn-at-talk (Table 2).

Table 1. Individual Interpreter's Ability to Mark the Speaker for Each Turn-at-Talk When Working in the Rotate Model.

Interpreter1	Interpreter2	Interpreter3	Interpreter4
94%	89%	88%	79%

Table 2. Individual Interpreter's Ability to Mark the Speaker for Each Turn-at-Talk When Working in the Remain Model.

Interpreter1	Interpreter2	Interpreter3	Interpreter4
97%	99%	98%	99%

Interpreter 1 improved to 97%; Interpreter 2, to 99%, Interpreter 3, to 98%; and Interpreter 4 to 99%. When working in the Remain Model, the interpreters did not have to remember to mark each turn-at-talk with a speaker identification marker because each time they raised their hands to interpret, they interpreted for an assigned speaker. The reason each interpreter did not mark 100% of the turns-at-talk was either one or more utterances were not interpreted or instead of an attorney talking with the English-speaking witness, the judge spoke to the witness and the interpreter forgot to identify the judge as the speaker.

Now to the second research question: How did the way the interpreters worked together as a team impact their ability to consistently identify the speaker at each turn-at-talk?

INTERPRETING THE ENGLISH-SPEAKING WITNESS' TESTIMONY

There was a total number of 1,752 dialogic/two-way discourse turns-at-talk across all of the mock trials. This correlates to 78% of the entire 2,237 turns-at-talk for the collection. Of the 1,752 dialogic/two-way turns-at-talk, 889 occurred when the interpreters were working in the Rotate Model, and 863 occurred when the interpreters were working in the Remain Model.

As a group, when working in the Rotate Model, the interpreters unambiguously marked the speaker for 770 out of 889 dialogic/two-way turns-at-talk (87%; see Figure 6). They clearly produced body movements, directional questions, indexing, and lexical markers, and interpreted from the neutral position. Although there were ambiguous body movements, directional questions, indexing, and "NEXT SPEAKER" markers for 13% of the underdetermined turns-

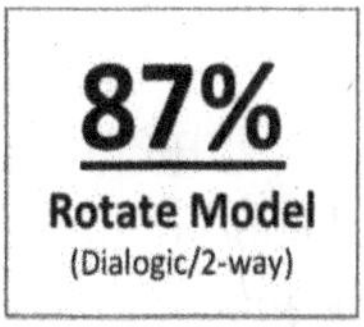

87%
Rotate Model
(Dialogic/2-way)

Figure 6. Unambiguous markings for the Rotate Model.

at-talk, over half of these interpretations were not clearly marked because the interpreters worked from the neutral position for the judge, prosecutor, defense attorney, and English-speaking witnesses, or the utterance was not interpreted at all.

The interpreter working alone in the "on" position is faced with at least four challenges relating to identifying the speaker at each turn-at-talk. First, they must remember to clearly and consistently mark the speaker for each turn-at-talk. Second, they must remember to use the correct placeholder set up by themselves or their teammate for each speaker.

Third, the handshape of the indexing speaker identification marker is the same handshape used for the American Sign Language sign you. This made deciphering the meaning of the pointing index finger a challenge, especially when the English utterance began with the word "YOU." For example, the attorney asks the English-speaking witness when they went to the police station by saying, "You said you went to the police. Do you remember the date?" When the interpreter begins the American Sign Language interpretation with "YOU" by pointing to the witness, this could be construed either as the first word of the interpretation or as a speaker identification marker. After all, the American Sign Language sign for "YOU" and the speaker identification marker indexing are similarly produced. Thus, there is potential for confusion in these situations possibly resulting in an unmarked turn-at-talk.

Fourth, when interpreting questions about the crime, for example, the interpreter may mark each speaker by body shifting from right (the attorney placeholder) to left (the witness placeholder). The challenge comes because the body movements into the right and left placeholder positions for the attorney and witness, respectively, can be very similar to the body movements used to depict characters and actions in the interpretation of the crime narrative. During my analysis, I found it difficult at times to decipher the intended purpose of a particular body movement.

Although the interpreters acknowledged during a debrief session that speaker identification was an important aspect of the interpretation, none of them corrected their own or their teammate's work when a marker was unclear or absent. Consequently, they left the dDeaf defendant having to perceive on their own who was speaking at each turn-at-talk during the sporadic unmarked utterances throughout the interpretation of the courtroom drama. An argument can be made that a missing speaker identification marker here and there during direct or cross-examination may have little impact on the dDeaf defendant because of the question–answer sequence pattern. But what if the interpreter misses or is unclear with multiple speaker identification markers? What if the interpreter incorrectly identifies the speaker as the witness and then self-corrects (without informing the dDeaf defendant of the correction) to indicate that the attorney is actually talking? In this instance, the dDeaf person would see two people talking, first the witness, then the attorney, when in reality the entire interpretation is for a single turn-at-talk by the attorney.

The dDeaf defendant actors explained that when speaker identification markers were incorrect, unclear, or absent, they were confused and found it harder to concentrate on the interpreted message. Now is the time to consider new possible solutions to increase the clear and consistent use of speaker identification markers for each turn-at-talk during an interpreted courtroom event.

POSSIBLE SOLUTIONS

One possible solution is to monitor and insist upon the interpreter's consistent and accurate use of speaker identification markers for each turn-at-talk when working alone in the "on" position in the Rotate Model. The interpreters in my study already knew how to identify the speaker at each turn-at-talk. But as one interpreter said,

98%
Remain Model
(Dialogic/2-way)

Figure 7. Unambiguous markings for the Remain Model.

"I know I identified the wrong person more than I want to admit" (Clark, 2018, p. 170).

Another possible solution is to test interpreting students and practitioners on their consistent use of speaker identification markers for each turn-at-talk. Since the topic of speaker identification has not been reported in the literature, it is possible that interpreter education is not teaching, or at least insisting, that students/practitioners must incorporate this vital component into the interpretation each time a change of speakers occurs. Also, at this time, the presence or absence of accurate speaker identification is not considered in the examination and certification process for interpreters by Registry of Interpreters for the Deaf (RID). So, since speaker identification is not being tested, it may not be taught or practiced as an essential skill.

A third possible solution is to change the way interpreters work together. The Rotate Model has become standard practice in the field, and, at this time, neither the RID nor National Consortium of Interpreter Education Centers (NCIEC) promotes teaming approaches other than the Rotate Model as a viable teaming option. However, as my study suggests, this practice does not always stand up to the demands for speaker identification in multiparty interactions. When interpreters work in the Remain Model for dialogic/two-way discourse, their ability to consistently and unambiguously identify the speaker at each turn-at-talk was 98% of the 863 turns-at-talk (see Figure 7). This allowed the dDeaf defendant an increased opportunity to follow the contributions to the conversation by each speaker.

Working in the Remain Model eliminates the need to add the speaker identification marker for each turn-at-talk because one interpreter is assigned to interpret for the attorney asking questions and the other interpreter is assigned to interpret the witness's response. The interpreters must inform the dDeaf defendant of their interpreting assignments so when the interpreter works from spoken English into American Sign Language for the attorney, the dDeaf defendant knows the attorney is speaking. Likewise, when the interpreter assigned to the English-speaking witness begins to interpret, the dDeaf defendant knows the witness is speaking. One of the dDeaf defendant actors said that when interpreters worked in the Remain Model, she could follow who was talking, as if this was a new experience. It appears knowing who is talking, even in a mock trial in which the dDeaf defendant actor was in no danger of losing personal liberties or freedoms, had a profound effect. It may be that because the dDeaf defendant actors had nothing to lose, they felt empowered to be completely forthright, preferring that interpreters work in the Remain Model. Their assertion leads to questions about what power lies in knowing who is talking during the complex social interactions in the courtroom.

I take the words of Wadensjö (1998) one step further by observing that the Rotate Model may not be ideal for dialogic/two-way discourse as the interpreters identify who is speaking at each turn-at-talk. She states:

> [i]n practice, there are no absolute and unambiguous criteria for defining a mode of interpreting which would be "good" across the board. Different activity-types with different goal structures, as well as the different concerns, needs, desires and commitments of primary parties, imply various demands on the interpreters. (p. 287)

Now backed by research, it is time for American Sign Language–English interpreting professors and practitioners to expand their understanding and choice of teaming approaches and choose the model that best supports the inclusion of speaker identification for each discourse type and for each turn-at-talk.

TEACHING TEAMING MODELS FOR INTERACTIVE CONVERSATIONS

The first consideration of teaching or practicing speaker identification is to recognize the different types of discourse: monologic, dialogic/two-way, and dialogic/three-way (which includes three or more interlocutors). The study concluded that either teaming model is appropriate for interpreting monologic discourse. However, when two interlocutors are engaged in conversation, the interpreters should work in the Remain Model. Yet, when three or more interlocutors are having a discussion, neither the Rotate Model nor the Remain Model adequately supports the interpreter's ability to identify the speaker at each turn-at-talk. For dialogic/three-way discourse, the interpreter's individual skill and ability to include the speaker identification markers for each turn-at-talk becomes paramount.

Rotate Model

- When teaching students/practitioners to work together in the Rotate Model for interactive conversations, teachers/instructors must insist that each turn-at-talk begins with a speaker identification marker as a component of a complete and accurate interpretation.
- While monitoring the interpretation, students/practitioners must devise culturally and setting-appropriate strategies for interrupting the interpretation when a speaker is not identified so the marker can be inserted for each turn-at-talk to complete the accurate interpretation.

Remain Model

At the time of this publication, I do not know of any scholarly or professional instructional materials for teaching students how to work in the Remain Model. To begin to fill this gap, I suggest the following mnemonic device—INTERACTIVE:

I. INTERPRETING MYTH
The myth of our profession is that best practices dictate that inter-

preters are to work alone in the "on" position for a given amount of time when interpreting interactive conversations must be dispelled. Neither Babbini Brasel (1976) nor Moser-Mercer et al. (1998) studied interpreters working as a team in interactive settings. In fact, both concluded that switching interpreters during a presentation/lecture "may appear disruptive" (Babbini Brasel, 1976, p. 48).

N. NOTIFY

One interpreter only interprets for the attorney asking questions while the second interpreter only interprets the answers given by the English-speaking witness on the stand. The interpreters must inform the dDeaf defendant of these assignments.

T. TEAMING TOGETHER

Both interpreters sit/stand in the "on" position throughout the dialogic/two-way conversation.

E. EYE GAZE TO EACH OTHER

The interpreters should sit/stand in the "on" position at an approximately 45° angle facing each other and with an unobstructed sight line to the dDeaf defendant. The interpreters should look at each other while they are interpreting the conversation between the attorney and witness. In addition, on occasion, one of the interpreters should look to the dDeaf defendant to check in.

R. REFLECTIVE INTERACTING

The interpreters "interact" with each other by mirroring the interactions of the English-speaking attorney and witness so the interpretation will include the conversation's pacing, interruptions, talking over each other, politeness, arguments, nuances, gestures, and so on.

A. ACTIVE MONITORING

When either interpreter notices an error, they can lean slightly toward the team interpreter and sign the corrected information to complete the interpretation.

C. CHANGE ROLES FOR EACH WITNESS

To mitigate fatigue, the interpreters can switch roles for each witness.

In other words, if Interpreter A interprets for the attorneys during direct and cross-examination and Interpreter B interprets for the first English-speaking witness, then for the second English-speaking witness, Interpreter B interprets for the direct and cross-examination questions and Interpreter A interprets for the second English-speaking witness's answers.

T. THIRD PERSON: ABOUT, NOT TO

The discourse during direct and cross-examination is often about the dDeaf defendant. The interpreters should not look at the dDeaf defendant when their name comes up in the conversation nor should they point to the dDeaf defendant. Both the eye gaze to the dDeaf defendant and the point toward the defendant indicate that the conversation is TO the defendant and welcomes participation in the discourse. This is not the case during this portion of the proceeding. So in order to avoid any misunderstanding about the nature of direct and cross-examination, the interpreters should not look at the dDeaf defendant, except to check in on occasion, and should use the dDeaf defendant's sign name (as a third-person reference) when their name comes up in the narrative.

I. INCORPORATE TO CATCH UP

If the interpretation lags behind the source conversation (perhaps because of a quick exchange between the attorney and the witness), the interpreted answer can incorporate several answers in one interpreted turn so the interpreters can catch up with the narrative.

V. VICINITY

1. Typically, the interpreter sitting/standing nearer the attorney will interpret for them and the interpreter sitting/standing nearer the witness will interpret for the witness.
2. Because the interpreters are sitting/standing near each other, they can share the same space one of them uses to set up referents/classifiers for people/places/things.

E. ENHANCEMENT

When interpreters work together in the Remain Model, their ability to consistently mark who is speaking at each turn-at-talk is greatly enhanced because they are assigned to a specific speaker. This in turn, enhances the opportunity for the dDeaf defendant to more easily track who is talking during the evidence collection phase of the court proceeding

CONCLUSION

It is clear that speaker identification in the interpreted message is not simply a luxury that brings some measure of value to the interpretation. Rather, it is a substantive matter of due process for the dDeaf defendant standing before the court ready to confront the witnesses who testify as afforded by the Constitution. This study scratches the surface of understanding the connection between teaming models, types of discourse, speaker identification, and the impact of ambiguous interpretations on the dDeaf defendant. Many questions are still unanswered, including how does the lack of speaker identification markers for each question–answer sequence impede the dDeaf defendant's right to confront a witness?

The results of this study may be best summarized in the comment made by a dDeaf defendant upon seeing interpreters working in the Remain Model (translation of the American Sign Language utterance), *Oh! That's much better! Now I can see who is talking!*

AUTHOR'S NOTE

For more information about working in the Remain Model, contact LeWana Clark at drlewanaclark@gmail.com.

QUESTIONS AND APPLICATION

1. The Remain Model proposed and studied by Clark is set in a courtroom. Are there other legal settings where this model might work? Where would it not work? Why?

2. Does, as Clark suggest, the Remain Model resolve the 6th Amendment right to confront witness issues?
3. Prepare an introduction to the judicial officer in a local court. In it, explain that your team will employ the Remain Model. Be sure to provide a rationale for this model.

REFERENCES

Arizona v. Natividad. (1974). 111 Ariz. 191 526 P.2d 730. http://law.justia.com/cases/arizona/supreme-court/1974/2854-0.html

Babbini Brasel, B. (1976). The effects of fatigue on the competence of interpreters for the Deaf. In H. Murphy (Ed.), *Selected readings in the integration of Deaf students at CSUN* (pp. 19–22). Center on Deafness. https://files.eric.ed.gov/fulltext/ED123812.pdf#page=23

Baker-Shenk, C., & Cokely, D. (1980). *American Sign Language: A teacher's resource text on grammar and culture*. Gallaudet University Press.

Berk-Seligson, S. (1990). The bilingual courtroom: Court interpreters in the judicial process. University of Chicago Press.

Clark, L. (2018). *The interactive courtroom: The Deaf defendant watches how the speaker is identified for each turn-at-talk during a team interpreted event* [Doctoral dissertation]. Department of Interpretation and Translation Research, Gallaudet University.

Cokely, D., & Hawkins, J. (2003). Interpreting in teams: A pilot study of requesting and offering support. *Journal of Interpretation*, 49–93. https://docs.google.com/viewer?a=v&pid=sites&srcid=ZGVmYXVs-dGRvbWFpbnxyaWRwdWJsaWNhdGlvbnNwcm9qZWN0fGd4O-jYzYTZjOWVhMmJlZDAyYjQ

Coulthard, M., & Johnson, A. (2007). Order in court. In A. Johnson & M. Coulthard (Eds.), *An introduction to forensic linguistics: Language in evidence* (p. 95–118). Routledge.

de Jongh, E. (2008). Court interpreting: Linguistic presence vs. linguistic absence. *The Florida Bar Journal*, *82*(7), 20. https://www.floridabar.org/the-florida-bar-journal/court-interpreting-linguistic-presence-v-linguistic-absence/

ELAN (Version 6.2) [Computer software]. (2021). Max Planck Institute for Psycholinguistics, The Language Archive. https://archive.mpi.nl/tla/elan

Federal Rules of Evidence, Rule 604, (Pub. L. 93–595, §1, Jan. 2, 1975, 88 Stat. 1934; Mar. 2, 1987, eff. Oct. 1, 1987; Apr. 26, 2011, eff. Dec. 1, 2011.).

Friedman, L. A. (1975). Space, time, and person reference in American Sign Language. *Language*, *51*(4), 940–961. http://doi.org/10.1371/

journal.pone.0005772

González, R., Vasquez, V., & Mikkelson, H. (1991). *Fundamentals of court interpretation, theory, policy and practice*. Carolina Academic Press.

Hale, S. (2001). Complexities of the bilingual courtroom. *Law Society Journal*, 39(6), 68–72. https://doi,org/10.3316/ielapa.200112383

Hale, S. (2002). How faithfully do court interpreters render the style of non-English speaking witnesses' testimonies? A data-based study of Spanish—English bilingual proceedings. *Discourse Studies*, 4(1), 25–47. http://doi.org/10.1177/14614456020040010201

Hoza, J. (2010). *Team interpreting as collaboration and interdependence*. RID Publications.

Lentz, E. (1986). Teaching role shifting. In C. Padden (Ed.), *Proceedings of the fourth national symposium on sign language research and teaching* (pp. 58–69). National Association of the Deaf.

Liddell, S. K., & Metzger, M. (1998). Gesture in sign language discourse. *Journal of Pragmatics*, 30(6), 657–697. http://doi.org/10.1016/S0378-2166(98)00061-7

Meier, R. (1990). Person deixis in American Sign Language. *Theoretical Issues in Sign Language Research*, 1, 175–190.

Merriam, S. B. (2009). *Qualitative research: A guide to design and implementation* (The Jossey Bass Higher and Adult Education Series, Vol. 2). Jossey Bass. http://doi.org/10.1097/NCI.0b013e3181edd9b1

Metzger, M. (1999). *Sign language interpreting: Deconstructing the myth of neutrality*. Gallaudet University Press.

Metzger, M. (2005). Interpreted discourse: Learning and recognizing what interpreters do in interaction. In C. Roy (Ed.), *Advances in teaching sign language interpreters* (pp. 100–122). Gallaudet University Press.

Mickelson, P., & Gordon, P. (2015). Intentional teaming: Experiences from the Second National Healthcare Symposium. *Journal of Interpretation*, 24(1), Article 5. https://digitalcommons.unf.edu/cgi/viewcontent.cgi?article=1048&context=joi

Mikkelson, H. (2010). Consecutive or simultaneous? An analysis of their use in the judicial setting. *Across the Board*, 5(1), 4–7. https://acebo.myshopify.com/pages/consecutive-or-simultaneous-an-analysis-of-their-use-in-the-judicial-setting

Milenkovski, K. (2012, March 29). Interpreter must take oath to make true translation. *Litigation News*. Mobile Edition. https://www.dropbox.com/s/g5g9kn11s8nannn/MilenkovskiInterpreterMustOath.pdf?dl=0

Moser-Mercer, B., Kunzli, A., & Korac, M. (1998). Prolonged turns in interpreting: Effects on quality, physiological and psychological stress (Pilot study). *Interpreting, International Journal of Research and Practice in Interpreting*, 3(1), 47–67. https://doi.org/10.1075/intp.3.1.03mos

Padden, C. (1986). Verbs and role-shifting in American Sign Language. In C. Padden (Ed.), *Proceedings of the fourth national symposium on sign language research and teaching, Las Vegas, Nevada, January 27-February 1, 1986* (pp. 44–57). https://quote.ucsd.edu/padden/files/2013/01/14.pdf

RID (Registry of Interpreters for the Deaf). (2007). *Standard practice paper: Team interpreting.* https://drive.google.com/file/d/0B3DKvZMfl-FLdVzZpaUtraW5xZG8/view?resourcekey=0-MzvKxpp1Ie1Dr7Vk-M_7yVQ

Roberson, L., Russell, D., & Shaw, R. (2011). American Sign Language/English interpreting in legal settings: Current practices in North America. *Journal of Interpretation, 21*(1), 64–79. http://digitalcommons.unf.edu/joi/vol21/iss1/6

Russell, D. (2000). *Interpreting in legal contexts: Consecutive and simultaneous interpretation* [Doctoral dissertation]. University of Calgary.

Russell, D. (2002). *Interpreting in legal contexts: Consecutive and simultaneous interpretation.* Linstok Press.

Russell, D. (2008). Interpreter preparation conversations: Multiple perspectives. *Studies in Interpretation, Issues in Legal Interpretation, 7,* 123–147.

Russell, D., & Hale, S. (2008). *Interpreting in legal settings.* Gallaudet University Press.

Shuy, R. (2001, 2003). Discourse analysis in the legal context. In D. Schiffrin, D. Tannen, & H. E. Hamilton (Eds.), *The handbook of discourse analysis* (pp. 441–442). Blackwell.

Stewart, K., Witter-Merithew, A., & Cobb, M. (2009). *Best practices.* National Consortium of Interpreter Education Center—Legal Interpreting Workgroup. http://www.interpretereducation.org/wp-content/uploads/2011/06/LegalBestPractices_NCIEC2009.pdf

van Herreweghe, M. (2002). Turn-taking mechanisms and active participation in meetings with Deaf and hearing participants in Flanders. In C. Lucas (Ed.), *Turn-taking, fingerspelling and contact in signed languages* (pp. 73–103). Gallaudet University Press.

Wadensjö, C. (1998). *Interpreting as interaction.* Longman.

Wiggins, G., & McTighe, J. (2006). *Understanding by design* (Expanded 2nd ed.). Association for Supervision and Curriculum Development.

10 TRAINING LEGAL INTERPRETERS TO WORK WITH DEAF JURORS

Jemina Napier, Debra Russell, Sandra Hale, David Spencer, and Mehera San Roque

EDITOR'S INTRODUCTION

Jurors are part of an important process in the legal system. In the United States, deaf citizens are able to sit as jurors. This means that they must have sign language interpreters who can effectively interpret trials, deliberations, and votes. The authors provide insight into another important part of the jury process, orienting potential jurors to their roles and responsibilities. Given that most people in the United States are familiar with the jury process through what they have seen in movies, this is an opportunity for the myths to be dispelled, and the weight of the responsibilities on the shoulders of the jurors is explained. The responsibility occurs as soon as potential jurors arrive on their assigned date. This contribution leads to discussions around best practices, not only vis-à-vis interpreting but also about scheduling interpreters.

AT PRESENT, the United States is the only country in the world that systematically allows deaf sign language users to perform their civic duty as jurors, but little is known about how interpreters work in this setting. This chapter provides an overview of key findings of studies that have explored ethnographic observations of an interpreted jury empanelment process in the United States (Napier & Russell, forthcoming), interviews with court judges and deaf people who have served on juries in the United States (Hale et al., 2017; Napier et al., 2019; Spencer et al., 2017), and examination of deaf juror participation in jury deliberations in a mock trial (Hale et al.,

2017; Napier et al., forthcoming). These interdisciplinary studies conducted by sign and spoken language interpreter researchers with law academics also pave the way for interdisciplinary curriculum development and evidence-based interpreting education. Professional development training recommendations are given for how training can be delivered to interpreters for working with deaf jurors based on the evidence acquired through the research studies. Although there is a long history of interpreters working with deaf jurors in the United States, there has never been any empirical evidence of how they work, and thus a framework for evidence-based, interdisciplinary training for interpreters in this context is much needed. In addition to providing training recommendations for interpreters in the United States who are already working with deaf jurors, the suggestions can also be used to train interpreters who may find themselves working in this context for the first time as new countries begin to change their legislation to allow deaf people to serve as jurors. In sum, this chapter will (1) explore effective strategies used by an interpreter in working with a deaf juror, (2) consider the perspectives of stakeholders on interpreters working with deaf jurors, and (3) explain how to apply theory into practice in the training of interpreters to work with deaf jurors.[1]

LEGAL INTERPRETING

There is an increasing amount of research on legal interpreting in spoken and sign languages, which serves as a solid evidence base for the training of legal interpreters. The first two decades of systematic research, starting from the early 1990s, predominantly focused on courtroom interpreting and investigated several issues. These earlier studies tended to focus on the interpreter's role and linguistic, ethical, and moral challenges for court interpreters. In particular, authors tended to concentrate on the tensions between the court's expectations that interpreters should be impartial and interpreta-

---

1. This chapter is an updated version of a paper that was previously published in Winston et al. (2019) and is published in this volume with permission from the Conference of Interpreter Trainers.

tions should be "as neutral as possible"; the reality of how interpreters face linguistic and ethical dilemmas in needing to add or omit information, give explanations, and relay cultural information; and the challenges that interpreters face when the strict protocols of courtroom interactions do not align with the need for interpreters to manage and coordinate communication with their clients and other stakeholders in the court proceedings. For this reason, the notion of court interpreters having much more rigid role boundaries than in other contexts has been promoted, in order to mitigate the risks involved when interpreters make errors in their interpretations (e.g., Edwards, 1995; Fenton, 1997; Fowler, 1997; Gonzalez et al., 1992; Mikkelson, 1998, 2000; Morris, 1995; Schweda Nicholson, 1994; Wilcox, 1995). Concerns about challenges for interpreters have been noted to be exacerbated when interpreting for people with limited access to conventional spoken and sign languages, either because they have limited fluency or use a rare language, because interpreters may feel even more compelled to give explanations or add information to ensure that legal instructions are understood (Cooke, 2002; Eades, 2003; Goldflam, 1995; McCay & Miller, 2001, 2005; Miller & McCay, 2001; Tuck, 2010). A plethora of later studies in the late 1990s and 2000s in spoken language legal interpreting focused on linguistic analyses of interpreters' output or interpreters' decision-making, through analyses of simulated or authentic courtroom interpreting data (Angelelli, 2004; Angermeyer, 2005, 2008, 2009; Berk-Seligson, 1990, 2002; Gallez & Maryns, 2014; Gallez & Reynders, 2015; Hale, 1996, 1997, 1999, 2002, 2004, 2008; Jacobsen, 2003, 2008; Lee, 2013, 2015; Liu & Hale, 2017; Martinsen & Dubslaff, 2010). During this era, there was a dearth of research on sign language legal interpreting, with two notable exceptions:

1. the Access to Justice project conducted in the UK, which conducted observations of British Sign Language (BSL)–interpreted trials and noted the difficulties for deaf people in accessing qualified, professional interpreters in court and also explored whether interpreters were available to deaf prisoners (Brennan, 1999; Brennan & Brown, 1997; Turner, 1995; Turner & Brown,

2001—see Napier et al., this volume, for more discussion of the findings of this project).

2. Debra Russell's research on American Sign Language (ASL)–English court interpreting, which compared interpreters working in simultaneous or consecutive mode, and found that interpreter renditions were more accurate when produced in consecutive mode (Russell, 2002).

Since that time, Russell has followed up her earlier study of a corpus of four mock-criminal trials, with analyses of the interpretation of question–answer statements in witness testimonies (Russell, 2004) and the perspectives of interpreters on how best to prepare for interpreting for trials and how to prepare legal personnel for how best to work with sign language interpreters in court (Russell, 2008).

All of these studies have provided an important foundation for the linguistic understanding of legal interpreting, but the courtroom is only one legal setting. The next two decades of research have seen explorations of legal interpreting covering a wider range of legal settings, including interpreting in war crimes tribunals (Elias-Bursac, 2015; Nicholson, 2010; Takeda, 2008), in refugee settings (Crezee et al., 2011; Gibb & Good, 2014), with minors in criminal proceedings (Böser & La Rooy, 2018; Salaets & Balogh, 2015), and in police–suspect interviews (Böser, 2013; Gallai, 2013, 2016; Lee, 2017; Määttä, 2015; Mason & Rock, 2019; Monteoliva, 2017; Mulayim et al., 2014; Nakane, 2014; see Napier et al., this volume, for a more detailed review of police interpreting literature). There is also an increasing amount of research that analyses the additional linguistic challenges that occur in the rising dependence on the use of videoconference technologies and remote interpreting of criminal proceedings, both court and police, which creates additional challenges for interpreters when they do not have proximity to their clients (Braun, 2013, 2014, 2017; Braun & Taylor, 2012; Braun et al., 2018; Devaux, 2017; Licoppe & Veyrier, 2017; Licoppe et al., 2018; Napier, 2013a; Napier & Leneham, 2011; Salaets & Balogh, 2018; Skinner et al., 2021). There are many more studies now that draw on sociological approaches to examine stakeholder perspectives of legal interpreting, including interpreters, lawyers, judges, and police officers (Braun, 2018; Goodman-Delahunty & Martschuk, 2016; Hale, 2011; Hale & Napier, 2016; Lee, 2009; Napier, 2012; Napier & Banna, 2018; Roberson et al., 2012a; Wakefield et al., 2015).

It could be said, therefore, that considerations of legal interpreting have achieved a "turning point" (Blasco Mayor & del Pozo Triviño, 2015) in that legal settings outside of the courtroom that were typically considered as a "gray zone" (Bancroft et al., 2013) have also begun to receive more attention. With this advent of more legal interpreting research, interpreter educators are therefore now in a position to develop evidence-based training for legal interpreting students.

TRAINING LEGAL INTERPRETERS

We have seen increasing scholarship in interpreter education and training, with more evidence-based pedagogy whereby research is "taking place in the classroom or in the educational context that provides us with the evidence for effectively making change in education. This growth is evidenced in all disciplines, not only interpreter education" (Napier, 2013b, p. 1). Furthermore, we are also witnessing a growth in interdisciplinary approaches to interpreter education, so that interpreter educators collaborate with experts in other disciplines to provide content-specific education and training opportunities, as evidenced, for example, by the volume on educating health care interpreters (Swabey & Malcolm, 2012) featuring articles by interpreter educators and medical professionals together.

When we consider the training of legal interpreters, research with legal interpreters about the training they have received or desire shows that interpreters struggle to obtain the standard of interpreting skills needed to interpret in court and often fail specialized certification tests (Wallace, 2015), and students often make typical errors in interpreting courtroom discourse (Burn & Crezee, 2017); therefore, training needs to be of the highest quality to ensure that legal interpreters are not set up to fail (Wallace, 2015). There is not a significant amount of evidence-based pedagogy for the training of legal interpreters, but when we review the evidence base of legal interpreting research, we can consider the implications for legal interpreter training (Ng, 2016) and ensure that trainers, as well as curricula, are updated to reflect that evidence base as well as changes in society (Monzo, 2015). In legal sign language interpreting, there have been calls for training for legal specialization (Roberson et al., 2012b; Witter-Merithew & Nicodemus, 2012), and to date legal interpreter training typically focuses on working in the courtroom. Inevitably, this training concentrates on interpreting for actors in the courtroom who are participating in a trial (predominantly accuser, defendant, and witness). However, for legal sign language interpreters, especially in the U.S. context, there is another "gray zone" that receives little attention.

A "GRAY ZONE" FOR LEGAL SIGN LANGUAGE INTERPRETERS

For deaf people encountering the justice system, the provision of sign language interpreters is a legal accommodation requirement (Brunson, 2008), which has led to increasing numbers of deaf interpreters working in court (Tester, 2018, 2021). One of the "gray zones" in legal sign language interpreting is the work with deaf people who are called for jury service. This type of work is well established in the United States, as deaf people have been permitted to serve as jurors since 1979 (Napier & McEwin, 2015), but in other countries with adversarial court systems deaf sign language users are typically excluded from jury duty. In Australia, for example, the relevant legislation in different states generally exempts deaf people from serving as jurors if they are unable, because of sickness, infirmity, or disability, to discharge the duties of juror.[2] Another argument that has been used is due to concerns about having an interpreter as a 13th person in the jury deliberation room because of

---

2. One deaf man served as a juror in New Zealand in 2005 shortly after the enactment of the New Zealand Sign Language (NZSL) Act, and, as a consequence of the research outlined in this study, a deaf woman was permitted to participate in the jury selection process in Western Australia in 2014, and a deaf man served on a jury in Ireland in 2017.

confidentiality issues or because they may impact on the flow of the deliberation process[3] (Hale et al., 2017; Napier, 2013c; Napier et al., 2019). Some time ago, Mather and Mather (2003) asserted that the role of interpreters for deaf jurors is different than interpreting for defendants and witnesses in court, because jurors need to have access to key points of information in order to make informed decisions as jurors. However, their assertions were based on experience and general observations, rather than empirical data.

As you can imagine, getting access to a jury deliberation room to empirically evaluate how the interpreting happens is not possible, mainly due to the fact that jury deliberations are not open to the public and also that deaf people are not always called to serve, and, when they are, they might not be selected during the empanelment process. Yet in order to address the concerns of the justice system about whether deaf people can serve as jurors and have interpreters in the deliberation room, an evidence base was needed.

INTERPRETING FOR DEAF JURORS: AN EVIDENCE BASE

A series of linked interdisciplinary research studies over a 10-year period in Australia were conducted by sign language interpreting, spoken language interpreting, and law academics,[4] in order to examine the feasibility of deaf people serving as jurors and the impact of having interpreters present in the deliberation room. The various studies revealed that deaf people can comprehend jury instructions through interpreters as well as those who access the information directly (i.e., "hearing" people; Napier & Spencer, 2007a, 2007b, 2008, 2017), and legal professionals and sign language interpreters feel that there is no impediment to deaf people serving as jurors (Napier, 2013a; Napier & McEwin, 2015). All of these studies were based on experimental tests, surveys, or interviews, but there was

---

3. The standard jury is made up of 12 people, except for Scotland where it involves 15 people.
4. Napier and Russell are sign language interpreting researchers, Hale is a spoken language interpreting researcher who specializes in legal interpreting, and Spencer and San Roque are law academics.

still no evidence for what *actually happens* when interpreting for deaf jurors and specifically in the deliberation room.

The next stage was to conduct a mock trial to simulate a court case involving 11 hearing jurors, a deaf juror, and two sign language interpreters (Hale et al., 2017; Napier et al., forthcoming). The trial took place in Sydney in July 2014 and replicated a real court case, involving barristers, solicitors, and a retired judge. The case was carried out over 1.5 days, and the jury deliberated for half-a-day before delivering their verdict. The whole proceedings and deliberations were filmed, the deliberations were analyzed for participant turn-taking, and the jurors were interviewed on completion of their trial about their perceptions of the presence of a deaf juror and the potential impact of interpreters on the deliberation process. The analysis of turn-taking (Hale et al., 2017) revealed that the deaf juror was able to participate in jury deliberations to the same degree as hearing jurors and that the interpreters were not active participants in the jury deliberations. The hearing jurors confirmed that they felt no negative impact from having interpreters in the room and quickly became accustomed to mediated communication with the deaf juror (see Hale et al., 2017, for more detail). The data are still being analyzed in relation to the interpreting strategies and interpretation accuracy.

Subsequent to the mock trial, focus groups were conducted with two stakeholder groups—a range of legal professionals and deaf community representatives—to discuss the outcomes of the mock trial findings and the implications for the provision of sign language interpreters for deaf jurors in Australia (Napier et al., 2019). After much discussion in both groups, there was agreement that the evidence confirmed that there is no question whether deaf people can participate as jurors by working with interpreters and that, in principle, deaf people should be permitted to do jury service in Australia. There were still some reservations from both stakeholder groups, however, on the logistics of providing adequate interpreting services to ensure that deaf jurors are not disadvantaged in carrying out the juror role.

We know that interpreting services for deaf jurors are provided regularly in various states throughout the United States. One study conducted as part of this deaf juror research involved nonparticipant observations of a jury empanelment process involving a deaf juror and interviews with legal personnel in the same courthouse in Rochester, New York. This chapter provides an overview of our, as yet unreported, findings from this observational study and then draws together this new evidence base with that from the previous studies, to reflect on the implications for training sign language interpreters to work with deaf jurors.

Doing a Case Study of the Monroe County Courts

For this project, we conducted a case study (Yin, 2003) of one court system: the Monroe County Courts in Rochester, New York in the United States. Given that the city of Rochester in the state of New York has the National Technical Institute for the Deaf (NTID) situated within the Rochester Institute of Technology, there is a large population of deaf ASL users living in that city who stay on after they graduate. There is estimated to be 90,000 deaf ASL users in a population of 700,000 living in Rochester.[5] As a consequence, the Monroe County Courts have a well-established system to provide interpreters as an accommodation to allow deaf ASL users to serve as jurors. This involves a process whereby citizens of the state who are called for jury service can tick a box to state that they need ASL–English interpreting on their return form. Once the form is received, the deaf person is allocated dates for summons and an interpreter is booked for their arrival, induction, and the jury selection process. A team of interpreters is also put on standby in case the deaf juror is empaneled for a full trial. This process is carefully managed by the jury commissioner, who has access to a pool of staff and freelance interpreters who regularly interpret in the Monroe County Courts and for deaf jurors in particular. Approximately six deaf ASL users

---

5. See http://www.nytimes.com/2006/12/25/nyregion/25deaf.html?_r=1&adxnnl=1&oref=slogin&adxnnlx=1193285123-Ewd7wx9A2T6Bl0hdYCOPKg.

are empaneled to serve on a jury every year. For these reasons, this city and court system were purposely selected for this case study.

The data were collected by Napier and Russell. Drawing upon our positions as sign language interpreters and researchers, we were able to utilize our professional networks of ASL interpreters in Rochester, and contact was made with the jury commissioner at the Monroe County Courts responsible for managing the process of recruiting jurors. We were invited to attend the Monroe County courts as nonparticipant observers to observe and talk to as many people as possible at the courts who are involved in the justice system and in relation to deaf people serving as jurors, in order to gain an in-depth overview of how deaf people are included as jurors. The jury commissioner set up meetings with a range of judges, lawyers, and administrators for the purpose of semistructured interviews, and as we walked around the court buildings he also introduced us to other key people, where we would engage in impromptu unstructured conversations about our research. The jury commissioner also identified deaf people in Rochester who had previously served as jurors and contacted them to ask if we were willing to be interviewed and arranged for them to meet. The observations and interviews were conducted in either spoken English or ASL over a 5-day period in the spring of 2014.

We observed three settings: (1) the Central Jury Room, (2) the waiting area outside the courtroom, and (3) a criminal courtroom. We took extemporaneous field notes of anything we observed of interest during the observations, as per ethnographic principles. The goal was to observe the processes, the interactions, and the communication between deaf people, sign language interpreters, and any court personnel. It was recognized that it was not possible to observe any actual jury deliberations in the Monroe County Courts, only the process leading up to jury empanelment and any trial that a deaf juror was selected for.

The Data

The participants in this study represent multiple stakeholders in the legal process. The age range of the participants is between 30 and 60 years, and those who were employed as lawyers and judges had between 10 and 15 years of experience. The ASL interpreter was certified by the national Registry of Interpreters for the Deaf (RID) and had nearly 40 years of experience, with almost 20 years of legal and court-related experience (including regular experience interpreting with deaf jurors).[6]

In addition to field notes from observations of the jury selection process, data also include semistructured interviews and unstructured conversations. The total data set includes 390 minutes (6.5 hours) of observations, 305 minutes (5.08 hours) of semistructured interviews, and 300 minutes (5 hours) of unstructured conversations. Field notes were taken during interviews and after unstructured impromptu conversations.

We were able to observe the jury panel induction and waiting period and the jury selection (empanelment) process that included one deaf person and an ASL interpreter, for the period of one full day. The remaining 4 days were taken up with interviews and conversations. While the deaf person was not, in the end, selected for the jury, the observations presented us with insight into how a deaf juror might participate in a trial process, what information they receive, and the strategies that an interpreter uses when working with a deaf juror.

Analysis

We analyzed the strategies used by the interpreter using Wadensjö's (1998) taxonomy of interpreter renditions (as outlined in Table 1). As we were not permitted to record the interpreter or interactions,

---

6. In our observation there was only one ASL–English interpreter present, which is the standard practice at Monroe County Courts for a jury selection process with one deaf juror. If selected for a full trial, a team of two interpreters is allocated. We acknowledge that this is a resourcing decision for the county court and actually goes against best practice.

Table 1. Wadensjö's Rendition Subcategories.

Rendition type	Definition
Close	Propositional content of original explicitly expressed in the rendition, style approximately the same.
Expanded	More explicitly expressed information in the rendition than the original.
Reduced	Less explicitly expressed information in the rendition than the original.
Summarized	Text that corresponds to two or more prior originals.
Non	Interpreter-initiated (e.g., to seek clarification or address a participant directly)
Zero	Original not translated

our analysis is restricted to what was captured in the field notes, rather than a fine-grained discourse analysis. The interpreting excerpts are presented using horizontal transcription (Gallez, 2010). The interview field notes were analyzed and coded using content and thematic analysis (Krippendorff, 2004), examining the content and emergent themes.

INTERPRETING STRATEGIES

The best practice for producing an effective interpretation in court and other legal settings is to achieve an accurate, meaningful, and effective interpretation that meets the cultural and linguistic needs of the deaf individual or party (NCIEC, 2009; Newby & Weald, 2015). Furthermore, the best practices framework asserts that court interpreters should ensure that minority language users can fully participate in the judicial process and gain access to justice. In discussing the strategies used by the interpreter in this case study, we can see that she did give the deaf juror access to justice and that he was able to participate in the judicial process. Her interpretations were accurate, meaningful, and effective. In all three settings, there is evidence that the interpreter used close, expanded, reduced, summarized non- and zero renditions, as shown in Table 2 and as observed by spoken and sign language interpreters in other contexts

Table 2. Summary of Interpreter Renditions.

Close	Expanded	Reduced	Summarized	Non	Zero
19	5	5	3	5	3

(cf. Major & Napier, 2012; Wadensjö, 1998). Wadensjö promotes the idea that it is not only the rendition that is significant but also the before and after of the rendition that should also be explored in order to truly understand the affect of the rendition, that is, that interpreting decisions are context-bound. So wherever possible we provide this information to contextualize the interpreter's decisions and our analysis. Here our discussion predominantly focuses on the interpreter renditions during question–answer sequences in the courtroom during the empanelment process and summarizes the pattern of renditions across all three settings (Setting 1: Central Jury Room, Setting 2: Waiting Area, Setting 3: Courtroom).

For this interpreter, the typical pattern was to produce close renditions. The interpreter provided extremely close renditions, typically for fingerspelling of names, key terms, and read-aloud text (e.g., the oath in Setting 1), but also when it was obvious that she was tiring (as she was rubbing her eyes and rotating her wrists). The interpreter was obviously comfortable with the language of the court and offered close renditions throughout.

But there was also evidence of several expanded renditions when she gave examples to elucidate concepts such as "perspective on the witness" where she signed "VIEW ON PERSON MISERABLE, FRIENDLY, WHATEVER . . . DOESN'T MATTER,"[7] based on her understanding of the term and her experience of frequently interpreting this term for other deaf jurors. Another example was when a juror was asked the question as to why family members might make up accusations, and the panelist response was that it might be due to "bitterness." The interpreter began to produce a close rendition by fingerspelling the

---

7. When our focus is on the specific items that were signed by the interpreter, we using sign glossing to represent a translation of the exact signs that were used. In other tables, we present a translation of the meaning of the signed renditions of the interpreter in order to illustrate how information was expanded or reduced or summarized.

Table 3. Examples of Expanded Renditions

Original Utterance	Interpreter Rendition
How people interact with each other . . .	*How do people interact?* <u>*Two people meet, say hello, and hug. Two people meet and shake hands. Then they talk.*</u>
You're in the jury deliberation room . . .	*You <u>all</u> are in the jury deliberation room <u>over there (behind you), 12 people</u> . . .*

term, but the deaf juror offered her a sign for the term. She then adopted this sign and thanked the deaf juror for his input. During this question–answer sequence, the interpreter produced frequent expanded renditions for terms such as "reliance" and "trust," and for phrases such as those illustrated in Table 3.

Examples of expanded renditions were also observed for specific legal phrases that may have been unfamiliar to the deaf client in Settings 1 and 3. This strategy has been identified as typical in courtroom interpreting when dealing with legal discourse (Brennan & Brown, 1997; Hale, 2004), although it can be a risky strategy if the interpreter inadvertently misinterprets the term, which can lead to evidence being challenged, regardless of whether it is a legal term (see example from Lee, 2009 in Korean–English interpreting). The types of expansions seen in Table 3 might be seen by the courts and attorneys as problematic, because it could be argued that the interpreter was adding information that is not in the original source text and, therefore, the interpreter is not retaining their neutrality. But to use Wadensjö's frame, we would assert that the interpreter is producing relative expansions that embody visual information for clarity that is the norm in sign language discourse (Major & Napier, 2012) and that making implicit information explicit by giving examples is a typical practice in ASL interpreting (Lawrence, 1995).

At times the interpreter would combine more than one rendition type into a sequence. For example, at one point in the courtroom, the judge explained that panel members in the box would be asked questions about their education, work, and so on but that the questionnaire form that they had previously been given would not be

Table 4. Example of Close Rendition Followed by Nonrendition

Interpreter: . . . *so you don't need the form*	
	DJ: (points to form) Don't need?
Interpreter: *No, you can put away, take home, tear up, whatever . . .*	

Table 5. Nonrenditions in Conversation

Juror	Interpreter	Deaf Juror
My hobby is fencing . . .	*My hobby is fencing* (fingerspelled).	
	Fencing (fingerspelled). Do you know what that is?	
		Yes I know. Fencing (offers sign).
	Yes, fencing (uses sign).	

referred to. The interpreter interpreted this instruction as a close rendition, but then produced a nonrendition as a consequence of an intervention by the deaf juror, as shown in Table 4. Another example was when a juror was asked about the difference between the words "burglary" and "robbery." Initially, the interpreter produced close renditions but then produced a nonrendition to explain that someone breaking into your house is legally called "burglary" not "robbery."

In another question–answer sequence, the interpreter produced nonrenditions and initiated a brief conversation with the deaf juror in relation to the content of a panelist response, as shown in Table 5. During this conversation, there were zero renditions of the continued interaction between the panelist and attorney.

There was evidence of the interpreter using reduced and summarized renditions, which has been observed as a strategy used by interpreters when they judge that there is no impact on the integrity of the message (see, for example, Major & Napier, 2012; Napier,

Table 6. Summarized Rendition of Question–Answer Sequence

Judge	Juror	Interpreter Rendition
Where do you live?		
	South West Rochester	
How long have you lived there?		
	27 years	
		I have lived in SW Rochester for 27 years.

2002). In Setting 1 for example, the interpreter decided that it was more important for the deaf person to know when his own name was called rather than all the names of jurors being read out. It may also have been a strategy used to conserve energy. Occasionally, there were also examples of the interpreter making decisions to produce reduced or summarized renditions during the questioning of an individual prospective juror, where she focused on the key points of a narrative answer. An example can be seen in Table 6.

It is possible to speculate as to why the interpreter made these decisions to produce nonrenditions or summarized renditions, as shown in Tables 4, 5, and 6. We perceive that she made judgments that the content of the interaction between the panelist and the attorney was not as important for the deaf juror to know. This was a process that all jurors were engaged in as part of the selection process. What was most important to the deaf juror was any questions addressed directly to him, and then obviously if selected, the content of the trial. Thus, by engaging the deaf juror in small talk, or summarizing the interaction, the interpreter was able to conserve energy in a different way. In Setting 3, as with Setting 1, the interpreter engaged in more informal conversation with the deaf juror, likely because they were together for a longer period of time, with occasional opinions. If the deaf juror initiated conversation, the interpreter always responded politely but did not prolong the conversation (nonrenditions).

Zero renditions were typically produced when panel members were asked to approach the bench to disclose information in a whispered conversation with the judge. At these times the interpreter would break eye contact with the deaf juror and get something out of her bag, drink water, or just look away. When zero renditions were produced, and the interpreter broke eye contact (e.g., during a whispered conversation at the bench), this was a strategic decision by the interpreter because she could not hear the whispered conversation, so therefore could not relay any information, and was also able to use the opportunity to manage her energy as she was working all day by herself. It could be argued that these were not nonrenditions, as the interpreter could not actually hear the source text, so it would not have been possible to produce any rendition. The breaking of eye contact could be regarded as problematic by some deaf clients, as they may not understand what she was doing, or that she actually cannot hear the spoken utterances. In this case study, the deaf juror did not make any comment when the interpreter looked away. There was limited interaction between the deaf juror and interpreter in the Setting 2 (Waiting Area). Although other hearing jurors engaged in casual conversation during the recess periods with each other, there was no attempt by either the deaf juror or other hearing jurors to interact with one another at any time, so there was no interpretation required (zero renditions). We did not perceive any negative impact from her decisions as the communication flowed smoothly, and the deaf juror was engaged in the process throughout.

In Setting 3 in particular, the interpreter demonstrated a typical sign language interpreting strategy: source attribution, for example, pointing behind her to the judge to stress that he was talking, and pausing to look at parties as they spoke, supporting the deaf person's ability to follow the multiple parties in the courtroom. This strategy has been found in previous research (see Marks, 2012, 2015; Metzger, 1999) when the interpreter is relaying the talk and making it clear who is speaking, often to distance themselves from the generator of the utterance or to facilitate rapport building directly between the deaf and hearing interlocutors.

In sum, it can be seen that the interpreter engaged in a variety of strategies to ensure that the deaf juror was able to access the proceedings of the empanelment process and did not overly assert her presence. The fact that she had a long track record of working in legal settings and with deaf jurors has obviously lent itself to working effectively in this setting. By conducting this type of analysis, we are able to demonstrate an evidence base for the typical rendition patterns and strategies used across the different settings when working with deaf jurors.

STAKEHOLDER PERSPECTIVES

The interviews and conversations with the legal and deaf stakeholders were analyzed for key themes, and here we provide a brief summary. Three of the themes that we address here include: (a) interpreters as gatekeepers; (b) interpreters as distraction; (c) interpreters as prima donnas; (d) and training. The reason we have chosen to highlight these themes is because they contrast with the evidence from our observations, which highlight the positive strategies used by the interpreter; whereas, the stakeholders tended to focus on negative aspects. However, there was one theme, (e) isolation, which tallied with our observations.

Interpreters as Gatekeepers

Court administrators and judges stated that they believe there are interpreter politics that lead to *gatekeeping* of the work with deaf jurors. For example, some interpreters who do work for the courts may put off other interpreters by telling them the work is challenging and the interpreters are not treated well, thus ensuring the pool of interpreters doing the work is small. Other ways of perceived, subtle gatekeeping are that interpreters may complain to their colleagues about the working conditions, in hopes of dissuading the interpreter from accepting work within the court system.

From our observations it could be seen that the working conditions were not ideal, as the interpreter worked all day by herself. This meant that the zero renditions produced often seemed to be on occasions when she could briefly rest (e.g., when other jurors were being questioned, or a long list of names was read out). The interpreter we observed frequently works with deaf jurors and told us that if the juror had been selected, a second interpreter would have been booked to work through the trial, so the working conditions would have improved. The interpreter told us that only a small number of interpreters in the area are willing to work with deaf jurors, as they find the context intimidating and would be nervous of making mistakes, which contrasts with the legal personnel's perspectives on why there are limited numbers of interpreters available.

Interpreters as Distraction

Some judges believed that there may be an overarching lack of appreciation for what an interpreter really does, which can feed misconceptions of interpreters as a *distraction*, as highlighted in the comments of this judge:

> A lot of people are nervous about having a deaf juror because it might be distracting. Or if an interpreter brings bias we don't really know. Some people are reluctant or have more concerns but I don't have a concern as we see regular interpreters, we trust that they are doing their job. People think it's going to be distracting for other jurors but it's not.

Another judge went further saying this:

> I worry about having the attention taken away from me and I wonder if it might undermine the process, based on a misconception that the interpreter can bring a bias into the trial.

Other lawyers and judges who had previous positive experiences did not report that it was distracting to have an interpreter at all, and especially when the interpreter is well trained as an interpreter and in the protocol of the courtroom. The lawyers expressed trust in the interpreters to do their job and reported that the legal processes have not been altered by the presence of the interpreting team, which we see in this quote:

> So many people have initially been distracted by an interpreter, but soon they become so absorbed in the case information that they pay no attention to the interpreter. People in Rochester are used to see-

ing deaf people with interpreters....

From our observations, we do not believe that the interpreter was perceived as a distraction. She was treated professionally by the jury commissioner, the court clerk, and the judge. The hearing jurors did not attempt to interact with the interpreter at all and did not watch her during the empanelment process.

Interpreters as Prima Donnas

The judges suggested that it is not generally the deaf juror that is the problem; rather, it is the interpreters not respecting the judicial space and the jurisdiction of the judge and behaving like prima donnas. Judges reflected on their past experiences with interpreters, raising the point that some interpreters can be very difficult to work with. In the words of one judge:

> Deaf people are not the problem, it's the interpreters who can be "prima donnas," with interpreters who think that the centre of my attention should be on the deaf person, but it is not and that is a complication. They need to be unobtrusive but they seem to want to be the centre of attention.

Several judges emphasized that they had witnessed interpreters who were acting as advocates for the deaf juror and behaving in ways that brought undue attention to their work and needs. As one judge stated:

> My concern is for the defendant—the deaf person may be upset for a day or two (by the trial content), but a defendant may be going to jail for the rest of their life. The focus has to be on the person who is charged with the crime.

> The interpreters need to be unobtrusive and let the court handle any issues that arise.

> Interpreters are used to being advocates for the deaf person and start by telling me where they need to sit. I don't care about the deaf person, my concern is for the defendant.

The interpreter in our observation did not advocate for the deaf juror, but through the use of expanded renditions and nonrenditions did provide information to the deaf juror to ensure that he understood what was going on or what key terms meant. It could be argued that this is a form of advocacy, but instead we see this as a form of "emancipatory interpreting" (Mole, 2018), whereby the interpreter is recognizing the power imbalance in this context and empowering the deaf juror with information that may not be generally accessible due to life experiences or literacy levels.

Training

The importance of specialized *training* was a theme that spanned judges, lawyers, court administrators and deaf consumers in our interview data. Across all stakeholders there is a perception that the interpreters may not be as well trained as compared to other cities, which then leads to problems. The deaf participants described the kinds of training opportunities that they believe would be useful, including an existing program in the United States that prepares interpreters for legal specialization work after an interpreter has completed a bachelor's degree in interpreting, holds national certification, and has a minimum number of years of experience. The training takes 2 years of part-time study, and then interpreters sit for a specialized skills and knowledge exam that leads to national RID certification as a legal interpreter (known as the SC:L).[8] It is interesting to note that not all states in the United States require the SC:L and there are courts that employ interpreters who therefore could potentially lack the specialized skills and knowledge needed for successful practice in legal settings.

The deaf participants reported that there is noticeable difference in quality of interpretation offered by interpreters who have RID legal interpreter certification, and not all of the local interpreters who provide service possess the national certification. The lack of training may also contribute to the issue raised by judges and ad-

---

8. This specialized certification was placed on a moratorium in January 2016 and is not currently available.

ministrators about difficulty recruiting interpreters for the court. It may be that interpreters fear the work, based on having no schema for the work because of the lack of specialized training in legal settings and with legal discourse.

From a deaf participant lens, there was also a desire to see greater training for the courts about what it means to be deaf and access proceedings via an interpreter. The need for judicial training about the nature of interpreting is apparent in the following remark from a judge, who sees interpreters as machines:

> Interpreters don't need to understand anything—they should be like court stenographers and should just record what is said.

The court administrators expressed a desire to work with local postsecondary institutions to develop a Legal Interpreting Certificate and provide a systemic approach to increasing the capacity of the courts and the interpreting community to respond to the work opportunities at the court.

> I think it would be helpful to collaborate with interpreter training programs to provide internship experiences within the court system.

Isolation

One theme that corresponded with our observations was that of *isolation*. The interviews with deaf jurors revealed a key issue in relation to isolation, as illustrated by the following quote:

> As a deaf juror it was a huge positive to have an interpreter, but the huge negative was the behaviour of interpreters (e.g. refusing to go into the deliberation room on breaks so deaf juror couldn't get to know other jurors). The interpreter established their role boundaries that were too extreme.

The court administrator also acknowledged the challenges for deaf jurors not having access to interpreters during breaks:

> It could be socially isolating if interpreters don't interpret during break times, such as lunch. Maybe this is a function of not managing a team well or when there is only one interpreter then they also need a break.

This is something we observed in our case study, as the interpreter asserted that she needed the time to rest during the breaks as she was working on her own all day. This meant that the deaf juror did not interact with the other jurors at all. If the juror had been selected, this could have become an issue if the trial lasted some time. Nonetheless, we also recognize that the interpreter may have made that decision in order to publicly confirm her lack of direct involvement in the jury panel—maintaining distance in order to ensure that her role solely as mediator of communication is recognized and understood. This strategy has been confirmed by other interpreters, who were interviewed about their experiences of working with deaf jurors (Napier, 2013c).

RECOMMENDATIONS FOR TRAINING LEGAL SIGN LANGUAGE INTERPRETERS TO WORK WITH DEAF JURORS

By conducting this type of analysis based on a case study of an interpreter working with a potential deaf juror, we are able to demonstrate the typical rendition patterns across the different legal settings when interpreters work with deaf jurors. Combining these results with the findings from a previous study that articulates turn-taking patterns in jury deliberations means that we have an evidence base to discuss with legal interpreters what strategies they can use when interpreting with deaf jurors. Furthermore, highlighting key issues raised by legal and deaf stakeholders based on their experiences of working with interpreters when deaf people are jurors is valuable for interpreters to reflect on the different perspectives, which could influence their decision-making when working in that context.

Although we were able to observe an interpreter who behaved professionally and had minimal impact on the proceedings,[9] it is interesting to contrast with the perceptions of stakeholders about the perceived inconsistencies across interpreter provision for deaf jurors, the behavior of interpreters in that context, and how it impacts

---

9. We acknowledge that the interpreter may have been on her "best behavior" because we were observing her, which is the nature of the researcher's "observer's paradox."

on other interlocutors. Turner and Best (2017) argued that interpreters who behave as the stakeholders report are engaging in "defensive" interpreting—making "self-preservation" decisions to suit their own needs rather than that of the people they are interpreting for. They suggest that in order to demonstrate professional practice, interpreters should engage in "expository interpreting" and be:

> willing to be "self-revealing, on display, open to critique" and, above all, open to collaboration with interlocutors. . . . The main guiding principles of expository interpreting are transparency and cooperation, grounded in the selfless de-prioritisation of the interpreter's immediate interests with an orientation not towards self-preservation, but to a broader and fundamentally more inclusive frame of reference.

We would suggest that the interpreter in this case study was engaged in a mix of expository and defensive interpreting. At times she made decisions for the best interests of the deaf juror (making sure he had access to information and could participate in the judicial process), and at other times for herself (conserving energy, avoiding being drawn into conversations with the deaf juror), both of which were justifiable. We believe that in training legal interpreters to be best prepared to work with deaf jurors, they need to be made aware of the types of renditions produced across different settings and why; the self-preservation strategies that are sometimes needed in order to contend with the working conditions; as well as awareness of the role of the juror, others' perceptions of their role and behavior as interpreters, and how to engage in expository interpreting so that deaf jurors can be effectively included in the jury empanelment and deliberation processes. Evidence from this case study has shown that the interpreter strategically used expanded renditions. So future legal interpreters need to be taught this strategy—when and how it is acceptable and/or important to use these features. Similarly, the interpreter in this case study also strategically broke eye contact with the deaf juror, in order to manage her fatigue, which is a strategy that new legal interpreters can be taught so that they can subtly manage their workload without offending the deaf jurors that they are working with. And finally, the interpreter in this case study did produce nonrenditions by occasionally engaging in conversation with the deaf juror. We deemed that this was an important part of her rapport-building strategy with the deaf juror but needs to be managed carefully so as not to confuse deaf jurors or any other court personnel about the role of the interpreter and the nature of their interactions. This tactic should be problematized as part of any training for legal interpreters who work with jurors so that they are mindful of the potential positive and negative consequences of engaging in conversation.

Training for legal personnel and deaf people would also be useful in ensuring that they understand the role and responsibilities of interpreters generally in court (see Napier & Banna, 2018) and, in contrast, when working with deaf jurors. The ideal would be for the training to be interdisciplinary—involving interpreting and law educators—in order to draw not only on the evidence base but also on the personal and professional practitioner experiences of those with relevant expertise.

QUESTIONS AND APPLICATIONS

1. Discuss the staffing of interpreters for the jury orientation explored in this study. Why do you think there is only one? Do you think there should be more? How might this be resolved in the future?
2. Interview interpreters who have experience interpreting for jurors in your area. What insight do they provide? Does their experience align with the interpreter in this study? How do they differ?
3. Given that at least one judge believes interpreters are like stenographers, prepare a script that will explain how they are not.

ACKNOWLEDGMENTS

The funding for this study was provided by the Australian Research Council Linkage Program 2012 Round 2 (LP120200261) for the project titled *Participation in the Administration of Justice: Deaf Citizens as Jurors*. The project obtained ethics approval from the University of New South Wales (UNSW) Research Human Ethics Committee. We would like to acknowledge the support and involvement of the New South Wales Attorney General's office, the Sheriff's Office, the District Court of New South Wales and Legal Aid New South Wales, and all of the participants who gave up their time to be involved in the mock trial, including Steven Doumit, Paul Johnson, Chris Geraghty, David Evenden, Tim Macintosh, Danny Eid, Jeff Ludkin, Eve Gerzabek, and Skye Southan. We also wish to acknowledge the support of the New York State Courts at Monroe County Hall of Justice in Rochester, New York, and in particular the jury commissioner Mr. Chuck (Charles) Perreaud for his time and efforts in ensuring we had such liberal access to the participants in this study. To the interpreter Rachel Rose and the deaf juror David Schiff (named here with permission), thank you for allowing us to observe you. Finally, thank you to Research Assistants Julie Lim, Gerry Shearim, and Silvia Martinez from UNSW, and Stacey Webb from Heriot-Watt University for support in organizing data collection, transcribing, and coding the data.

REFERENCES

Angelelli, C. (2004). *Revisiting the interpreter's role: A study of conference, court, and medical interpreters in Canada, Mexico, and the United States.* John Benjamins.

Angermeyer, P. S. (2005). Who is "you"? Polite forms of address and ambiguous participant roles in court interpreting. *Target, 17*(2), 203–226. https://doi.org/10.1075/target.17.2.02ang

Angermeyer, P. S. (2008). Creating monolingualism in the multilingual courtroom. *Sociolinguistic Studies, 2*(3), 385–403. https://doi.org/10.1558/sols.v2i3.385

Angermeyer, P. S. (2009). Translation style and participant roles in court interpreting. *Journal of Sociolinguistics, 13*(1), 3–28. https://doi.org/10.1111/j.1467-9841.2008.00394.x

Bancroft, M., Bendana, L., Bruggeman, J., & Feurle, L. (2013). Interpreting in the gray zone: Where community and legal interpreting intersect. *International Journal of Translation & Interpreting Research, 5*(1),

94–113. https://doi.org/10.12807/ti.105201.2013.a05

Berk-Seligson, S. (1990). *The bilingual courtroom: Court interpreters in the judicial process.* University of Chicago Press.

Berk-Seligson, S. (2002). The impact of politeness in witness testimony: The influence of the court interpreter. In F. Pöchhacker & M. Shlesinger (Eds.), *The interpreting studies reader* (pp. 278–292). Routledge.

Blasco Mayor, M. J., & del Pozo Triviño, M. (Eds.). (2015). Legal interpreting at a turning point. *MonTI, 7.* https://doi.org/10.12807/ti.108201.2016.r01

Böser, U. (2013). "So tell me what happened!": Interpreting the free recall segment of the investigative interview. *Translation & Interpreting Studies, 8*(1), 112–136. https://doi.org/10.1075/tis.8.1.06bos

Böser, U., & La Rooy, D. (2018). Interpreter-mediated investigative interviews with minors: Setting the ground rules. *Translation & Interpreting Studies, 13*(2), 208–229. https://doi.org/10.1075/tis.00012.bos

Braun, S. (2013). Keep your distance? Remote interpreting in legal proceedings. A critical assessment of a growing practice. *Interpreting, 15*(2), 200–228. https://doi.org/10.1075/intp.15.2.03bra

Braun, S. (2014). Comparing traditional and remote interpreting in police settings: Quality and impact factors. In C. Falbo & M. Viezzi (Eds.), *Traduzione e interpretazione per la società e le istituzioni* (pp. 161–176). Edizioni Università di Trieste.

Braun, S. (2017). What a micro-analytical investigation of additions and expansions in remote interpreting can tell us about interpreters' participation in a shared virtual space. *Journal of Pragmatics, 17,* 165–177. https://doi.org/10.1016/j.pragma.2016.09.011

Braun, S. (2018). Video-mediated interpreting in legal settings in England: Interpreters' perceptions in their sociopolitical context. *Translation & Interpreting Studies, 13*(3), 393–420. https://doi.org/10.1075/tis.00022.bra

Braun, S., Davitti, E., & Dicerto, S. (2018). Video-mediated interpreting in legal settings: Assessing the implementation. In J. Napier, R. Skinner, & S. Braun (Eds.), *Here or there? Research on interpreting via video link* (pp. 144–182). Gallaudet University Press.

Braun, S., & Taylor, J. L. (Eds.). (2012). *Videoconference and remote interpreting in criminal proceedings.* University of Surrey.

Brennan, M. (1999). Signs of injustice. *The Translator, 5*(2), 221–246. https://doi.org/10.1080/13556509.1999.10799042

Brennan, M., & Brown, R. (1997). *Equality before the law: Deaf people's access to justice.* Deaf Studies Research Unit, University of Durham.

Brunson, J. (2008). Your case will now be heard: Sign language interpreters as problematic accommodations in legal interactions. *Journal of*

Deaf Studies & Deaf Education, 13(1), 77–91. https://doi.org/10.1093/deafed/enm032

Burn, J. A., & Crezee, I. (2017). "That is not the question I put to you, officer": An analysis of student legal interpreting errors. *International Journal of Interpreter Education, 9*(1), 40–56. http://www.cit-asl.org/new/an-analysis-of-student-legal-interpreting-errors/

Cooke, M. (2002). Indigenous interpreting issues for courts [Unpublished research report]. Australian Institute of Judicial Administration. http://www.aija.org.au/ac01/Cooke.pdf

Crezee, I., Jülich, S., & Hayward, M. (2011). Issues for interpreters and professionals working in refugee settings. *Journal of Applied Linguistics & Professional Practice, 8*(3), 253–273. https://doi.org/10.1558/japl.v8i3.253

Devaux, J. (2017). *Technologies in interpreter-mediated criminal court hearings: An Actor-Network Theory account of the interpreter's perceptions of her role-space* [Unpublished doctoral dissertation]. University of Salford.

Eades, D. (2003). Participation of second language and second dialect speakers in the legal system. *Annual Review of Applied Linguistics, 23*, 113–133. https://doi.org/10.1017/S0267190503000229

Edwards, A. B. (1995). *The practice of court interpreting.* John Benjamins.

Elias-Bursac, E. (2015). *Translating evidence and interpreting testimony at a war crimes tribunal: Working in a tug-of-war.* Palgrave.

Fenton, S. (1997). The role of the interpreter in the adversarial courtroom. In S. E. Carr, R. Roberts, A. Dufour, & D. Steyn (Eds.), *The critical link: Interpreters in the community* (pp. 29–34). John Benjamins.

Fowler, Y. (1997). The courtroom interpreter: Paragon and intruder? In S. E. Carr, R. Roberts, A. Dufour, & D. Steyn (Eds.), *The critical link: Interpreters in the community* (pp. 191–200). John Benjamins.

Gallai, F. (2013). "I'll just intervene whenever he finds it a bit difficult to answer": Exploding the myth of literalism in interpreted interviews. *Investigative Interviewing: Research and Practice (II-RP), 5*(1), 57–78. https://iiirg.org/wp-content/uploads/2021/02/II-RP-Volume-5-Issue-1-Gallai.pdf

Gallai, F. (2016). Point of view in free indirect thought and in community interpreting. *Lingua, 175–176,* 97–121. https://doi.org/10.1016/j.lingua.2015.08.012

Gallez, E. (2010, July 26–30). *Advantages of a horizontal transcription format for interpreter-mediated interactions* [Paper presentation]. Critical Link 6 Conference, Aston University, Birmingham.

Gallez, E., & Maryns, K. (2014). Orality and authenticity in an interpreter-mediated defendant's examination: A case study from the Belgian Assize Court. *Interpreting, 16*(1), 49–80. https://doi.org/10.1075/

intp.16.1.04gal

Gallez, E., & Reynders, A. (2015). Court interpreting and classical rhetoric ethos in interpreter-mediated monological discourse. *Interpreting, 17*(1), 64–90. https://doi.org/10.1075/intp.17.1.04gal

Gibb, R., & Good, A. (2014). Interpretation, translation and intercultural communication in refugee status determination procedures in the UK and France. *Language and Intercultural Communication, 14*(3), 385–399. https://doi.org/10.1080/14708477.2014.918314

Goldflam, R. (1995). Silence in court! Problems and prospects in Aboriginal legal interpreting. In D. Eades (Ed.), *Language in evidence: Issues confronting aboriginal and multicultural Australia* (pp. 28–54). University of New South Wales Press.

Gonzalez, R. D., Vasquez, V. F., & Mikkelson, H. (1992). *Fundamentals of court interpretation: Theory, policy, and practice*. Institute for Court Interpretation, University of Arizona.

Goodman-Delahunty, J., & Martschuk, N. (2016). Risks and benefits of interpreter-mediated police interviews. *ARSTVOSLOVJE, Journal of Criminal Justice and Security, 18*(4), 451–471. https://www.fvv.um.si/rV/arhiv/2016-4/05_Goodman-Delahunty%20_Martschuk_rV_2016-4.pdf

Hale, S. (1996). Pragmatic considerations in court interpreting. *Australian Review of Applied Linguistics, 19*(1), 61–72. https://doi.org/10.1075/aral.19.1.04hal

Hale, S. (1997). The interpreter on trial: Pragmatics in court interpreting. In S. E. Carr, R. Roberts, A. Dufour, & D. Steyn (Eds.), *The critical link: Interpreters in the community* (pp. 201–211). John Benjamins.

Hale, S. (1999). The interpreter's treatment of discourse markers in courtroom questions. *Forensic Linguistics, 6*(1), 57–82. https://doi.org/10.1558/sll.1999.6.1.57

Hale, S. (2002). How faithfully do court interpreters render the style of non-English speaking witnesses's testimonies? A data based study of Spanish-English bilingual proceedings. *Discourse Studies, 4*(1), 25–48. https://doi.org/10.1177/14614456020040010201

Hale, S. (2004). *The discourse of court interpreting: Discourse practices of the law, the witness and the interpreter*. John Benjamins.

Hale, S. (2008). Controversies over the role of the court interpreter. In Valero-Garcès (Ed.), *Crossing borders in community interpreting: Definitions and dilemmas* (pp. 99–121). John Benjamins.

Hale, S. (2011). *Interpreter policies, practices and protocols in Australian courts and tribunals: A national survey*. Australian Institute of Judicial Administration (AIJA). http://www.aija.org.au/online/Pub%20no89.pdf

Hale, S., & Napier, J. (2016). "We're just kind of there": Working conditions and perceptions of appreciation and status in court interpreting. *Target, 28*(3), 351–371. https://doi.org/10.1075/target.28.3.01hal

Hale, S., San Roque, M., Spencer, D., & Napier, J. (2017). Deaf citizens as jurors in Australian courts: Participating via professional interpreters. *International Journal of Speech, Language & the Law, 24*(2), 151–176. https://doi.org/10.1558/ijsll.32896

Jacobsen, B. (2003). Pragmatics in court interpreting: Additions. In L. Brunette, G. L. Bastin, I. Hemlin, & H. Clarke (Eds.), *The critical link 3: Interpreters in the community* (pp. 223–238). John Benjamins.

Jacobsen, B. (2008). Interactional pragmatics and court interpreting: An analysis of face. *Interpreting, 10*(1), 128–158. https://doi.org/10.1075/intp.10.1.08jac

Krippendorff, K. (2004). *Content analysis: An introduction to its methodology* (2nd ed.). Sage Publications.

Lawrence, S. (1995). Interpreter discourse: English to ASL expansion. In E. A. Winston (Ed.), *Mapping our course: A collaborative venture, Proceedings of the Tenth National Convention of the Conference of Interpreter Trainers* (p. 15). Conference of Interpreter Trainers.

Lee, J. (2009). Conflicting views on court interpreting examined through surveys of legal professionals and court interpreters. *Interpreting, 11*(1), 35–56. https://doi.org/10.1075/intp.11.1.04lee

Lee, J. (2013). A study of facework in interpreter-mediated courtroom examination. *Perspectives: Studies in Translatology, 21*(1), 82–99. https://doi.org/10.1080/0907676X.2011.629729

Lee, J. (2015). Evaluation of court interpreting: A case study of metadiscourse in interpreter-mediated expert witness examinations. *Interpreting, 17*(2), 167–194. https://doi.org/10.1075/intp.17.2.02lee

Lee, J. (2017). A case study of interpreter-mediated witness statement: Police interpreting in South Korea. *Police Practice and Research, 18*(2), 194–205. https://doi.org/10.1080/15614263.2016.1248840

Licoppe, C., Verdier, M., & Veyrier, C. A. (2018). Voice, power, and turn-taking in multilingual, consecutively interpreted courtroom proceedings with video links. In J. Napier, R. Skinner, & S. Braun (Eds.), *Here or there? Research on interpreting via video link* (pp. 299–322). Gallaudet University Press.

Licoppe, C., & Veyrier, C. A. (2017). How to show the interpreter on screen? The normative organization of visual ecologies in multilingual courtrooms with video links. *Journal of Pragmatics, 107*, 147–164.

https://doi.org/10.1016/j.pragma.2016.09.012

Liu, X., & Hale, S. B. (2017). Facework strategies in interpreter-mediated cross-examinations: A corpus-assisted approach. *The Interpreter's Newsletter, 22*, 57–77. https://doi.org/10.13137/2421-714X/20738

Määttä, S. K. (2015). Interpreting the discourse of reporting: The case of screening interviews with asylum seekers and police interviews in Finland. *International Journal of Translation & Interpreting Research, 7*(3), 21–35. https://doi.org/10.12807/ti.107203.2015.a02

Major, G., & Napier, J. (2012). Interpreting and knowledge mediation in the healthcare setting: What do we really mean by "accuracy"? In V. Montalt & M. Shuttleworth (Eds.), *Linguistica antiverpiesa: Translation & knowledge mediation in medical and health settings* (pp. 207–226). Artesius University College.

Marks, A. R. (2012). Participation framework and footing shifts in an interpreted academic meeting. *Journal of Interpretation, 22*(1), 4. https://digitalcommons.unf.edu/joi/vol22/iss1/4/

Marks, A. R. (2015). Investigating footing shifts in video relay service interpreted interaction. In B. Nicodemus & K. Cagle (Eds.), *Signed language interpretation and translation research: Selected papers from the First International Symposium* (pp. 71–96). Gallaudet University Press.

Martinsen, B., & Dubslaff, F. (2010). The cooperative courtroom: A case study of interpreting gone wrong. *Interpreting, 12*(1), 21–59. https://doi.org/10.1075/intp.12.1.02mar

Mason, M., & Rock, F. (Eds.). (2019). *The discourse of police interviews.* University of Chicago Press.

Mather, S., & Mather, R. (2003). Court interpreting for signing jurors: Just transmitting or interpreting? In C. Lucas (Ed.), *Language and the law in deaf communities* (pp. 60–81). Gallaudet University Press.

McCay, V., & Miller, K. (2001). Linguistic incompetence to stand trial: A unique condition in some deaf defendants. *Journal of Interpretation, 11*, 99–120.

McCay, V., & Miller, K. (2005). Obstacles faced by deaf people in the criminal justice system. *American Annals of the Deaf, 150*(3), 283–291. https://doi.org/10.1353/aad.2005.0036

Metzger, M. (1999). *Sign language interpreting: Deconstructing the myth of neutrality.* Gallaudet University Press.

Mikkelson, H. (1998). Towards a redefinition of the role of the court interpreter. *Interpreting, 3*(1), 21–46. https://doi.org/10.1075/intp.3.1.

02mik
Mikkelson, H. (2000). *Introduction to court interpreting*. St Jerome Publishing.
Miller, K. (2001). Access to sign language interpreters in the criminal justice system. *American Annals of the Deaf, 146*(4), 328–330. https://doi.org/10.1353/aad.2012.0188
Miller, K. R., & McCay, V. (2001). Linguistic diversity in Deaf defendants and due process rights. *Journal of Deaf Studies and Deaf Education, 6*(3), 226–234. https://doi.org/10.1093/deafed/6.3.226
Mole, H. (2018). *Narratives of power: Critical reflections on signed language interpreting* [Unpublished doctoral dissertation]. Heriot-Watt University.
Monteoliva, E. (2017). *The collaborative construction of the stand-by mode of interpreting in police interviews with suspects* [Unpublished doctoral dissertation]. Heriot-Watt University.
Monzo, E. N. (2015). Understanding legal interpreter and translator training in times of change. *The Interpreter and Translator Trainer, 9*(2), 129–140. https://doi.org/10.1080/1750399X.2015.1051766
Morris, R. (1995). The moral dilemmas of court interpreting. *The Translator, 1*(1), 25–46. https://doi.org/10.1080/13556509.1995.10798948
Mulayim, S., Lai, M., & Norma, C. (2014). *Police investigative interviews and interpreting: Context, challenges, and strategies*. CRC Press.
Nakane, I. (2014). *Interpreter-mediated police interviews: A discourse-pragmatic approach*. Palgrave MacMillan.
Napier, J. (2002). *Sign language interpreting: Linguistic coping strategies*. Douglas McLean.
Napier, J. (2012). Exploring themes in stakeholder perspectives of video remote interpreting in court. In C. J. K. Bidoli (Ed.), *Interpreting across genres: Multiple research perspectives* (pp. 219–254). EUT Edizioni Universtà di Trieste.
Napier, J. (2013a). "You get that vibe": A pragmatic analysis of clarification and communicative accommodation in legal video remote interpreting. In L. Meurant, A. Sinte, M. Van Herreweghe, & M. Vermeerbergen (Eds.), *Sign language research uses and practices: Crossing views on theoretical and applied sign language linguistics* (pp. 85–110). De Gruyter Mouton and Ishara Press.
Napier, J. (2013b). Evidence-based pedagogy. *International Journal of Interpreter Education, 5*(2), 1–3.
Napier, J. (2013c). Legal interpreting, deaf people and jury service: A happy union? *Newsli: Magazine of the Association of Sign Language Interpret-*

ers of the UK, 6(December Issue), 6–12.

Napier, J., & Banna, K. (2018). Walking a fine line: The legal system, sign language interpreters, roles and responsibilities. *Journal of Applied Linguistics & Professional Practice, 13*, 109–129. https://doi.org/10.1558/japl.31859

Napier, J., & Leneham, M. (2011). "It was difficult to manage the communication": Testing the feasibility of video remote signed language interpreting in courts in NSW, Australia. *Journal of Interpretation, 21*(1), 53–62. https://digitalcommons.unf.edu/joi/vol21/iss1/5/

Napier, J., & McEwin, A. (2015). Do deaf people have the right to serve as jurors in Australia? *Alternative Law Journal, 40*(1), 23–27. https://doi.org/10.1177/1037969X1504000106

Napier, J., & Russell, D. (forthcoming). The presence and impact of interpreters in court: An ethnographic sociolinguistic case study of sign language interpreting for a deaf juror.

Napier, J., & Spencer, D. (2007a). A sign of the times: Deaf jurors and the potential for pioneering law reform. *Reform, 90*, 35–37. http://classic.austlii.edu.au/au/journals/ALRCRefJl/2007/35.pdf

Napier, J., & Spencer D. (2007b, March). *Deaf jurors' access to court proceedings via sign language interpreting: An investigation* [Unpublished research report]. NSW Law Reform Commission, Research Report No. 14.

Napier, J., & Spencer, D. (2008). Guilty or not guilty? An investigation of deaf jurors' access to court proceedings via sign language interpreting. In D. Russell & S. Hale (Eds.), *Interpreting in legal settings* (pp. 71–122). Gallaudet University Press.

Napier, J., & Spencer, D. (2017). Jury instructions: Comparing hearing and deaf jurors' comprehension via direct or interpreter-mediated communication. *International Journal of Speech, Language & the Law, 24*(1). https://doi.org/10.1558/ijsll.30878

Napier, J., Spencer, D., Hale, S., San Roque, M., Shearim, G., & Russell, D. (2019). Changing the international justice landscape: Perspectives on deaf citizenship and jury service. *Sign Language Studies, 19*(2), 240–266. https://doi.org/10.1353/sls.2018.0034

Napier, J., Strong, S., Spencer, D., Hale, S., & San Roque, M. (forthcoming). Sign language interpreting: Presence, performance & impact in jury deliberations.

NCIEC. (2009). *Best practices: American sign language and English interpretation within legal settings*. National Consortium of Interpreter Education Centers.

Newby, K., & Weald, J. (2015). *Best practices for BSL-English interpreters working in legal settings*. Legal Interpreting Standards Group, Association of Sign Language Interpreters UK. https://zakon.co.uk/admin/resources/downloads/asli-best-practice-for-bsl-interpreting-in-legal-settings.pdf

Ng, E. (2016). Interpreter intervention and participant roles in witness examination. *International Journal of Interpreter Education, 8*(1), 23–39. Available: http://www.cit-asl.org/new/interpreter-intervention-participant-roles-witness-examination/

Nicholson, N. S. (2010). Interpreting at the International Criminal Tribunal for the Former Yugoslavia. In H. Tonkin & M. E. Frank (Eds.), *The translator as mediator of cultures* (pp. 37–52). John Benjamins.

Roberson, L., Russell, D., & Shaw, R. (2012a). American Sign Language/English interpreting in legal settings: Current practices in North America. *Journal of Interpretation, 21*(1), 6. https://digitalcommons.unf.edu/joi/vol21/iss1/6/

Roberson, L., Russell, D., & Shaw, R. (2012b). A case for training signed language interpreters for legal specialisation. *International Journal of Interpreter Education, 4*(2), 52–73. https://www.cit-asl.org/new/a-case-for-training-signed-language-interpreters-for-legal-specialization/

Russell, D. (2002). *Interpreting in legal contexts: Consecutive and simultaneous interpretation*. Sign Media.

Russell, D. (2004, May). *Interpreting strategies in legal discourse* [Paper presentation]. Critical Link 4: The 4th International Conference on Interpreting in Legal, Health and Social Service Settings, Stockholm, Sweden.

Russell, D. (2008). Interpreter preparation conversations: Multiple perspectives. In D. Russell & S. Hale (Eds.), *Interpreting in legal settings* (pp. 123–147). Gallaudet University Press.

Salaets, H., & Balogh, K. (2015). *Children and justice. Overcoming language barriers: cooperation in interpreter-mediated questioning of minors*. Intersentia.

Salaets, H., & Balogh, K. (2018). Videoconferencing in legal context: A comparative study of simulated and real-life settings. In J. Napier, R. Skinner, & S. Braun (Eds.), *Here or there? Research on interpreting via video link* (pp. 264–298). Gallaudet University Press.

Schweda Nicholson, N. (1994). Professional ethics for court and community interpreters. In D. L. Hammond (Ed.), *Professional issues for translators and interpreters* (pp. 79–98). John Benjamins.

Skinner, R., Napier, J., & Fyfe, N. (2021). The social construction of 101 non-emergency video relay services for deaf sign language users. *Policing: An International Journal of Police Strategies and Management, 23*(2), 145–156. https://doi.org/10.1177/1461355720974703

Spencer, D., Napier, J., San Roque, M., & Hale, S. (2017). Justice is blind as long as it isn't deaf: Excluding deaf people from jury duty—an Australian human rights breach. *Australian Journal of Human Rights, 23*(3), 332–350. https://doi.org/10.1080/1323238X.2017.1392479

Swabey, L., & Malcolm, K. (2012). (Eds.). *In our hands: Educating healthcare interpreters*. Gallaudet University Press.

Takeda, K. (2008). Interpreting at the Tokyo war crimes tribunal. *Interpreting, 10*(1), 65–83. https://doi.org/10.1075/intp.10.1.05tak

Tester, C. (2018). How American Sign Language-English interpreters who can hear determine need for a deaf interpreter for court proceedings. *Journal of Interpretation, 26*(1). https://digitalcommons.unf.edu/joi/vol26/iss1/3

Tester, C. (2021). *Intralingual interpreting in the courtroom: An ethnographic study of Deaf interpreters' perceptions of their role and positioning*. [Unpublished doctoral dissertation]. Heriot-Watt University.

Tuck, B. M. (2010). Preserving facts, form, and function when a deaf witness with minimal language skills testifies in court. *University of Pennsylvania Law Review, 158*(3), 905–956. https://doi.org/10.2307/20698348

Turner, G. H. (1995). The bilingual, bimodal courtroom: A first glance. *Journal of Interpretation, 7*(1), 3–34.

Turner, G. H., & Best, B. (2017). From defensive interpreting to professional interpreting practices. In M. Biagini, M. S. Boyd, & C. Monacelli (Eds.), *The changing role of the interpreter: Contextualising norms, ethics and quality standards* (pp. 102-121). Routledge.

Turner, G. H., & Brown, R. (2001). Interaction and the role of the interpreter in court. In F. J. Harrington & G. H. Turner (Eds.), *Interpreting interpreting: Studies and reflections on sign language interpreting* (pp. 152–167). Douglas McLean.

Wadensjö, C. (1998). *Interpreting as interaction*. Longman.

Wakefield, S., Kebbell, M., Moston, S., & Westera, N. (2015). Perceptions and profiles of interviews with interpreters: A police survey. *Australian & New Zealand Journal of Criminology, 48*(1), 53–72. https://doi.org/10.1177/0004865814524583

Wallace, M. (2015). A further call to action: Training as a policy issue in court interpreting. *The Interpreter & Translator Trainer, 9*(2), 173–187.

https://doi.org/10.1080/1750399X.2015.1051769

Wilcox, P. (1995). Dual interpretation and discourse effectiveness in legal settings. *Journal of Interpretation, 7*(1), 89–98.

Winston, E. A., Monikowski, C., & Lee, R. G. (Eds.). (2019). *Reaching new heights in interpreter education: Mentoring, teaching, and leadership, proceedings of the 2018 Biennial conference of interpreter trainers.* Conference of Interpreter Trainers.

Witter-Merithew, A. & Nicodemus, B. (2012). Toward the international development of interpreter specialization: An examination of two case studies. *Journal of Interpretation, 20*(1), Article 8. http://digitalcommons.unf.edu/joi/vol20/iss1/8

Yin, R. (2003). *Case study research: Design and methods* (3rd ed.). Sage.

11 PRACTICAL PROFESSIONAL TRAINING: BUILDING CAPACITY IN OUR INTERPRETING COMMUNITIES

Debra Russell

EDITOR'S INTRODUCTION

> *Dr. Debra Russell's contribution shows the importance of community building. Rather than relying on what she and others might know and understand about legal interpreting, Dr. Russell gathers information from people for whom she is developing a training—interpreters. Using a community-building approach, she creates a potential template for training. How might a grassroots training for sign language interpreters take shape? Who should be involved and how much? These are some of the answers we glean from Dr. Russell's contribution.*

ALL CANADIANS REGARDLESS of ethnicity, age, gender, or disability may be involved in court proceedings of some kind. It is of fundamental importance that the Canadian justice system be accessible to all citizens. Legislation in Canada has ensured that this right has been both ratified and enforced. From the perspective of Canadian law, Section 15 of the Canadian Charter of Rights and Freedom compels accessibility for all individuals:

> Every individual is equal before and under the law and has the right to equal protection and benefit of the law without discrimination and, in particular, without discrimination based on race, national or ethnic origin, colour, religion, sex, age or mental or physical disability.

Section 14 of the charter mandates accessibility for the American Sign Language (ASL) and *La Langue Signes Québécoise* (LSQ) deaf communities who represent Canadian cultural and linguistic minorities:

> ... a party or witness in any proceedings who does not understand or speak the language in which the proceedings are being conducted or who is deaf has the right to the assistance of an interpreter.

This jurisprudence is critical, and, as in many other countries, is fundamental to the right to full access in society. Hence, the training of interpreters who can work effectively with legal discourse and in legal settings is an important issue in many countries, and Canada is no exception.

Roberson et al. (2012) conducted a survey of 1,800 interpreters in the United States and Canada, finding that the most pressing need identified by interpreters working in legal settings was the lack of ongoing professional development for this specialized form of interpreting. In addition, among interpreters who reported not working in legal settings, the most frequent response for not accepting work in this area was that they had no training. These findings echo earlier work by Brunson (2008), Witter-Merithew and Johnson (2005), and Bontempo and Napier (2007), suggesting that training is insufficient for generalist practitioners, let alone interpreters working in specialized areas such as medical and legal. Witter-Merithew and Nicodemus (2012) argue that interpreters working in legal settings require access to training that is situationally relevant.

Napier et al. (see this volume) reviews the research on interpreting in legal settings, with both spoken and sign language interpreters, identifying the solid evidence base for training interpreters who can work with legal discourse and in legal settings. The topics that have been addressed in the literature cover examinations of the role of interpreters working in courtrooms and linguistic analysis of interpreting (Angelelli, 2004; Angermeyer, 2005, 2008, 2009; Berk-Seligson, 1990, 2002; Gallez & Maryns, 2014; Gallez & Reynders, 2015; Hale, 1996, 1997, 1999, 2001, 2002, 2004, 2008; Jacobsen, 2008; Lee, 2013, 2015; Leung & Gibbons, 2008; Liu & Hale, 2017;

Martinson & Dubslaff, 2010; Morris, 1995; Russell, 2002, 2005), ethical challenges (Vernon & Miller, 2001, 2005; Miller & Vernon, 2001), policy development (Wallace 2015), working with deaf interpreters (Boudreault, 2005; Forestal, 2005, 2014; Tester, 2018; Wilcox, 1995), deaf juror studies (Napier & Spencer, 2008; Napier et al., 2018), and the perspectives of interpreters on how best to prepare for interpreting for trials and how to prepare legal personnel for how best to work with sign language interpreters in court and other settings where legal discourse may occur (Robertson et al., 2012; Russell, 2008; Russell & Shaw, 2016).

Drawing on the available research, the following training program was created to support the professional development of sign language interpreters, followed by spoken language interpreters.

NEEDS ASSESSMENT

The need for advanced national training was identified by a group of Canadian interpreters[1] attending a workshop prior to a national conference of the Association of Visual Language Interpreters of Canada (AVLIC).[2] That workshop was cofacilitated by Dr. Risa Shaw and Dr. Debra Russell. The 30 participants were from several provinces across Canada, and all reported that they had participated in short-term training; however, the demand for interpreting legal discourse and working in legal settings was insufficient to warrant any significant training in some provinces. This was especially true for provinces and communities with smaller deaf communities. Similar to the findings of Roberson et al. (2012), many of the participants indicated they did not feel comfortable working in both police and courtroom settings and desired more intensive learning experiences.

Four Canadian interpreter referral services report having video screening tools that require interpreters to demonstrate their inter-

---

1. The chapter chooses to refer to interpreters, who may be deaf or nondeaf, rather than to use the convention of deaf interpreters and hearing interpreters.
2. AVLIC ratified a name change in 2016 to the Canadian Association of Sign Language Interpreters (CASLI).

preting competencies, and all of them have one simulated scenario involving legal discourse (e.g., a police interview or a lawyer–client meeting). In addition, the province of Ontario has a Ministry of the Attorney General (MAG) test specific for ASL interpreters. However, less than five interpreters have passed the MAG, and the interpreter referral services report that typically the interpreter candidates do not do well on the legal scenarios used in the in-house testing (personal correspondence, Sheila Johnston, May 1, 2019). Based on the expressed desire of the Canadian interpreters participating in that initial two-day workshop, the following intensive training program was created.

THE TRAINING MODEL

A number of decisions were made that shaped the model of training, including assembling a team of two lead instructors, one of whom was deaf. This would ensure that the training reflected the perspectives of interpreters who are themselves deaf and that the face-to-face education would be delivered in ASL. In addition, an administrative coordinator was secured in order to manage the logistics of hosting both online and face-to-face delivery.

Given the solid body of research evidence that has emerged in the area of legal interpreting, the instructional team determined the key studies that would serve as the foundation of the curriculum. We wanted to also ensure that all participants had a common frame of reference prior to engaging in the intensive learning, and hence the "flipped instruction" model that required prereading, pre-assignments, and opportunities for participants to engage with each other online prior to travelling to the training site to participate in mock trials and other authentic learning events.

The instructors drew on a theoretical approach to interpreting in legal settings that was based on Wadensjö's (1998) seminal work, *Interpreting as Interaction*. Within Wadensjö's model, she draws our attention to the concept that all parties contribute to meaning-making in contrast to understanding interpreting as the interpreter's sole responsibility. Furthermore, her use of the phrases "interpreting as text (or talk)" and "interpreting as interaction" helps to further examine the role and decisions that interpreters make in an interpreter-mediated interaction. Using this theoretical approach, we then reviewed the literature framing legal interpreting and chose materials and articles that aligned with that approach. These articles addressed aspects of the Canadian legal system, processes used in criminal and family law, legal terminology, ethical decision-making, interpreting techniques of notetaking, consecutive and simultaneous interpreting, working effectively in situations where there is more than one interpreter required, power and privilege as applied to legal interpreting, and so on.

There were 30 participants who met the prerequisites of having a minimum of five years of experience as a community interpreter, having completed a formal interpreter program, and being members of their provincial and national organizations. The invited participants were from seven provinces and one territory,[3] and the group included five interpreters who were deaf. The Association of Sign Language Interpreters of Alberta (ASLIA) hosted the training and covered the administrative costs. Community partnerships were a key aspect both in terms of being able to reduce the fees paid by the participants and in demonstrating the support for the specialized training. For example, one community interpreter referral service in Alberta reimbursed interpreters on their roster for taking the training, and other referral services donated refreshments for the five-day learning event. Based on the relationships of the primary instructors and administrator, we were able to secure a professional learning classroom through IBM at no cost, and the Alberta chief justice, Judge Ann Brown, worked with us to secure courtrooms, and judges and lawyers donated their time to participate in the trials. We chose to deliver the training in a year when the Canadian national interpreter association—Canadian Association of Sign Language Interpreters (CASLI)—was not hosting their biennial conference, so that interpreters would not have to choose between training and attending their national conference. In order to access courtrooms

---

3. Participants hailed from British Columbia, Alberta, Manitoba, Yukon Territory, Ontario, Quebec, Nova Scotia, and New Brunswick.

for the simulated trials, we identified that July was the least busy month for the Calgary courthouse where we hosted the mock trials.

Phase One: Flipped Instruction to Build a Common Foundation

The instructors chose a number of key readings in order to build a common understanding among the participants prior to attending the face-to-face training. The readings, prerecorded videos, and webinars included the following topics and resources:

- the foundation of the Canadian legal system (with the exception of Quebec, which uses the French civil code);
- the progression of legal steps in criminal, family and youth, and civil matters;
- the Ontario *Court Interpreter's Handbook* (Ministry of the Attorney General, 2017);
- *Ethical Decision-Making and the Demand Control Schema* (Dean & Pollard, 2005);
- *Interpreting Techniques—Consecutive and Simultaneous Interpreting* (Russell, 2002, 2005);
- *Power and Privilege* (Russell & Shaw, 2016);
- preparation among interpreters (Russell, 2008);
- *The Context-Based Ethical Reasoning: Demand Control Schema* (Dean & Pollard, 2011);
- *Interpreting Legal Discourse and Working in Legal Settings:* AVLIC Position Paper (2010); and
- structured observation form (adapted from Dean & Pollard, 2005).

The materials were available to the participants eight weeks in advance of the face-to-face learning event, through a file-sharing service known as Dropbox. In addition, a private Facebook group was created to encourage conversations and dialogue among the cohort. The participants were assigned two courtroom observations to be conducted in their home communities. The structured observations were to be of courtroom events where there were no interpreters working, and this allowed the interpreters to focus on the legal processes, language use, and interactions among the courtroom participants, contrasting, for example, docket court and the federal drug court, or a criminal trial summation and jury instructions. The other assignment was to note questions on the legal system and processes that stemmed from thereadings, in order to prepare for the first day of classroom instruction that included a presentation by the chief crown prosecutor for Calgary.

During Phase 1 we also began to assemble the mock trial materials; confirm lawyers, judges, and deaf community members who would play the role of witnesses and/or the accused; and confirm guest speakers for the one-week intensive summer institute.

Phase 2: Direct Experience in the Courtroom

The second phase of learning was designed to offer the practical authentic experience of working with legal discourse and working in courtrooms. The association collaborated with members of the legal profession in order to offer a five-day intensive learning experience, using the provincial court building to host a series of mock trials. Similar to the findings of Russell and Shaw (2016) who identified the advantage of interpreters developing long-term professional relationships with those in the legal system, we were able to capitalize on long-term existing relationships that the facilitator and administrator had with the legal community. For example, one lawyer had participated in a similar mock trial as part of my PhD study. One of the judges chaired a court interpreting committee of which I was a part, and she "championed" the training event to her colleagues on the bench, encouraging participation.

The multiple mock trials were conducted using lawyers who practice criminal law or family law, provincial court judges, and deaf community volunteers who played roles in the trials. By recruiting lawyers and judges, we were assured that the discourse and processes used would be as authentic as possible. The lawyers had from five to 25 years of experience, and two of the lawyers also had their senior articling students participate as junior counsel. The judges who participated had served on the bench for over 10 years, which again added to the authenticity of the trials. In addition, the judges had their own clerks perform in the mock trials. One of the trials required an expert witness with a psychology background, and we were able to recruit a hearing psychologist for this role. We also were successful in recruiting a police officer who played the role of the arresting officer in the impaired driving matter, and he was helpful in modifying the mock trial details for the impaired driving trial. On the day of the trial he arrived in full uniform, which again supported the simulation.

In terms of deaf actors, we recruited from various parts of the local deaf community, choosing a deaf senior to play the role of a grandparent testifying in a custody matter, a 17-year-old deaf youth with additional learning challenges to play the role of a student witness in a teacher assault case, a 25-year-old deaf woman with some significant vision loss as a witness in a sexual assault case, a 30-year-old male as the accused in the same trial, and a 40-year-old male to play the role of an accused in an impaired driving case. In this way, we incorporated diversity of language use and style that would be paramount in challenging the interpreter's linguistic and interpreting skills.

The scenarios were based on mock trial materials used by the British Columbia Criminal Trial Lawyers Association, which ensured that the simulations stemmed from actual cases that had been tried in the Canadian courts. The roles of each participant were described within the mock trial materials; however, there were no scripts, allowing for natural discourse to emerge during the trial. We distributed the mock trial materials to all participants playing a role, and we offered the interpreters an overall description of the trial, similar to the type of information they might receive when accepting the assignment.

The deaf participants were all users of ASL, and as such written English was not their first language. After they received the mock trial materials, they met individually with the workshop administrator who was also an interpreter, to ensure that they were comfortable with the assigned role and had an overall sense of the trial parameters. In the case of the youth with additional learning challenges, we asked his deaf-supported roommate to help him to prepare for the role. All of the deaf participants were very comfortable playing the roles, and in reacting in spontaneous ways to the events that unfolded in the trials, which added to the naturalness of the interpreting and interaction demands that the interpreters faced.

Interpreting and Language Specialists

One aspect to this learning model was that we also retained the services of two additional specialists who could offer linguistic and interpreting-related feedback. The ASL specialist is a deaf ASL instructor and has considerable experience working with deaf people from other countries. This meant he was in a position to comment on language structure and lexical choices from the perspective of what might work best for the deaf person involved in the individual trials. The other specialist is an interpreter who also managed a provincial internship program. She was invaluable in offering feedback based on comparisons between the source language and target language choices. Both specialists worked with the primary facilitators, and we rotated among the trials so that the participants could access feedback based on multiple perspectives. We used a structured feedback form in terms of trying to ensure that team members were commenting consistently on key language and interpreting features. This same form was used by any interpreters who were observing the trial, when it was not their turn to actively interpret, in order to capture peer feedback.

When each trial was concluded, the facilitators and language specialists debriefed with the participants, seeking observations from the judges and lawyers first, prior to moving into reflective conversations with the working interpreters. Some of the interpreters asked their peers to videotape them while working as an additional tool for analysis; however, this was not a requirement.

The Five-Day Schedule

The first day began with an opportunity to ask questions based on theprereadings and courtroom observations, as we invited a senior crown prosecutor to join us. He was able to address questions of legal process and law and specific aspects that emerged through the pre-observations. This was followed by a webinar with Karen Malcolm, a Canadian interpreter educator well versed in the Demand-Control Schema (Dean & Pollard, 2005), and this set the context for how the framework could be applied to the decision-making that would be required in the trials and throughout an interpreter's practice. The first day also involved direct instruction focused on co-interpreting between deaf–nondeaf teams, as that would be one key aspect of the upcoming mock trials as we built the schedule to include the deaf interpreters participating in the training.

The second day involved practical application of the interpreting legal discourse with a number of role-plays that centered on legal interaction. We invited deaf community members to join us, and they performed in role-plays that involved a police interview regarding theft in the workplace, a social work investigation of child abuse, a lawyer interview to respond to a civil lawsuit, a police interview with a senior regarding elder abuse, and filing a police report about a hit-and-run accident. These role-plays were opportunities for the facilitators and specialists to begin observing the linguistic and interaction decisions that the interpreter made and for peers to observe and offer feedback as well. Participants rotated through each of the scenarios, which were designed to allow for the blended use of simultaneous and consecutive interpreting. After each 15-minute role-play, the deaf and hearing participants offered comments on their experience and any feedback they might have for the interpreter(s) and then took short breaks while the interpreters and facilitators/specialists debriefed with them. Of note is that we were able to offer an honorarium to all deaf participants, acknowledging their time.

Later that day, the schedule for mock trial assignments was released, and teams then had time to prepare how they would work with each other during the trial and to prepare for the specifics of the case, seeking information from the facilitators by using the internet, and other resources available in the same way they might in a real scenario.

Over the next 2 days, the eight mock trials were conducted, using two courtrooms that allowed for two trials to run simultaneously both morning and afternoon. The administrator managed the logistics related to the trials, including checking in each of the volunteer participants, ensuring they were ready for the assigned trial. Each trial had a team of active interpreters, and if there were deaf defendents and deaf witnesses then there were multiple teams working. Each team had time to meet the crown prosecutors and defense lawyers prior to the trials and ask questions that would support their work. The administrator also had file information that some teams accessed and others did not. Deaf actors were paid an honorarium, and lawyers and judges were also offered this; however, they declined. We were able to offer lawyers gift certificates to a book store and those were accepted.

We did not prescribe a time for interpreters to arrive for their assigned trial, and it was interesting to note that some teams arrived last minute, while others arrived very early and took advantage of meeting and garnering as much information as possible. The quality of the interpreting was affected positively for those teams that researched the charges, met with crown and defense lawyers, and sought file information like witness lists, dates, locations where the alleged crimes took place, and so on, and this was noted later as significant learning for those teams that chose not to prepare in similar ways.

The final day was a further opportunity for the interpreters to debrief learning within the teams that had worked the trial and to explore challenges that arose. There was also time for individual reflection, examining the aspects of their professional practice that had worked well and should be maintained or amplified, as well as identifying features of their interpreting skills, knowledge, and decisions that need to be improved. This led to the interpreters working on professional development plans and identifying resources that could support that growth.

REFLECTIONS ON THE TRAINING FROM PARTICIPANTS

The participants were asked to reflect on the learning approximately one week after the event, and the following quotes demonstrate the kind of impact that such training can have on the interpreting participants, deaf community members, and members of the legal profession.

In their words:

> This training allowed me to put the theory into practice in a safe and supportive environment, and has given me the confidence to begin accepting assignments in legal settings.—Interpreter B

Another interpreter stated:

> I hadn't worked with a Deaf interpreter before so this was amazing to see what they bring to the work—I would love to work with them again but our community doesn't have anyone qualified. . . .—Interpreter L

Another interpreter stated:

> Getting the feedback was the best part of the training for me—I have done a lot of legal interpreting and never have I had this depth of analysis of my work—makes me far more aware of my patterns and what I need to do differently. —Interpreter D

While the feedback was overwhelmingly positive about the training, there were some difficult learning moments that also taught lessons. For example, one deaf and hearing team completely broke down when the deaf interpreter could not understand the hearing interpreter, and in the process of seeking clarification, the team was singled out by the judge as disrupting the process. This mirrors the authentic world, in that many deaf interpreters report challenges working with the hearing colleagues (Russell & Shaw, 2016), and, during the debriefing sessions, both interpreters reflected on what they each could have done differently to address this breakdown:

> I wish we would have had clearer signals between us for how we would handle it if I didn't understand the hearing interpreter's feed, and I wish we would have asked for a break when it was clear we weren't communicating effectively, let alone working well for the court. I am not proud of how we handled it, and worry that we left the judge with a negative view of co-interpreting.—Interpreter G

During the large group debrief, all the participants reflected on the ways that the interpreting profession needs to do a better job of describing the co-interpreting relationship and the benefits to the court, so that judges and lawyers who may be experiencing its use for the first time can remain open to the necessity and importance. This was supported in the perspective of one of the judges:

> I question the role of the interpreter who was Deaf and the interaction between the two interpreters. I believe that the integrity of the judicial process and the rules of evidence was altered by this process.—Justice T

The crown prosecutors and lawyers commented on several key aspects, including this point of view:

> I found the professionalism of the sign language interpreters to be very high—which has not always been our experience with the community [of] spoken language interpreters. I was impressed with their skills and felt that I was communicating effectively with the witnesses who were hearing impaired or deaf.—Crown Prosecutor N

In addition, one lawyer stated the following:

> This was an incredible training opportunity and our legal community should be doing more to ensure the interpreters are well trained. I am very pleased I participated and will certainly recommend this approach to other lawyers should the opportunity arise again. We need to know more about interpreting across many languages and this training served as a great example of how to do that well. This could happen in law school or our moot courts. . . .—Lawyer O

The week intensive ended with a social event, which was a perfect way to celebrate the accomplishments of the participants and relieve any tension that may have arisen among the teams of interpreters.

Given that we were dealing with attendees from across Canada, it would have been useful to have offered a similar event on the first evening as well, in order to allow the participants more time to become acquainted with each other.

ADAPTING THE PROGRAM: MEETING THE NEEDS OF SPOKEN LANGUAGE INTERPRETERS

Given the success of the training model with sign language interpreters, the Alberta Court Interpreters Association (ACIA) invited me to deliver the same type of training for spoken language interpreters working within Alberta. Together with a Spanish–English interpreter who had operated a part-time court interpreting program at a college, we developed an adapted program for community interpreters whose languages included Turkish, French, Spanish, Mandarin, and Russian.

With support from the Court Interpreting Committee, and Judge Ann Brown, ACIA was able to plan for a similar program. We began by sharing the readings and webinars with the registrants, allowing for a much longer period of time to absorb the material than that of the sign language interpreting cohort. This decision was based on the demographics of the group in that only two of the 25 participants had formal training as an interpreter, despite having worked as interpreters in a variety of settings. Many of them had taken a series of two-hour information workshops through ACIA on topics such as notetaking to support consecutive interpreting, ethical standards, memory development, simultaneous interpreting strategies, legal terminology, and the role of interpreters working in the legal system. However, the majority of the cohort had no experience reading research or academic articles, and the materials proved to be very challenging for them. One sign language interpreter returned to take the program again, indicating that the more experience she had, the more tools she would take to the courtroom and legal work.

The process was adapted to offer three half-day preworkshops where the facilitators taught the content found in the readings through the use of visual presentations with slides, mini-lectures, small group discussions, and case studies where the group applied the concepts from the articles.

The participants completed the same preassignment observations as the sign language interpreters, observing the docket court and the domestic violence courtroom, accessing public trials that involved impaired driving, assault with a weapon, and watching a bail hearing. These assignments were handed in for grading on the first day of the summer institute.

We drew upon our same networks within the legal commuity to secure teaching space at the Calgary Court Centre. For this summer institute we were able to use the First Nations courtroom, which is a teaching space that allowed for all participants to be seated in a circle with the facilitators in the center of the room. The design of the courtroom allows for smudging ceremonies as well, and there are First Nations artifacts on display in the room. The room was very suited to adult learning needs. The use of this room also allowed for easy access to the courtrooms that we used for the mock trials and facilities at the courthouse, including the cafeteria, law library, legal aide offices, and the court management offices.

The provincial court judges and many of the lawyers who participated in the previous year joined us again for this institute, and other slots were filled with legal professionals who were referred to us from the crown prosecutors' office. In terms of having witnesses who matched the language combinations of the interpreters, we asked the participants to use their personal contacts to recruit volunteers for the trials, and that was successful. We used the same mock trials, and the two facilitators prepared the witnesses for the roles that they would play. While I do not share any of the spoken languages that we were using for the trials, I was able to provide feedback on interpreting decisions, use of notetaking, the aspects of consecutive and simultaneous interpreting that worked well, the interpreting when the target language was spoken English, and so on. For the sign language interpreter who worked two of the trials, I was able to provide her with feedback that may have been even more helpful to her in that my attention was on one ASL interpreter, not several, as it had been in the previous institute. My cofacilitator was the language specialist for the Spanish trial, and a Mandarin interpreter with a great deal of court and government experience joined us for the specific Mandarin trial. We also secured the services of a Russian interpreter who was not attending the workshop and was willing to serve as the language specialist on that particular trial. The Turkish interpreters received feedback from the other Turkish-speaking participants, and once again, the facilitators were able to comment on the interpreting where the target language was English and other aspects of the interpreting process.

We chose to alter the schedule for the mock trials so that the trials took place over three mornings, and the afternoons were used as opportunities for longer reflective conversations and to offer direct instruction to address any of the challenges that had arisen in the trials. We made the decision based on the challenges that the group had in reading the prematerials and the lack of in-depth formal training. A simple example of direct instruction based on "teachable moments" that occurred in the mock trials will demonstrate why this was necessary. Despite having read the court interpreting manual prior to the institute, two of the interpreters arrived in clothing that was inappropriate for a courtroom. This led to an opportunity to deal in more depth with protocol, expectations of professionals, and how each decision an interpreter makes has an impact on how others perceive our profession and our competence. We also spent afternoons in practical exercises designed to strengthen their understanding of interpreting as an act of co-construction of meaning, versus the dominant habit of trying to transcode without understanding the deeper meaning behind a question, or not understanding narrative structures well enough to see how an answer brought forward previously shared information in order to address the question.

As with the sign language summer institute, the participants were asked to reflect on the learning approximately one week after the event, and the following quotes demonstrate the kind of impact that such training can have on the interpreting participants and members of the legal profession. In their words:

> I didn't realize that there was so much to know about interpreting prior to coming to this training—I will carefully consider whether I should be doing court at this time. I think I need to learn a lot more about legal terminology and processes before I will feel comfortable. . . . .—Interpreter Y

Another interpreter stated:

> The mock trials were amazing—it brought to life the readings and preworkshops. I am less scared now to do the assignments when offered as I know what to expect and how to be in the role of a court interpreter. . . .—Interpreter G

In the words of another participant:

> I will use this experience to continue to grow—I have set goals now and want to meet with other interpreters to practice and come to observe in court more often.—Interpreter M

The sign language interpreter that took the institute for the second time shared her thoughts:

> It was wonderful to come back and re-do the learning, which gave me more time to absorb the intense experience. I also learned a great deal from the spoken language interpreters and think we need to do more combined training. There is much to learn from each other in order to have consistent ethical and competent practice across all language communities working in courts.

The crown prosecutors and lawyers commented on several key aspects, including this point of view:

> This was a different experience than last year with the sign language interpreters. I can see the differences in skill levels and I didn't feel confident at times that my questions were interpreted properly as the witness provided answers that didn't make sense. The positive aspect is that they are here taking training and again, there is such a need for more of it.—Crown Prosecutor Q

In addition, one lawyer stated the following:

> I speak some Mandarin so it was interesting to listen to the witness and then hear the interpreting. I think the interpreters are doing

their best however I think bilingual lawyers also need to play a role in bringing errors to the attention of the court. When I did that I sensed the interpreter was very unhappy but the error was significant. In what ways can we help the interpreters with terminology?—Lawyer G

Last, we created two social opportunities for the participants, with one held immediately after the first day and the final one occurring after the last afternoon. These were helpful in building a sense of trust among the group and starting to align the interpreters as a community of practice.

DISCUSSION

This form of situated learning based on authentic experiences can be a significant approach for advancing interpreter skills and knowledge. What we learned by offering the two institutes will shape future training. The blended model of prereadings and assignments, and cohort conversations about those readings via a private Facebook group worked well for the sign language interpreters, while proving much more challenging for the spoken language interpreters. While we attempted to mitigate the reading challenges by offering the preworkshops about the readings, it may have been more useful to blend the content of the articles into a series of webinars and then provide the readings after the webinar. In that way there would have been a greater conceptual framework for all the interpreters to draw upon as they read the materials. However, it also begs the question for courts about proficiency standards for spoken language interpreters working in courtrooms and how best to assess core language abilities.

The mock trials, role-plays, and case studies were powerful ways to engage the participants and ensure that research and practice were bridged in effective ways. Involving the deaf community in the role-plays and mock trials also had some unforeseen benefits, in that it fostered a greater understanding of the complexity of interpreting in general and the demands that are present in a courtroom environment. It is also clear that the mock trials fostered mutual learning within the legal community as well. We have stronger allies now in our court system given their experiences working with both spoken and sign language interpreters, and there are more frequent informal and formal conversations among judges, crown prosecutors, and defense lawyers about the value of well-trained interpreters for legal settings and ways that they can support effective interpreting.

It is also clear that interpreters and educators are well-served by developing professional relationships with members of the legal community, as they are willing collaborators in wanting to support quality interpretation and they understand the value of professional development. They facilitated the introductions to potential participants, opening doors that allowed us to secure judges and lawyers for the trials and access courtroom facilities for the training at no cost.

As identified by one participant, moot court experiences are something that all faculties of law use in training lawyers, and there may be value in reaching out to explore how our training could be strengthened by working some of those moot court trials.

One of the challenges in planning for curricular resources was to obtain video materials that reflect the Canadian judicial system. There are many materials that are U.S.-based that can be adapted while the Canadian materials that we did locate had greater impact. However, one aspect that we needed to consider more carefully was the potential of vicarious trauma. During the training for spoken language interpreters, we used a publicly available video of a Canadian police interrogation of a suspected serial killer. The video is an excellent example of the stages of an effective police interview and the kinds of information that can emerge in a lengthy interview with a very intelligent suspect. However, during the confession portion of the video, there accused gave disturbing descriptions of the killings, and it had a negative impact on two of our participants. This led to greater conversations among the group about how to determine whether you should accept a court assignment that may involve content that is violent and disturbing, and the ways in which professional interpreters need to practice self-care in order to stay emotionally healthy to interpret in legal settings.

During one of the trials, our judge had to be reassigned to an actual court appearance so we used one of the very experienced crown prosecutors, which worked well, but it did alter the authenticity as he was not robed as a judge, and the interpreters had already been exposed to him as a lawyer. It would have been better to have had a backup list of legal professionals, including a third judge who might have stepped in for us.

Having a workshop administrator for the sign language interpreter institute was essential to its success and allowed the facilitators to focus solely on the teaching and learning environment. Due to financial reasons, we did not have an administrator for the spoken language interpreter institute, and that created an additional workload for thecofacilitators prior to, and during, the intensive experience.

During the summer institute we hosted a social event on the first evening and the final day, which created comfort among the group who had not been together before and facilitated easier interactions. It also serves to create a sense of professional collegiality among those interpreters who may see each other again in the courthouse when working.

Both institutes started with seed money from interpreter professional associations and then operated as a cost-recovery program. It would be useful to explore financial support for those traveling from out of town to support travel and accommodation costs. Some of the sign language interpreters were able to billet with friends and colleagues that they knew, and others bore the costs of hotels for the week. This additional cost may prohibit participants attending from greater distances.

Based on these initial program options, the following recommendations emerged:

1. Ensure that the model is sufficiently funded to hire a coordinator or administrator for the program, especially during the intensive week. There are a number of aspects of volunteer

management and preparation that require attention that is best handled by a person not facilitating.
2. Build in prelearning materials about vicarious trauma or compassion fatigue as experienced by interpreters.
3. Work with Canadian universities and their faculty of law programs to consider partnership opportunities during moot court experiences with senior law students.
4. Work with Canadian universities and their Faculty of Law programs to identify Canadian curricular resources that may be suitable for the program.
5. Require videotaping for all interpreters working the mock trials as portfolio material suitable for self and peer analysis.
6. Facilitators create materials in which they are able to model interpretation and that these be used as part of the teaching resources.
7. Model how to prepare for trials in the prelearning webinars in order to stress the importance of preparation and to expose the participants to the multiple resources that can support effective interpretation.

SUMMARY

While it is time-consuming and costly to plan such an extensive program of professional practice, the evaluations from both sign and spoken language interpreters demonstrated that the program built a foundation of knowledge, skills, and confidence among the participants while building a community of support among interpreters. In addition, the learning institutes had the unexpected advantage of building greater awareness among lawyers, crown prosecutors, and judges about the challenges of interpretation and the ways in which members of the judicial community can support the advancement of interpreter training, resulting in more effective courtroom interpretation when working with either spoken and sign language interpreters.

QUESTIONS AND APPLICATION

1. What organizations in your area could you partner with to develop needed training?
2. Provide some talking points for your discussions with these partners.
3. Make two lists of readings. The first list consists of key readings every legal interpreter should read before accepting legal work. The second list consists of key readings that a legal interpreter should read after they have some experience interpreting in a legal setting.
4. In what ways can training both spoken and sign language interpreters in the same events benefit our shared profession? Are there potential drawbacks? How might those be addressed?

REFERENCES

Angelelli, C. (2004). *Revisiting the interpreter's role: A study of conference, court, and medical interpreters in Canada, Mexico, and the United States.* John Benjamins.

Angermeyer, P. S. (2005). Who is "you"? Polite forms of address and ambiguous participant roles in court interpreting. *Target, 17*(2), 203–226. https://doi.org/10.1075/target.17.2.02ang

Angermeyer, P. S. (2008). Creating monolingualism in the multilingual courtroom. *Sociolinguistic Studies, 2*(3), 385–403. https://doi.org/10.1558/sols.v2i3.385

Angermeyer, P. S. (2009). Translation style and participant roles in court interpreting. *Journal of Sociolinguistics, 13*(1), 3–28. https://doi.org/10.1111/j.1467-9841.2008.00394.x

Association of Visual Language Interpreters of Canada. Interpreting legal discourse and working in legal settings: An AVLIC Position paper. http://www.avlic.ca/sites/default/files/docs/AVLIC-Interpreting_Legal_Discourse%26Working_in_Legal_Settings.pdf

Berk-Seligson, S. (1990). *The bilingual courtroom: Court interpreters in the judicial process.* University of Chicago Press.

Berk-Seligson, S. (2002). The impact of politeness in witness testimony: The influence of the court interpreter. In F. Pöchhacker & M. Shlesinger (Eds.), *The interpreting studies reader* (pp. 278–292). Routledge.

Bontempo, K., & Napier, J. (2007). Mind the gap: A skills analysis of sign language interpreters. *The Sign Language Translator 1*(2), 275–299.

Boudreault, P. (2005). Deaf interpreters. In T. Janzen (Ed.), *Topics in signed language interpretation: Theory and practice* (pp. 323–355). Lawrence Erlbaum.

Brunson, J. L. (2008). Your case will now be heard: Sign language interpreters as problematic accommodations in legal interactions. *Journal of Deaf Studies and Deaf Education, 13*(1), 77–91.

Dean, R. K., & Pollard, R. Q. (2005). Consumers and service effectiveness in interpreting work: A practice profession perspective. In M. Marschark, R. Peterson, & E. Winston (Eds.), *Sign language interpreting and interpreter education: Directions for research and practice* (pp. 259–282). Oxford University Press.

Dean, R. K., & Pollard, R. Q. (2011). Context-based ethical reasoning in interpreting: A demand control schema perspective. *The Interpreter and Translator Trainer, 5*(1), 155–182. https://doi.org/10.1080/13556509.2011.10798816

Forestal, E. M. (2005). The emerging professionals: Deaf interpreters and their views and experiences on training. In M. Marschark, R. Peterson, & E. Winston (Eds.), *Sign language interpreting and interpreter education: Directions for research and practice* (pp. 235–258). Oxford University Press. https://doi.org/10.1093/acprof/9780195176940.001.0001

Forestal, E. M. (2014). Deaf interpreters: The dynamics of their interpreting processes. In R. Adam, C. A. Stone, S. D. Collins, & M. Metzger (Eds.), *Deaf interpreters at work: International insights* (pp. 29–50). Gallaudet University Press.

Gallez, E., & Maryns, K. (2014). Orality and authenticity in an interpreter-mediated defendant's examination for the Belgian Assiz Court. *Interpreting, 16*(1), 49–80. https://doi.org/10.1075/intp.16.1.04gal

Gallez, E., & Reynders, K. (2015). Court interpreting and classical rhetoric: Ethos in interpreter-mediated monological discourse. *Interpreting, 17*(1), 64–90. https://doi.org/10.1075/intp.17.1.04gal

Hale, S. (1996). Pragmatic considerations in court interpreting. *Australian Review of Applied Linguistics, 19*(1), 61–72. https://doi.org/10.1075/aral.19.1.04hal

Hale, S. (1997). The interpreter on trial: Pragmatics in court interpreting. In S. E. Carr, R. Roberts, A. Dufour, & D. Steyn (Eds.), *The critical link: Interpreters in the community* (pp. 201–211). John Benjamins.

Hale, S. (1999). The interpreter's treatment of discourse markers in courtroom questions. *Forensic Linguistics, 6*(1), 57–82. https://doi.org/10.1558/sll.1999.6.1.57

Hale, S. (2001). How are courtroom questions interpreted? An analysis of Spanish interpreters' practices. In I. Mason (Ed.), *Triadic exchanges:*

Studies in dialogue interpreting (pp. 21–50). St. Jerome.

Hale, S. (2002). How faithfully do court Interpreters render the style of non-English speaking witnesses's testimonies? A data based study of Spanish-English bilingual proceedings. *Discourse Studies, 4*(1), 25–48. https://doi.org/10.1177/14614456020040010201

Hale, S. (2004). *The discourse of court interpreting: Discourse practices of the law, the witness and the interpreter.* John Benjamins.

Hale, S. (2008). Controversies over the role of the court interpreter. In C. Valero-Garcès & A. Martin (Eds.), *Crossing borders in community interpreting: Definitions and dilemmas* (pp. 99–121). John Benjamins.

Jacobsen, B. (2008). Interactional pragmatics and court interpreting: An analysis of face. *Interpreting, 10*(1), 128–158. https://doi.org/10.1075/intp.10.1.08jac

Lee, J. (2013). A study of facework in interpreter-mediated courtroom examination. *Perspectives: Studies in Translatology, 21*(1), 82–99. https://doi.org/10.1080/0907676X.2011.629729

Lee, J. (2015). Evaluation of court interpreting: A case study of metadiscourse in interpreter-mediated expert witness examinations. *Interpreting, 17*(2), 167–194. https://doi.org/10.1075/intp.17.2.021ee

Leung, E. & Gibbons, J. (2008). Who is responsible? Participant roles in legal interpreting cases. *Multilingua 27*, 171–191. https://doi.org/10.1515/MULTI.2008.010

Liu, X., & Hale, S. (2017). Facework strategies in interpreter-mediated cross-examinations: A corpus-assisted approach. *The Interpreter's Newsletter, 22*, 57–77. https://doi.org/10.13137/2421-714X/20738

Martinson, B. & Dubslaff, F. (2010). The cooperative courtroom: A case study of interpreting gone wrong. *Interpreting, 12*(1), 21–59.

Miller, K. (2001). Access to sign language interpreters in the criminal justice system. *American Annals of the Deaf, 146*(4), 328–330. https://doi.org/10.1353/aad.2012.0188

Miller, K., & Vernon, M. (1994). Qualifications of sign language interpreters in the criminal justice system. *Journal of Interpretation*, 111–124.

Miller, K. R., & Vernon, M. (2001). Linguistic diversity in Deaf defendants and due process rights. *Journal of Deaf Studies and Deaf Education, 6*(3), 226–234. https://doi.org/10.1093/deafed/6.3.226

Ministry of the Attorney General. (2017). Court interpreter's handbook. ttps://www.municipalcourts.on.ca/court-interpreter-folder/court-interpreters-handbook/Interpreter_Handbook_Apr2011_1975571.doc/view

Ministry of the Attorney General. (2021). *Become a court interpreter.* https://www.attorneygeneral.jus.gov.on.ca/english/courts/interpreters/

rules_of_professional_conduct.php

Morris, R. (1995). The moral dilemmas of court interpreting. *The Translator, 1*(1), 25–46. https://doi.org/10.1080/13556509.1995.10798948

Napier, J., Skinner, R., & Böser, U. (in preparation). "*He said I will ask you questions. . . .* " *Shifts of footing and rapport building in sign language interpretation of a suspect interview.*

Napier, J., & Spencer, D. (2007a). A sign of the times: Deaf jurors and the potential for pioneering law reform. *Reform, 90,* 35–37. https://search.informit.org/doi/10.3316/ielapa.200708802

Napier, J., & Spencer, D. (2007b). *Deaf jurors' access to court proceedings via sign language interpreting: An investigation* [Unpublished research report]. NSW Law Reform Commission, Research Report No. 14, March.

Napier, J., & Spencer, D. (2008). Guilty or not guilty? An investigation of deaf jurors' access to court proceedings via sign language interpreting. In D. Russell & S. Hale (Eds.), *Interpreting in legal settings* (pp. 71–122). Gallaudet University Press.

Napier, J., Spencer, D., Hale, S., San Roque, M., Shearim, G., & Russell, D. (2018). Changing the international justice landscape: Perspectives on Deaf citizenship and jury services. *Sign Language Studies, 19*(2), 240–266. https://doi.org/10.1353/sls.2018.0034

Roberson, L., Russell, D., & Shaw, R. (2012). American Sign Language/English interpreting in legal settings: Current practices in North America. *Journal of Interpretation, 21*(1), 6. https://digitalcommons.unf.edu/joi/vol21/iss1/6

Roberson, L., Russell, D., & Shaw, R. (2013). A case for training signed language interpreters for legal specialisation. *International Journal Interpreter Education, 4*(2), 52-73. https://digitalcommons.unf.edu/eexc_facpub/1

Russell, D. (2002). *Interpreting in legal contexts: Consecutive and simultaneous interpretation.* Sign Media.

Russell, D. (2005). Consecutive and simultaneous interpreting. In T. Janzen (Ed.), *Topics in signed language interpretation: Theory and practice* (pp. 135–164). John Benjamins.

Russell, D. (2008). Interpreter preparation conversations: Multiple perspectives. In D. Russell & S. Hale (Eds.), *Interpreting in legal settings* (pp. 123–147). Gallaudet University Press.

Russell, D., & Shaw, R. (2016). Power and privilege: An exploration of decision-making of interpreters in legal settings. *Journal of Interpretion, 25*(1), Article 7. https://digitalcommons.unf.edu/joi/vol25/iss1/7

Tester, C. (2018). How American Sign Language-English interpreters who can hear determine need for a deaf interpreter for court proceedings. *Journal of Interpretation, 26*(1), Article 3. https://digitalcommons.unf.edu/joi/vol26/iss1/3/

Turner, G. H., & Best, B. (2017). From defensive interpreting to professional interpreting practices. In M. Biagini, M. S. Boyd, & C. Monacelli (Eds.), *The changing role of the interpreter: Contextualising norms, ethics and quality standards.* Routledge.

Turner, G. H., & Brown, R. (2001). Interaction and the role of the interpreter in court. In F. J. Harrington & G. H. Turner (Eds.), *Interpreting interpreting: Studies and reflections on sign language interpreting* (pp. 152–167). Douglas McLean.

Vernon, M., & Miller, K. (2001). Linguistic incompetence to stand trial: A unique condition in some deaf defendants. *Journal of Interpretation,* 99–120.

Vernon, M., & Miller, K. (2005). Obstacles faced by deaf people in the criminal justice system. *American Annals of the Deaf, 150*(3), 283–291. https://doi.org/10.1353/aad.2005.0036

Wadjensö, C. (1998). *Interpreting as interaction.* Addison Wesley Longman.

Wallace, M. (2015). A further call to action: Training as a policy issue in court interpreting. *The Interpreter & Translator Trainer, 9*(2), 173–187. https://doi.org/10.1080/1750399X.2015.1051769

Wilcox, P. (1995). Dual interpretation and discourse effectiveness in legal settings. *Journal of Interpretation, 7*(1), 89–98. https://citeseerx.ist.psu.edu/viewdoc/download?doi=10.1.1.584.6090&rep=rep1&type=pdf

Witter-Merithew, A., & Johnson, L. (2005). *Towards competent practice: Conversations with stakeholders.* RID Publications.

Witter-Merithew, A., & Nicodemus, B. (2012). Toward the international development of interpreter specialization: An examination of two case studies. *Journal of Interpretation, 20*(1), Article 8. http://digitalcommons.unf.edu/joi/vol20/iss1/8

CONTRIBUTORS

Natalie Atlas, B.A., CI, CT, SC:L, is a legal interpreting specialist with nearly 30 years of experience in legal, corporate, government, technical, entertainment, conference, postsecondary education, medical, and mental health settings. As an interpreter educator, she has facilitated and cofacilitated trainings including interpretation of jury instructions, integration of consecutive and simultaneous interpreting, interpreting the Miranda warning, overview of legal interpreting, Deaf/hearing team interpreting, and interpreting psychological evaluations. Atlas is also committed to life-long learning—seeking out and completing trainings, graduate school courses, and mentorship opportunities to bring new skills and perspectives to her work. She graduated from Rutgers College with a bachelor's in English and completed Union County College's interpreter training program. Most recently, Atlas had the privilege of interpreting full-time at Yale Law School, which brought together her loves of language, law, and justice.

Michèle Berger received her teacher's diploma in 1990. In 1991, she graduated from the sign language interpreting program in Zurich. Additionally, she received her certificate in legal interpreting from the Cantone of Zurich in 2001. Since 1994, she has been teaching in the sign language interpreters' program at the University of Applied Sciences for Special Education in Zurich, Switzerland. For 30 years now, she has been working nationally and internationally as a sign language interpreter in a variety of different settings. She also has been a board member and vice president of the European Forum of Sign Language Interpreters (efsli) for 10 years.

JEREMY L. BRUNSON, Ph.D., SC:L, is the executive director of the Division of Equity, Diversity, and Inclusion at Gallaudet University. He holds graduate degrees in social justice, social inquiry, and sociology from Arizona State University and Syracuse University, respectively. He earned his doctorate at Syracuse University as well as a Certificate of Advanced Studies in Disability studies. His book, *Video Relay Service Interpreters: Intricacies of Sign Language Access*, was published by Gallaudet University Press in 2011. He also coauthored (with Drs. Cynthia B. Roy and Christopher A. Stone) *The Academic Foundations of Interpreting Studies: An Introduction to Its Theories* (2018). His research interests are in the broad area of the sociology of interpreting and live at the intersection of sociology work and the professions, sociology of disability, critical theory. His interpreting practice is primarily in the legal arena. He has published and presented about video relay service, educational interpreting, the invisible labor deaf people perform, professionalization of sign language interpreting, and ethics. He earned The Irving K. Zola Award for Emerging Scholars in Disability Studies in 2009 and was named a Fulbright Specialist in 2017 and spent six weeks in Ulaanbaatar, Mongolia, helping to establish the country's first interpreter training program.

BARBARA BUCHER is a lecturer in the bachelor of sign language interpreting program at the University of Applied Sciences in Special Needs Education in Zurich, Switzerland. She has a diploma in sign language interpreting and a Swiss Federal Diploma for Trainer of Higher Education. She works since 2000 mainly as a professional Sign Language interpreter in Switzerland in various settings such as the judiciary, the media, politics, education, etc. In this context she took part in researches in sign language interpreting.

LEWANA CLARK, M.Ed, Ph.D., CSC, CI, CT, SC:L/Master Mentor, works as a nationally certified American Sign Language interpreter specializing in court/legal settings, teaches interpreter education and professional development workshops, and mentors new and experienced interpreters. Adding to her many accomplishments, she has completed the master mentorship program in 2005, then graduated from Lesley University in Cambridge, Massachusetts, with her master's degree in 2011: Independent Degree Study Program, Specialization: Transformative Learning for ASL/English Interpreters. Her thesis was titled *Beyond ASL Vocabulary: Towards Bicultural and Bilingual Proficiencies for ASL/English Interpreters*. She completed her doctorate studies at Gallaudet University in 2018 with a dual concentration of pedagogy and research from the Interpretation and Translation Department. Her doctorate, *The Interactive Courtroom: The Deaf Defendant Watches How the Speaker Is Identified for Each Turn-At-Talk During a Team Interpreted Event*, focused on the effects of teaming on the identification of speakers during a court proceeding. She is a coauthor of the new textbook *You Want to Be an Interpreter* (5th ed.). Clark continues to work as a private practice interpreter and teaches at Northern Essex Community College in Haverhill, Massachusetts.

JÉRÔME DEVAUX is a lecturer in French at the Open University (UK). Prior to joining academia, he worked for several years as a freelance translator and conference/public service interpreter. His areas of research lie in the use of technologies in public service interpreting, and their effect on the interpreter-mediated interaction.

CAROLIEN DOGGEN is a lecturer at the Katholieke Universiteit Leuven, Faculty of Arts in Antwerp, Belgium where she teaches courses in sign language proficiency, deaf studies, and sign language interpreting. Doggen is also a practicing sign language interpreter and translator, working between Dutch, Flemish Sign Language, English, and International Sign, having graduated from the European master's in sign language interpreting program.

GINO S. GOUBY, B.A., CDI, SC:L, is a nationally certified staff interpreter with Gallaudet University. He brings over 20 years of interpreting in generalist and specialized settings including legal proceedings. His areas of interests include translanguaging, DI/DI teams, and International Sign interpreting.

SANDRA HALE, Ph.D., is a professor of interpreting and translation and program convenor at the University of New South Wales. She is a National Accreditation Authority for Translators and Interpreters' accredited Spanish-English translator and conference interpreter. Her qualifications include a B.A. in interpreting and translation, a Dip. Ed. (Spanish and Italian), a master's of applied linguistics, and a Ph.D. in court interpreting/forensic linguistics. She was conferred a Doctorate Honoris Causa by the University of Antwerp in April 2014. She is a fellow of the Australian Institute of Interpreters and Translators and a fellow of the Australian Academy of the Humanities.

She is the sole author of the books: *The Discourse of Court Interpreting* (2004/2010) and *Community Interpreting* (2007), translated into Spanish and Japanese, and coauthor of four other books, including the latest one with Jemina Napier, *Research Methods in Interpreting* (2013). She has also written numerous journal articles and book chapters.

TOBIAS HAUG, Ph.D., studied sign linguistics at Hamburg University and Deaf education at Boston University, where he received his master's degree in 1998. In 2009, he earned his Ph.D. at Hamburg University. From 1998 to 2004, he worked as a sign language interpreter and researcher. Since 2004, he has been the program director of the sign language interpreter program at the University of Applied Sciences for Special Education in Zurich, Switzerland. In 2017, he completed his master's in language testing from Lancaster University. Among his research interests are sign language assessment and sign language interpreting.

FLURINA KRÄHENBÜHL received her undergraduate degree in translation and her postgraduate degree in conference interpreting from the Zurich University of Applied Sciences in Winterthur (Switzerland) in 2008 and 2010 respectively. Since 2010, she has been working as a translator, both in-house and freelance, and as a freelance interpreter. In 2015 and 2016, she was employed as a research assistant in interpreting studies at the University of Applied

Sciences in Winterthur with a focus on interpreting in criminal proceedings and community interpreting.

ROBERT G. LEE has been interpreting, teaching, and researching for more than 30 years. He is currently the course leader of the M.A. and postgraduate diploma in the British Sign Language/English Interpreting and Translation program at the University of Central Lancashire (UK). He has previously taught both interpreting and linguistics at Northeastern University in Boston as well as having presented workshops and conference papers in North America, South America, and Europe. In collaboration with Peter Llewellyn-Jones, Robert developed the role-space model of interpreted interaction.

LORRAINE LEESON, Ph.D., is professor in Deaf studies at the Centre for Deaf Studies, and currently serves as associate dean of research (2018-) at Trinity College Dublin in Ireland. Her research work is multidisciplinary in nature, influenced by her background in deaf studies, gender studies, and linguistics. she has published widely on aspects of the linguistics and applied linguistics of signed languages with a specific interest in Irish Sign Language and in the area of sign language interpreting. Lorraine was a member of the first cohort of professionally trained Irish Sign Language–English interpreters in Ireland, and she continues to interpret occasionally. She has engaged in pan-European research work with academic institutions, Deaf communities, and interpreting organizations for over two decades. Recent publications include *Sign Language in Action* with Jemina Napier (2016) and *Interpreting and the Politics of Recognition*, coedited with Christopher Stone (2018).

SCOTT ROBERT LOOS has worked in the field of translation and interpreting for over 40 years, both as an interpreter/translator and a trainer of interpreters. He holds a B.A. in education from Arizona State University and an M.A. in intercultural communication from the Monterey Institute. Loos has certifications in court interpreting from the Administrative Office of United States Courts and the Supreme Court of Arizona. During his time as supervisory interpreter at the Superior Court of Arizona in Maricopa County (1979-2018), he also taught as adjunct faculty at Arizona State University, Montclair State College, the University of Houston, and the College of Charleston, where he also participated in the curriculum planning for the M.A. program in judiciary interpreting. He devised and administered qualifying exams for interpreters of Spanish from 1983 to the time of his retirement in 2018. Beginning in 1982 and periodically till 2005, Loos worked on panels for the administration and scoring of the AOUSC's Federal Court Interpreters' examination for Spanish-English interpreters. Loos is the coauthor, with Virginia Benmaman and Norma Connolly, of the *Bilingual Dictionary of Criminal Justice Terms*.

TERESA LYNCH is a part-time assistant professor at the Centre for Deaf Studies at Trinity College Dublin in Ireland, where she teaches courses on Irish Sign Language (ISL) and interpreting. She holds an MSc in Deafhood studies (University of Bristol), a diploma in ISL Teaching, and a community management diploma. She has presented on deaf interpreter training, Deafhood, ISL, issues relating to Deaf women, and interpreting in many domains. Lynch has been an accredited Deaf interpreter for more than 20 years. She has also worked with external bodies that hire interpreters/translators. She is a member of the Council of Irish Sign Language Interpreters and is a founder member of The Council of Irish Sign Language Teachers, established in 2018.

CARLA M. MATHERS, Esquire, SC:L, practiced law in Maryland and the District of Columbia for over 20 years. She currently is an independent consultant teaching legal interpreters and interpreting in legal settings. Mathers's law degree is from Howard University School of Law. Her interpreting degree is from the College of Southern Idaho. She currently serves on the District of Columbia Courts Language Access Advisory Committee, the Registry of Interpreters for the Deaf Legal Interpreting Credential Task Force, and the National Association of the Deaf's Video Remote Interpreting in Court Task Force. She previously sat on the Advisory

Group for Language Access to develop standards for language access in courts for the American Bar Association. She also sat on the Maryland Administrative Office of the Courts' Advisory Committee on Interpreters Subcommittee on Ethics and Subcommittee on Testing and Training. Mathers formerly served as the legal program coordinator for MARIE Center/DOIT Center at the University of Northern Colorado. She serves as an adjunct instructor for the Gallaudet University Department of Interpretation teaching legal interpreting. She also served as vice president for the Conference of Interpreter Trainers and sat on the board of directors for the Deaf Abused Women's Network in Washington, D.C. Mathers is the author of *Sign Language Interpreters in Court: Understanding Best Practices*, a text for interpreters, attorneys, and courts to understand the principles underlying ASL court interpreting.

GENE MIRUS is an associate professor in the Department of Deaf Studies at Gallaudet University. As a linguistic anthropologist, he takes interest in understanding how understudied groups take advantage of various linguistic and paralinguistic resources for the purposes of communication, and how they creatively incorporate them in their communicative interactions among themselves.

JEMINA NAPIER, Ph.D., is a professor of intercultural communication and director of the Centre for Translation & Interpreting Studies at Heriot-Watt University in Edinburgh, Scotland, where she is also the director of research for the School of Social Sciences. She is an interpreter researcher, educator, and practitioner and has practiced as a sign language interpreter since 1989. She works between English and British Sign Language, Australian Sign Language, or International Sign. Napier is a fellow of the Association of Sign Language Interpreters and the Chartered Institute of Linguists in the UK, and an honorary life member of the Australian Sign Language Interpreters Association. She's also a visiting professor at the Centre for Deaf Studies, Trinity College Dublin, and an adjunct professor at Macquarie University in Sydney. She is the sole author of the books *Linguistic Coping Strategies in Sign Language Interpreting*

(2016, 2nd ed.) and *Sign Language Brokering in Deaf-Hearing Families* (in press), coauthor of three other books: *Research Methods in Interpreting* (2013) with Sandra Hale, *Sign Language Interpreting: Theory and Practice* (2018, 3rd ed.) with Rachel McKee and Della Goswell, and *Sign Language in Action* (2016) with Lorraine Leeson. She has also coedited several books on interpreting research and interpreter education and has published more than 150 journal articles and book chapters.

BARBARA ROSSIER is a lecturer in the Bachelor of Sign Language Interpreting program at the University of Applied Sciences for Special Education in Zurich, Switzerland. She has a certificate in sign language teacher and is a Swiss federal specialist trainer. Since 2010 she has been working mainly as a professional sign language teacher and has a lot of experience in raising awareness of issues concerning sign language and deaf people in German-speaking Switzerland (and parts of French-speaking Switzerland) in various areas such as the judiciary, media, politics, schools, museums, and public authorities. In addition, she also works as an independent professional translator of German texts into German-Swiss Sign Language or from English into International Sign for various private and public providers (TV programs, websites, and social media).

DEBRA RUSSELL, Ph.D., is a Canadian certified interpreter, educator, and researcher. As the previous David Peikoff Chair of Deaf Studies at the University of Alberta, her research interests include mediated education with interpreters, interpreting in legal settings and with legal discourse, and Deaf–hearing interpreter teams. She has published extensively in the field of interpretation. Her interpreting practice spans more than 30 years, and continues to focus on medical, legal, mental health, and employment settings. She has had a long history of leadership positions at the local, national, and international levels, serving with several volunteer organizations. She is the past president of the World Association of Sign Language Interpreters, and a commissioner for the Commission on Collegiate Interpreter Education. She loves to travel and has presented in 62 countries while maintaining a committed yoga practice over the past 40 years.

HEIDI SALAETS, Ph.D., currently is the head of the Interpreting Studies Research Group at the University of Leuven. At the Antwerp campus, she teaches interpreting studies and trains interpreters (Italian-Dutch) in the Master of Interpreting program. Salaets's research mainly focuses on community interpreting (health care) and legal interpreting (for the police, in languages of lesser diffiuson, in law clinics, for minors, etc.). Since 2012, she and Dr. Katalin Balogh coordinated different European Union DG-Justice projects.

MEHERA SAN ROQUE, Ph.D., is an associate professor in the faculty of law, University of New South Wales (UNSW) Sydney. She teaches courses on evidence and criminal procedure, and also teaches in the postgraduate forensic psychology program at UNSW. She researchs in the areas of identification evidence and expertise, feminist legal theory, acoustic justice and surveillance studies, and has a particular interest in developing critical, cross-disciplinary analyses of criminal trial processes. She is a member of the Evidence-Based Forensics Initiative and is on the Council of the Australian Academy of Forensic Sciences.

RISA SHAW, Ph.D., is a professor of linguistics at Gallaudet University; a working interpreter for more than 35 years with CSC, CI, SC:L certifications; an interpreter educator and trainer with a specialization in legal settings and discourse; a researcher focusing on interpreting in legal settings, power and privilege, narratives, and trauma (applied sociolinguistics research).

HAARIS SHEIKH is the chief executive of Interesource Group (Ireland) Limited. He is also an adjunct assistant professor in Deaf studies, Trinity College Dublin, where he is pursuing a Ph.D., funded by an Irish Research Council scholarship, exploring the Deaf community's experiences in employment. He has an undergraduate degree in business studies and human resource management, and a master's degree in business, both from the University of Limerick, Ireland.

He is a chartered fellow of the Chartered Institute of Personnel and Development and a member of the Institute of Management Consultants and Advisers. He specializes in human resource management, business strategy, and policy and is retained is a consultant to several private and public sector organizations. He also specializes in digital media and is involved in content creation in the field of sign languages and interpreting. He has successfully delivered on 17 European Commission projects in over 16 countries to date.

ROBERT SKINNER, Ph.D., is a qualified British Sign Language–English interpreter and researcher. In 2014, Skinner joined the BSL team at the Centre for Translation & Interpreting Studies in Scotland at Heriot-Watt University working various projects including the Insign project on video remote interpreting access to European institutions, the Justisigns project on police interpreting and the Translating the Deaf Self project on deaf people's experiences of being interpreted. Skinner subsequently completed his Ph.D. at Heriot-Watt University in 2020. The focus of his thesis was on video-mediated interpreting in frontline policing contexts. The study investigated how rights and duties were shared and negotiated between participants to complete a frontline policing task. The scholarship was jointly funded by the Scottish Graduate School for the Arts and Humanities and the School of Social Sciences at Heriot-Watt University. The Ph.D. project partners included Police Scotland and SignVideo. Skinner has coedited the volume *Here or There: Research on Interpreting via Video Link* (2018) with Jemina Napier and Sabine Braun, and has coauthored several published peer-reviewed articles and book chapters from the various projects he has been involved in.

DAVID SPENCER is an attorney admitted to the Supreme Court of New South Wales and the High Court of Australia in 1992. Spencer is also an academic and in 2008 was appointed a professor moving from Macquarie University in Sydney to La Trobe University in Melbourne. He now teaches law at the Australian Catholic University in Melbourne. He has won numerous university, awards, a national teaching award, and several competitive research grants. As a result of a recent Australian Research Council grant to investigate whether deaf people can serve as members of a jury, he was the lead author of an article that won the inaugural Andrea Durbach Award for Human Rights Scholarship awarded by the Australian Human Rights Institute and the *Australian Journal for Human Rights*.

He began researching and writing about dispute resolution in the mid-1990s and is currently one of Australia's leading authorities on the theory, philosophy, and practice of alternative dispute resolution. He is the author of seven books and research monographs; five book chapters; 22 articles and 90 case notes in refereed publications; and more than 100 articles in other journals and conference presentations. He is the chief editorial consultant for the *Australasian Dispute Resolution Journal*.

CHRISTOPHER STONE is a reader in translation and interpreting whose research interests include multimodal interaction in interpreter-mediated events, multimodal enrichment in sign language interpreting and translation in the media, sign language interpreting history, and the sociology of interpreting. He maintains an interpreting practice and serves on the Research Committee of the International Association of Conference Interpreters and at the time of writing is the president of the World Association of Sign Language Interpreters.

CHRISTOPHER TESTER, Ph.D., CDI, SC:L, is Deaf and is an actor, consultant, educator, and interpreter. As a seasoned presenter, he specializes in workshop and seminar facilitation on topics (not limited to) disability rights and laws, Deaf and hard of hearing awareness, and interpreting. He is a former adjunct instructor for CUNY's ASL/English Interpreter Education Program. Additionally, he has interpreted for several off and on Broadway shows, national and international conferences, at the United Nations and specializes in legal interpreting. His recent research focuses on Deaf interpreters' work within the court of law.

GRAHAM H. TURNER joined the Department of Languages and Intercultural Studies at Heriot-Watt University in 2005 as chair of Translation & Interpreting Studies and, focusing on British Sign Language, has been working full-time in academia since 1988. He has published widely, editing international journals in Deaf studies and in translation and interpreting studies, and served for many years as a board member and policy advisor to governmental, parliamentary, and community organizations. In well over 200 publications and presentations, supported by ESF, ESRC, Leverhulme, and others, he has pursued issues of social and applied linguistics centered upon the nature of signed language, and the linguistic identity of its users.

MYRIAM VERMEERBERGEN, Ph.D., is an associate professor at the Department of Linguistics at KU Leuven, Campus Antwerpen, where she teaches courses on linguistic aspects of Flemish Sign Language (VGT), general linguistics, and sign linguistics. She is also a research associate with the Department of Dutch and Afrikaans, Stellenbosch University, South Africa. In the early 1990s, Myriam pioneered sign language research in Flanders, Belgium, and in 1996, she obtained a Ph.D. with a dissertation on morphosyntactic aspects of VGT. From 1997 until 2007 she was a postdoctoral research fellow, continuing to work on the grammar of VGT and studying the similarities between the grammars of different signed languages and between signed languages and other forms of gestural communication. She is also involved in sociolinguistic studies and lexicographical work related to VGT. Her current research interests include the linguistics of VGT, the genesis and development of signed languages, and the linguistic aspects of (Flemish) sign language interpreting.

INDEX

Figures, notes, and tables are indicated by f, n, *and* t *following the page number..*

Access to Justice project, 159, 248
ACIA (Alberta Court Interpreters Association), 295
Actor-Network Theory, 205
Administrative Office of the United States Courts (AOUSC), 112
AdonSoto, Commonwealth v. (2016), 90, 95
agency
    interpreter as authorized or joint agent, 83–86
    language-conduit-agency theory, 84
    liability and, 83
Aguilar, People v. (1984), 22

Alberta Court Interpreters Association (ACIA), 295
Alvarez, United States v. (1985), 84
Ambriz-Arguello, State v. (2017), 93
American Sign Language (ASL)
    Canadian Charter of Rights and Freedom and, 283
    deaf attorneys and, 138
    deaf interpreters and, 48–49
    monitoring interpretations and, 25
    research on legal interpreting and, 249
    speaker identification and, 220–21, 227, 235
Anderson, L. W., 211–12
AOUSC (Administrative Office of the United States Courts), 112
Araujo, M., 22
Arizona v. Natividad (1974), 220
ASL. *See* American Sign Language
ASLIA (Association of Sign Language Interpreters of Alberta), 286
Association of Sign Language Interpreters of Alberta (ASLIA), 286
assessments, 106–27
    curriculum development and, 108–17, 125t
    language equivalence assumptions and, 109–10
    subject-matter challenges, 117–26, 125t
Association of Sign Language Interpreters (ASLI), 173–74
Association of Visual Language Interpreters of Canada (AVLIC), 284, 284n2, 287
Atlas, Natalie, 46
attorneys
    deaf attorneys, 132–50. *See also* deaf attorneys
    IRAC framework and, 52–61,

53f. *See also* IRAC (Issue, Rule, Application/Analysis, Conclusion) framework
   logic and language of, 46–66
   recommendations for monitoring interpretations, 40–41
Australia, deaf jurors in, 251, 251n2, 253
Australian Research Council, 271
AVLIC. *See* Association of Visual Language Interpreters of Canada

Babbini Brasel, B., 226, 239
backchanneling, 203
back-translation, 99–100
BDA (British Deaf Association), 173
Begum, Iqbal, 193
BEI (Board of Evaluators of Interpreters), 8, 10
Bélanger, D-C., 202
Belgium, *Justisigns* project in, 155, 158, 167t
Bel-Iran, United States v. (1985), 84
Berger, Michèle, 154
Berk-Seligson, S., 159–60
Best, B., 2679
Board of Evaluators of Interpreters (BEI), 8
Bontempo, K., 283
Braun, V., 165
British Columbia Criminal Trial Lawyers Association, 289
British Deaf Association (BDA), 173
British Sign Language (BSL)
   Access to Justice project and, 248
   in police settings, 159, 162, 165n5, 169–72
   training for legal interpreters, 199–200
Brown, Ann, 286, 295
Brunson, Jeremy L., 3, 4, 283
Bucher, Barbara, 154
Bullcoming v. New Mexico (2011), 89–90
Burton, K., 53
Butt, P., 7

California State Interpreter Certification, 107, 111
Campos, P. F., 6
Canada
   Charter of Rights and Freedom, 282–83
   credentialing of legal interpreters in, 285
   training for legal interpreters in, 282–302
Canadian Association of Sign Language Interpreters (CASLI), 284n2, 286
Carreon, People v. (1984), 22
Certified Deaf Interpreter (CDI), 8
Chang, W., 22
Chao v. State (1985), 84
Charles, United States v. (2013), 94
Chartered Institute of Linguists (CIoL), 198
civil cases, courtroom rules for, 8–9
Clarion UK, 200
Clark, LeWana, 219
Clarke, V., 165
close renditions, 257t, 258, 260t
code-blends, 137–38
Code of Conduct for legal interpreters (EU), 156
Code of Professional Conduct (RID), 75, 96

Cokely, D., 30n8, 31
Commonwealth v. See name of opposing party
compounding, 142–45, 145t
conference interpreting, 112–13
confessions, 82, 82n4
confidentiality issues
   deaf jurors and, 252
   expert witnesses and, 75–76
   trust and, 75–76, 102
Confrontation Clause, 78, 86, 88–91, 93–96
continuing professional development (CPD) training. *See also* training
   Justisigns training courses, 173–82, 175–76t, 179–81t
   for police settings, 165
contract law, 5–6
Cooperative Principle (Grice), 204
Cordero, United States v. (1994), 84
Correa v. Superior Court (2002), 84
Coulthard, M., 224
Court Interpreters Act of 1979 (U.S.), 112
courtroom rules, 8–9
covert interaction management, 202
covert participant alignment, 203
CPD. *See* continuing professional development training
Crawford v. Washington (2004), 88
credentialing. *See also specific credentialing organizations*
   assessments and, 106–7
   in Canada, 285
   curriculum development and, 111
   organizations, 8
criminal cases. *See also* police settings; *specific cases*

accuracy of interpretation in, 97
courtroom rules, 8–9
Cruz-Reyes v. State (2003), 84
Cuberlo, United States v. (2003), 90
cultural literacy
   assessments of, 107–8
   curriculum development and, 113–14
   in police interviews, 162–63, 169–70
   semantics and, 117–26
Curbelo, United States v. (2003), 93
curriculum development
   assessments and, 108–17, 125t
   credentialing and, 111
   cultural literacy and, 113–14
   Justisigns project online curriculum, 177–82, 179–81t
   physical appearance terminology, 118–26
   science terminology, 117
   subject-matter challenges, 117–26, 125t
   technology terminology, 117–18

DaSilva, United States v. (1983), 84
Daubert v. Merrell Dow Pharms., Inc. (1993), 98
deaf attorneys, 131–50
   co-occurrence of linguistic features used by, 141–45
   compounding, 142–45, 145t
   fingerspelling, 141–42, 142t
   mouthing, 144–45
   interviews with, 138–49
   language ideologies and, 133–41
   languaging as education and embodied learning for, 146–48

languaging strategies of, 138–41
preferred interpreters for, 148–49
deaf interpreters (DIs), 4
    credentialing of, 8
    literature review, 10–11
    partnering with, 47
    role of, 48–50
deaf jurors, 246–70
    as "gray zone" for legal interpreters, 251–52
    interpreting strategies for, 257–63
    isolation experienced by, 267–68
    research on legal interpreting for, 247–50, 252–57
    stakeholder perspectives, 263–68
    training to work with, 266–67, 268–70
Dean, R. K.
    The Context-Based Ethical Reasoning: Demand Control Schema (with Pollard), 287
    Ethical Decision-Making and Demand Control Schema (with Pollard), 287
defensive interpreting, 267
Demand-Control Schema, 287, 291
Devaux, Jérôme, 191, 192, 205, 207–8
DIMA language school, 177
Diploma in Public Service Interpreting (DPSI), 198, 198n4, 214
DIs. *See* deaf interpreters
Doggen, Carolien, 154

Doumit, Steven, 271
Dreyfus's model of skill interaction, 212
Durbin v. Hardin (1989), 84, 93
Dutch/Sign Language of the Netherlands, 212
efsli (European Forum of Sign Language Interpreters), 157n2, 163
Eid, Danny, 271
ELAN, 138, 139, 224, 224n4
emancipatory interpreting, 266
England. *See* British Sign Language; United Kingdom
errors
    additions, 32
    anomalies, 34
    deceptiveness, 34
    impact assessment, 30, 34–38
    monitoring interpretations for, 30–38
    omissions, 31–32
    options for dealing with, 30, 34–38
    remedies for, 30–31
    source language intrusions, 33
    substitutions, 32–33
    types of, 30, 30n8, 31–34
ethical standards
    for attorneys, 40
    for interpreters, 39
    Model Code of Professional Responsibility for Interpreters in the Judiciary, 57
EUD (European Union of the Deaf), 163
European Commission Directorate General for Interpretation, 156
European Commission for Life-

long Learning, 155
European Convention for the Protection of Human Rights and Fundamental Freedom, 194–95
European Forum of Sign Language Interpreters (efsli), 157n2, 163
European Union
   Code of Conduct for legal interpreters, 156
   Directive 2010/64/EU on right to interpretation and translation in criminal proceedings, 155–56, 178, 195
   Directive 2012/29/EU on rights, support, and protection of victims of crime, 155, 178, 195
Evenden, David, 271
expanded renditions, 257t, 258–59, 259t, 266, 269
expert witnesses
   basis of opinion for, 99–100
   confidentiality issues, 75–76
   consulting experts, 98
   interpreters as, 73–103
   legal basis for requiring interpreters to testify, 76–86
   personal knowledge standard and, 76–78, 77n3
   protocol for, 98–99
   reasonable interpreter standard, 96–100
   subpoena responses by interpreters, 100–102
   testifying experts, 98
expository interpreting, 269

Federal Rules of Evidence, 57, 76

Rule 104(a), 84, 85
Rule 601, 77n3
Rule 602, 77
Rule 702, 98
Rule 703, 98
Rule 801, 82
Rule 805, 80
Felton, State v. (1992), 84
Fifth Amendment, 81, 82
fingerspelling, 137, 141–42, 142t
Foley, T., 11
Forestal, E., 11
Fowler, Y., 12

Gallai, F., 156
Garcia-Trujillo, State v. (1997), 84
gatekeeping, 263–65
Geraghty, Chris, 271
Gerzabek, Eve, 271
Goffman, E., 203
González, E., 197, 198, 214
Gonzalez, R. D., 108, 112
Gordon, P., 227
Gouby, Gino S., 3
Gregerson, Judge, 222
Grice's Cooperative Principle, 204
Gutierrez, People v. (1995), 84

Hale, Sandra, 51, 197, 198, 214, 246, 252n4
Hammer, A., 212
hard of hearing interpreters (HIs), 10
Haug, Tobias, 154
hearsay
   Confrontation Clause and, 78, 86, 88–91, 93–96
   double hearsay rule, 80
   necessity test, 81
   opposing party's statement,

82–83
  reliability test, 81–82
  second-hand nature of interpreted renditions of testimony, 78–80
  Supreme Court cases on, 89–93
Heriot-Watt University, 174
Hinojas-Mendoza, People v. (2005), 84
Hirsch, E. D., 124
HIs (hard of hearing interpreters), 10
Hogue, T., 162

idioms, 123
IEPs (Individual Education Plans), 6
impartiality, 195–96, 203, 223, 248, 259
Institute of Linguists Educational Trust (IoLET), 198, 199
INTERACTIVE mnemonic for Remain Model of team interpreting, 239–41
Interesource Group (Ireland) Ltd., 157n2
International Organization for Standardization (ISO), 182, 192, 196, 199, 2035, 211, 215
International Red Cross, 182
interpersonal skills
  monitoring interpretations and, 24, 25
  rapport-building and, 196
  role-space theory and, 204, 211
  standards for legal interpreters and, 196
  training and, 191–92
interpreter preparation program (IPP). *See also* training
  assessments and, 106–27

curriculum development, 108–17
instructors requesting legal interpreting training, 3–4
language ideologies in, 135–36
recommendations for monitoring interpretations, 40
"in-vision" interpreters, 11
IoLET (Institute of Linguists Educational Trust), 198, 199
IPP. *See* interpreter preparation program
IRAC (Issue, Rule, Application/Analysis, Conclusion) framework, 47–48, 52–61, 52*f*
  application to interpreters, 57–60
  critiques of, 58
  defined, 54–57
  language modeling and samples for, 61–64
  practice scenario, 65–66
Ireland
  deaf jurors in, 251n2
  Justisigns project in, 155, 158, 167*t*
ISO. *See* International Organization for Standardization

Johnson, A., 224, 283
Johnson, Paul, 271
Johnston, Sheila, 285
Jones, J., 124
jurors. *See* deaf jurors
Justisigns project, 154–83
  authentic interpreter-mediated police interview, 169–72
  focus groups, 164–69, 167–69*t*
  interviews, 164–69, 167–69*t*
  masterclass, 173–77, 175–76*t*, 177*t*

methodology, 158–59, 164–73, 167–68t
online curriculum, 177–82, 179–81t
questionnaire, 163–64
research findings, 163–72
training courses, 173–82, 175–76t, 179–81t

Krähenbühl, Flurina, 154
Krathwohl, D. R., 211–12
Kruglov, A., 161
Kumho Tire Co. v. Carmichael (1999), 98
Kusters, A., 148

language-conduit-agency theory, 84
language ideologies, 133–38
 in deaf communities, 135–36
 in interpreter training, 134–35
 layering of linguistic resources and, 136–38
Langue Signes Québécoise (LSQ), 283
LaVigne, M., 23
law enforcement. *See* police settings
Lee, J., 12
Lee, Robert G., 191, 200, 205, 208
Leeson, Lorraine, 154
legalese, 7–8
legal interpreting
 accuracy, 9
 assessments, 106–27. *See also* assessments
 attorney logic and language, 46–66. *See also* attorneys
 competencies of, 50–52, 54
 courtroom rules, 8–9

credentialing bodies, 8
deaf attorneys, 131–50. *See also* deaf attorneys
deaf jurors, 246–70. *See also* deaf jurors
defining "legal," 5–6
literature review, 6–13
monitoring interpretations, 17–42. *See also* monitoring interpretations
police settings, 154–82. *See also* police settings
responsibilities of, 11–12
role of, 9–10, 11–12, 18–19, 18n3
speaker identification. *See* speaker identification
training for, 191–215, 282–302. *See also* training
witness testimony, 73–103. *See also* witness testimony
Leung, M., 156
Lim, Julie, 271
Llewellyn-Jones, Peter, 200, 205, 208
Loos, Scott Robert, 106
Lopez, United States v. (1991), 84
Lopez-Ramos, State v. (2018), 90
LSQ (*Langue Signes Québécoise*), 283
Ludkin, Jeff, 271
Lujan v. United States (1953), 22
Lynch, Teresa, 154

Macintosh, Tim, 271
Malcolm, Karen, 291
Martinez, Silvia, 271
Martinez-Gaytan, United States v. (2000), 84, 93
materiality issues with monitoring interpretations, 29, 30, 36,

37–38
Mathers, C., 49, 73
  The Deaf Interpreter in Court: An Accommodation That Is More Than Reasonable, 57
Melendez-Diaz v. Massachusetts (2009), 89, 90
Mendes, People v. (1950), 22
Merriam, S. B., 221–22
Metzger, M., 226
Mickelson, P., 227
Miranda warnings, 10, 161, 161n4
Mirus, Gene, 131
mock trials
  monitoring interpretations and, 22
  speaker identification research via, 221–25, 230, 234, 238
  training of legal interpreters via, 285, 287–92, 296–99, 302
Model Code of Professional Responsibility for Interpreters in the Judiciary, 57
monitoring interpretations, 17–42
  authority supporting, 21–23
  collaborative approach required for, 23–24, 42
  defined, 18
  ethical duties for, 26–27
  less-than-ideal circumstances, 27–29
  preconditions for, 23–24
  process of, 29–31
  protocol for, 26–27
  qualifications for, 25–26
  recommendations, 39–41
  role of, 18–19, 41–42
  team interpreting vs., 19n5
Monroe County Courts (Rochester, New York), 254–57, 271

Monteoliva-Garcia, E., 5
Montoya-Franco, State v. (2012), 79, 92, 93
morphemes, 136
Morris, R., 193n1
Moser-Mercer, B., 226, 239
mouthing, 135, 137, 140–46, 145*t*

Napier, Jemina, 7, 30n8, 31, 154, 246, 252n4, 255, 283
National Center for State Courts (NCSC), 57
National Institute of Trial Advocacy (NITA), 221
National Occupational Standards in Interpreting (NOSI, UK), 199
National Register of Public Service Interpreters, 205
National Registers of Communication Professionals Working with Deaf and Deafblind People (NRCPD), 200
National Vocational Qualification (NVQ, UK), 199
Nazemian, United States v. (1991), 84–85, 90, 92, 94
NCIEC (National Consortium of Interpreter Education Centers), 237
NCSC (National Center for State Courts), 57
Neumann, R. K., 54
neutrality. *See* impartiality
New Zealand, deaf jurors in, 251n2
Nicodemus, B., 283
NITA (National Institute of Trial Advocacy), 221
nonrendition, 257*t*, 260–62, 260*t*, 266, 270
NOSI (National Occupational

Standards in Interpreting, UK), 199
NRCPD (National Registers of Communication Professionals Working with Deaf and Deafblind People), 200
NTID (National Technical Institute for the Deaf), 254
NVivo, 2057
NVQ (National Vocational Qualification, UK), 199

Ohio v. Roberts (1980), 89
Ontario Court Interpreters Handbook, 287
overt interaction management, 202
overt participant alignment, 203

Patino, State v. (1993), 84
People v. See name of opposing party
Perez, I. A., 173
Perez-Lastor v. INS (2000), 97
Perreaud, Charles, 271
phonemes, 136–37
Police and Criminal Evidence Act (England), 195
Police Link Officers for the Deaf, 165n5
Police Scotland
 authentic interpreter-mediated police interview by, 169–72
 Justisigns Masterclass and, 173–74
police settings, 154–83. *See also Justisigns* project
 interview discourse in, 160–61
 power dynamics in, 161–62
 research findings on interpreting in, 159–62

training courses for, 173–82, 175–76t, 179–81t
training-to-practice gap in, 169
Pollard, R. Q
 The Context-based Ethical Reasoning: Demand Control Schema (with Dean), 287
 Ethical Decision-making and Demand Control Schema (with Dean), 287
privilege defense, 73–74, 74n1
proceedings interpreters, monitoring interpretations for, 19–20, 23–24, 27–28
prosodic markers, 11
proverbs, 123

Race, L., 162
Ramsey, C., 10
Randolph, State v. (1985), 84
rapport-building, 41, 196, 202
Reagan, H. E., 22–23
reasonable interpreter standard, 75n2, 96–100
reduced renditions, 172, 257t
refugees, legal interpreting for, 249
Registry of Interpreters for the Deaf (RID)
 Code of Professional Conduct, 75, 96
 credentialing by, 8
 interpreters as witnesses and, 87
 resources for citing rules in IRAC, 65
 team interpreting and, 237
 training of legal interpreters and, 256, 266
relay interpreting, 113
Remain Model of team interpreting, 223, 227–29, 228f,

233–34, 234t, 237–341, 237f
INTERACTIVE mnemonic
for, 239–42
renditions
close renditions, 258t, 258, 261t
expanded renditions, 257t,
258–59, 259t, 266, 268
nonrendition, 257t, 260–62,
258t, 267, 270
reduced renditions, 172, 257t
summarized renditions, 257t,
260–61, 259t
zero renditions, 171, 257, 257t,
260–63
Resendes, People v. (1985), 22
Ressler, C., 10
RID. *See* Registry of Interpreters
for the Deaf
Roberson, L., 12, 283, 284
Rochester Institute of Technology,
252
Rodriguez-Castillo, State v. (2008),
80, 91, 93
role-space theory, 191–215
Interaction Management axis,
200, 201–202, 201f, 209,
212–13
legal interpreting applications,
205–11
Participant Alignment axis, 200,
201f, 202–203, 209, 213
Presentation of Self axis, 200,
201f, 203–6, 208, 213–
125
training of legal interpreters
through, 211–15
Rose, Rachel, 271
Rossier, Barbara, 154
Rotate Model of team interpreting, 223, 225–27, 226f, 230,
233–35, 233t, 235f, 237–39

Russell, Debra, 10, 22, 52, 227, 248,
251, 252n4, 255, 282, 284,
288
*Interpreting Techniques—Consecutive and Simultaneous
Interpreting*, 287
Power and Privilege (with Shaw),
287

Saavedra v. State (2009), 84, 85
Salaets, Heidi, 154
Sanchez-Godinez, United States v.
(2006), 84
San Roque, Mehera, 246, 252n4
Santana, United States v. (1974), 84
Schiff, David, 271
SC:L (Specialist Certificate—Legal), 8, 222, 266
Scottish Association of Sign Language Interpreters (SASLI),
173–74, 200
Scottish Collaborative of Sign Language Interpreters, 173n6
Scottish Register for Language
Professionals with the Deaf
Community, 173n6
semantics
matching semantic value of
source language, 108
in police settings, 182
semantic bridging, 182
subject-matter challenges,
117–26
target-language familiarity and,
110
Sforza, S., 10
Shaw, Risa, 17, 52, 284, 288
Power and Privilege (with Russell), 287
Shaw, S., 12
Shearim, Gerry, 271

Sheikh, Haaris, 154
Shuy, Roger, 220
Silverstein, M., 135
similes, 123
simultaneous interpretation, 114
Sixth Amendment Confrontation
    Clause, 78, 86, 88–91, 93–96
Skinner, Robert, 154, 163
SLLS (Sign Language Linguistics
    Society), 163
snowball sampling, 163
soft skills. *See* interpersonal skills
source attribution, 260. *See also*
    speaker identification
Source Language (SL)
    accuracy of interpretation and,
        9
    matching register and tone of,
        108
Southan, Skye, 271
Spanish language interpreters,
    112–14, 117–26
speaker identification, 219–42
    for dialogic/two-way discourse,
        224–25, 225*f*, 233–34,
        233*t*
    discourse types during mock
        bench trials, 224–25, 225*f*
    for English-speaking witness
        testimony, 234–36, 235*f*
    markers for, 230, 231–32*f*
    monologic discourse, 224–25,
        225*f*
    possible solutions, 236–37, 237*f*
    Remain Model, 223, 227–29,
        228*f*, 233, 233*t*, 234–35,
        237–38, 237*f*, 239–41
    Rotate Model, 223, 225–257
        226*f*, 230, 233, 233*t*,
        234–35, 235*f*, 237–39
    study methodology, 221–24

teaching teaming models for
    interactive conversations,
    238–41
team interpretation and,
    225–30, 226*f*, 228–29*f*
for turn-at-talk discourse,
    224–25, 225*f*, 230–32,
    231–32*f*, 234*t*
Specialist Certificate—Legal
    (SC:L), 8, 222, 266
Spencer, David, 7, 246, 252n4
Spivey, State v. (1986), 84
State v. See name of opposing party
Stone, Christopher, 4, 11, 131
summarized renditions, 257*t*,
    260–61, 261*t*
Survey Monkey, 164
Switzerland, *Justisigns* project in,
    156, 159, 168*t*, 179

Target Language (TL) listeners, 9
Taylor, M. M., 30n8, 31
Taylor v. Maryland (2016), 79,
    86–89, 90–93, 94–95
team interpreting
    deaf-hearing teams, 49, 50
    INTERACTIVE mnemonic
        for, 239–41
    monitoring vs., 19n5
    Remain Model, 223, 227–29,
        228*f*, 233–35, 233*t*,
        237–41, 237*f*
    Rotate Model, 223, 225–27,
        226*f*, 230, 233–35, 233*t*,
        235*f*, 2357–39
    speaker identification and,
        225–30, 226*f*, 231–32*f*,
        238–41
Tester, Christopher, 46, 50
TL (Target Language) listeners, 9
training, 12–13, 191–215. *See also*

continuing professional development
   adaptation of programs, 295–99
   community building approach for, 282–302
   courtroom experience, 288–90
   deaf jurors, training to work with, 266–67, 268–70
   "flipped instruction" model, 285, 287–88
   international standards for, 196
   Justisigns training courses, 172–82, 175–76t, 179–81t
   language specialists and, 290
   legal interpreting requirements and, 194–200
   model for, 285–92
   needs assessment, 284–85
   recommendations for, 301–2
   research on, 250–51
   testing and, 198–99
translanguaging strategies, 132, 135, 137, 138–39
triadic exchanges, 79, 178, 180–81t, 182–83
trust
   confidentiality and, 75–76, 102
   monitoring legal interpreting and, 39, 40, 42
   Participant Alignment and, 202–3
   Presentation of Self and, 203–4
   rapport-building and, 41, 202
   role-space theory and, 203–4, 209
Turner, Graham H., 154, 269

United Kingdom. *See also* BSL (British Sign Language)
   Justisigns project in, 155, 158, 167t, 173–77, 175–76t
   legal provisions for legal interpreters in, 195
   Police Link Officers for the Deaf, 166n5
   police setting interpretation in, 166n5, 169–70
   spoken languages interpreters in, 197–200
   training of legal interpreters in, 173–77, 175–76t, 193, 197–99
United States v. See name of opposing party
Universal Declaration of Human Rights, 194, 195
University of Applied Sciences of Special Needs Education, 177
University of New South Wales, 271
Ushakow, United States v. (1973), 84

Van den Bogaerde, B., 212
Vermeerbergen, Myriam, 154
Vernon, M., 23
Vvidacak, United States v. (2009), 84
videoconference interpreting (VCI), 205
Villagomez, People v. (2000), 93

Wadensjö, C., 224, 238
   Interpreting as Interaction, 285–86
   taxonomy of interpreter renditions, 256–58, 257t
Walker, J., 12
war crimes tribunals, 249
Webb, Stacey, 271
Wilson, C. W., 173
Wilson, W., 123
Winston, E. A., 247n1
witness testimony, 73–103. *See also* expert witnesses
   deaf-hearing team interpreting

for, 50
dialogic/two-way discourse and, 224
double hearsay rule and, 80
hearsay exceptions, 78–83. *See also* hearsay
interpreted renditions as inherently second-hand, 78–80
interpreter as authorized or joint agent, 83–86
language-conduit-agency theory and, 84
legal basis for requiring interpreters to testify, 76–86
personal knowledge standard for, 76–78
reasonable interpreter standard, 96–100
rules of evidence and, 80–82
subpoena responses by interpreters, 100–102
Witter-Merithew, A., 49, 281

zero renditions, 171, 257, 257t, 260–62